The Crum
Inside the Crumlin Road Prison

The Crum

Inside the Crumlin Road Prison

Patrick Greg

Glen Publishing

'A life spent making mistakes is not only more honourable, but more useful than a life spent doing nothing.'

GEORGE BERNARD SHAW

Contents

Acknowledgments   xi

1.   Baptism of Fire   1

2.   Yesterday and Today   15

3.   Swift Retribution   36

4.   Cons and Screws   82

5.   Screws and Cons   136

6.   Over the Wall   187

7.   Trial and Error   213

8.   Looking Back   227

Index   235

Acknowledgments

With many thanks to those who made writing this book more a labour of love than a task to be endured—Mark Devenport, for his encouragement, and Susan Dalzell, for her patience. Thanks also to the late David Ervine, along with Lord Maginnis, Gusty Spence, Martin Meehan, Gerry Anderson, Dessie O'Hagan, and all those others who made time out of their busy schedules to indulge me. Also to all of those former colleagues, ex-prisoners and friends whose doors I knocked upon and coerced into sharing their own experiences and thoughts with me, and to Jane Campbell and the First Minister's Office for allowing me a trip down memory lane. Thanks also to the keeper of the records at PRONI, the Linenhall Library, the *Belfast Telegraph* and the *Newsletter*, all invaluable sources for research.

Most importantly, to my wife and kids and my mum, for giving me space and time to 'play' with my laptop—I hope I wasn't too difficult to live with.

Chapter 1
Baptism of Fire

I will never forget the first time I walked through the gates of Belfast Prison—'The Crum'. It was July 1985, and I had joined the ranks of the Northern Ireland Prison Service just a few days earlier. As was the practice, I was sent to Crumlin Road for two weeks to begin my training.

This was the ultimate baptism of fire. Untrained and unprepared, I was to shadow experienced officers throughout the course of the next fourteen days whilst they carried out their daily duties. I would have no responsibility, and was apparently only there to absorb the atmosphere, and gain a valuable insight into what may have been expected of me as a trained officer.

I suspect the truth of the matter was somewhat different. No better way to sort the wheat from the chaff. This was my opportunity to suck it and see. To evaluate and be evaluated. If I had decided, as some had, that the job was not for me, then no harm was done. I could walk away without having committed to a lengthy training programme, saving myself time and the Northern Ireland Office some money.

From the moment I stepped inside the main prison, with its highly polished floors, and myriad of iron gates, I was captivated. The noise, the smells, the organised confusion. It was seven-thirty in the morning, and the tension emanating from the wings was almost palpable as I entered the large circle area where the day staff were being paraded. There was a constant stream of officers milling around, some with obvious purpose, and others grudgingly heading to take up a post somewhere in the bowels of the jail. Chains were clanking and keys jangling, a cacophony of metal on metal, deeply unsympathetic to the ear at such an early hour.

I was directed to assist in D-wing during the course of my first day, and as I worked my way through the air-lock grill system into the wing, I was to learn that patience is a virtue in such a secure environment. To move throughout the jail, you relied on the person holding the keys at each gate to facilitate your entry and exit. The feeling that it was not just the inmates who were the prisoners in this environment soon became clear, to me at least.

I quickly learned that D-wing was specifically for sentenced prisoners, housing the top-security 'red books' and lifers on the top landing—the threes—whilst the ones and the twos were reserved for prisoners serving shorter terms or approaching the end of their sentence. Various orderlies used throughout different areas in the prison resided amongst the inmates on D1 and D2, holding their positions based on trust, and a low-risk security clearance.

Finally, at eight o'clock in the morning, when the numbers were counted and returned to the senior officer, and in turn to the chief officer in the circle, the order to unlock was given. As the forbidding green Belfast doors were opened and locked back, the drama unfolded, and the nameless, faceless bogeymen ventured out. Never have I experienced such a tangible atmosphere of hopelessness, drudgery and despair, laid bare by the expressions on the inmates' faces and those of their keepers. It was clear that for some inmates this was the ultimate low point in their lives, but for others it was merely an occupational hazard to be endured. For all, however, this place was a great leveller.

As I walked around the landings peering into the cells, I was shocked at how bleak and depressing they were. No amount of wall decoration, pornographic or otherwise, would have redeemed them. Simple, basic furniture and fittings added to the picture of a harsh and antiquated regime. The smells were much more potent here, an acrid concoction of urine, tobacco and body odour, pushing its way out through the doors into the landings as if attempting to make good its own escape.

I briefly stepped inside a cell, and immediately felt a sense of panic starting to rise in me. The mere idea of the door being closed behind me was unthinkable, and I knew then that a person would have to be in total resignation to accept such a fate; hope would only frustrate and agitate. Although there was a barred window in the cell, it was set high up and did not afford a view unless you were to climb up on the bed and stretch. The sounds of the city still filtered through, tantalising and beckoning, yet unattainable.

It struck me as being rather more torturous to have an institution such as this within a mile of the city centre. All who resided within were constantly reminded of day to day life on the outside, a mere stone's throw from their cells.

But life inside soon began to take on a shape of sorts, as I watched the cons performing their ablutions and preparing for breakfast in the dining hall in D-wing. As I took up a position beside one of the high chairs in the dining hall, I immediately grasped just how vulnerable the screws were. I was only one of four men inside an area holding about one hundred prisoners at mealtimes. My fate, and that of my fellow screws, lay in the hands of the cons, a very unnerving shift of trust for me to accept at first. The high chairs were just as you would imagine: hard-backed seats set on tall metal legs, providing a view over the whole room. I felt terribly self-conscious as I climbed into one at the behest of the senior officer on duty. I sensed, wrongly of course, that all the cons were watching me, and would be trying to test me, fully aware that I had no notion as to what I was meant to be observing. I summoned my most steely of looks and settled into a rigid pose, looking at everyone and no one. As the minutes ticked by and my nerves subsided somewhat, I began to pick up on a subtle change in the atmosphere. Here in the dining hall the noise was deafening, yet the mood of the majority of the inmates appeared rather more upbeat. I could only think that the interaction between themselves and other individuals after several hours of confinement and solitude was a welcome relief, and afforded some cause for celebration. Another day over, as it were, or another night at least.

As I moved around the dining hall between posts, I began to look more closely at the faces of the men as they breakfasted. The ages of the cons ranged from early twenties right up to what appeared to be men in their sixties. For some reason I found it hard to accept that some of these men were, for want of a better description, 'senior citizens'. I had a pre-conceived idea of the type of person whom I would find languishing in jail: young, fit, street-wise and always confrontational. I couldn't have been further off the mark. There was certainly an element of truth to my stereotyping, but they were clearly in the minority. Half of these men looked like anyone's uncle, dad or grandad. The fascinating question for me thereafter remained, exactly what crimes had these men committed and in what circumstances to end up serving a prison sentence?

Like many people growing up in Northern Ireland at the time—a country with a narrow, parochial attitude—I took a keen interest in local issues and events, in particular the many terrorist incidents that we all came to accept as the norm. Informed and aware, I later found myself trawling the landings of D-wing, putting faces to names, and names to events. I was genuinely caught up in the gruesome celebrity of some of these people. Faced with a renowned bomber or gunman, I would search their faces for a common trait: a bloodthirsty lust in their eyes or a psychopathic demeanour. I rarely found either. I can honestly say that I was in awe of this whole experience. I felt that it was utterly surreal to be walking amongst a community of criminals, and in some cases sophisticated terrorists, in a backdrop taken straight from Dickensian times. I couldn't shake the feeling that in some small way, I was standing watching history unfold. Not international, front page news, but a little bit of the history of Northern Ireland, where the people making the headlines were right in front of me.

For a few days, I struggled with many aspects of the job, none more so than actually shutting the doors at lock-up. Although it was to become an automatic response to the command at the end of association time, and was generally accepted and adhered to by most inmates without any great drama, at first I felt a terrible guilt about locking anyone away, regardless of their crimes. Over time, however, I could see that the inmates hardly glanced at the person banging them up. The system worked by totally institutionalising them, taking them to a point where they conformed to a routine and lived within that routine. All decisions were made for them and any independence was removed.

Moving throughout the jail, from wing to wing and post to post, gave new recruits like me an opportunity to experience every gate and grill which was operational on a day to day basis. Some were obviously more unpleasant than others, but I can honestly say that I found none of the duties terribly taxing. I frequently saw inmates engage staff in what I perceived to be good-natured banter, and to a degree I found some comfort in this. Maybe it was not nearly as daunting as it first seemed. Maybe 'screws' and 'cons' happily co-existed, and the great machine which was prison life was well oiled and maintenance-free. I was to learn through experience, though, that the screws were always the common enemy, and that some hapless officers were destined to become victims of 'conditioning' by inmates, whereby they would let down their guard and compromise either themselves or others. Of course the cons were not all out to exploit you at every turn. Some screws and cons had an unspoken understanding, which still fell slightly short of friendship, but nevertheless was comfortable for both of them. Still, even with arrangements such as these existing, it paid to remember that a high percentage of those serving sentences inside Northern Ireland's prisons at the time, constituted some of the most hardened terrorists in Europe, having committed despicable acts for whatever causes they felt justified them.

Nearly everyone I was to meet over the next few weeks would share a personal word or two of wisdom with me on such issues as conditioning. Some, it seems, genuinely wanted to guide me on the right path, and unfortunately others wanted to level criticism at fellow officers or authorities, who they continually blamed for implementing a 'holiday camp' regime. If ever there was a workplace where division amongst the workforce was evident, this was it. The disillusioned and the deluded, as I liked to refer to them, worked alongside each other in relative harmony but undermined each other at every opportunity. I felt, however, that as a 'red arse' (as the new staff were referred to by cons and screws alike), I would be obliged to humbly accept all advice from whatever source, and form my own opinions when I had established myself in the rank of officer. From what I could determine, there appeared to be some fairly young 'veterans' in the job, barely out of their probationary period themselves, who had quickly acquired the lethargy and acerbic tongue of their more truculent seniors. Gone were the days when one could identify the longer-serving officers by the length of their key chain, or the wear and tear on their baton strap. I blamed the job itself for injecting more cynicism into young men than would normally be found. Old before their time would be an apt description of many of the twenty-somethings working in the jails at the time.

*   *   *

One duty which I was never particularly comfortable with, either during those first two weeks, or indeed anytime after, was in the visits area. The visits took place in separate areas for each wing, and consisted of either open tables or enclosed booths. Neither of these afforded any great privacy for the inmates and their visitors, and, to add injury to insult, there were patrol officers continually walking up and down observing the actions of both parties. I spent at least two days in visits, in different wings, and always found it unpleasant to watch the fumbled attempts at intimacy as you passed a table. All coyness and embarrassment appeared to go out the window, and the sexual tension emanating from the room was palpable.

Of course, the cons were in some ways happier in creating an uncomfortable aspect to observing visits, and, by continually labelling the screws as voyeurs, it provided the perfect environment for smuggling contraband. I was continually warned about items, particularly drugs, being passed from mouth to mouth in the form of a kiss, and was encouraged to enforce the rules as much as possible. Prisoners have always been ingenious and have learned numerous ways to smuggle goods in and out of jail by trial and error. Kissing was just another opportunity. Many an item was passed through the handling of babies by doting daddy, where he was supposedly making up for lost hugs and cuddles, whilst rummaging around in the child's nappy for a ten deal of cannabis.

The food and clothing parcels sent into jail also provided an opportunity to smuggle prohibited items, and these could not always be picked up by the X-ray machines. One incident which sticks in my head was when a bag of oranges was found to have been injected with straight vodka, which would have provided a fun night in for the recipient had it not been twigged by a screw with an acute sense of smell.

Every day of that two weeks launched me on a steep learning curve into the many aspects of the cat and mouse game played out by screws and cons. And every post within the jail was continually being tried and tested, poked and prodded, in an attempt to find the chink. When you came to realise that, your senses were sharpened and you began to think like a con, which was the most valuable lesson of all.

If the object of the two-week trial period was to whittle down the new recruits to a more manageable number, then it succeeded, as two casualties fell by the wayside at the end of the first week. I would never remember their names, as I spoke with them rarely, and even then only in passing. At least they had not made any major commitment in terms of time, and in that sense the system was a fair one.

The remainder of my trial period went by in the blink of an eye, and after my period of training at Millisle Prison Service College, I was posted to Magilligan Prison in the north-west of the Province.

Magilligan was a whole different kettle of fish. The complex was a mixture of Nissen huts and H-blocks, vast open phase areas, and work compounds. The prison population was comprised of sentenced prisoners only, whereas the Crum held many who were on remand or awaiting trial. It wasn't long before

I realised that the regime was more stringent in its approach to prison discipline and retaining a general work ethic. Prisoners were encouraged to work in the metal workshops or learn a trade, as well as being given the opportunity to attend evening classes in various subjects, taught by qualified teachers who visited the jail regularly.

All the wings in the three H-blocks were mixed, Catholics and Protestants together, with sex offenders amongst them. Although this attempt at inducing normality was to be praised on many occasions, the reality of daily life on the wing was contradictory. Both factions introduced a form of self-segregation, occupying opposite sides of the integral dining halls and alternating exercise and ablution routines by agreement.

The environment was arguably more modern and comfortable to work in, but the blocks were just as imposing and restrictive as the Crum had been. I began to see that the buildings themselves played a major part in defining the space as being one of containment and punishment, and appeared to have an effect not only on the inmates, but also on the officers. Part of the disadvantage for me was the fact that because of the location of the jail on the northernmost tip of the Province, I had little choice but to live in the official accommodation provided. This consisted of a small room in a pre-fabricated building known as a terrapin, situated within the old prison area, and around 500 metres from the main gate of the new prison. The room was dank and dingy, and had seen better days, and the ablution area was equally as depressing. At first I was deflated at the prospect of having to live in this hole for at least two weeks at a time. And I could not get my head around the fact that I had to come and go through a set of secure outer gates, which gave me more of a sense of being a prisoner than a screw. As with many things in Magilligan, though, the reality of living and working in virtually the same place became less of a problem, and I began to accept the discomfort of my room and adjust to the positives about living in a jail.

I settled into life in the prison very easily, and became an avid runner in my spare time, clocking up around fifty to sixty miles a week, taking in the sumptuous scenery around the base of

Benevenagh, and thriving in the good country air. Of the live-in staff (of whom there were around fifteen to twenty), at least ten of us were single, and our entertainment was self-generated, often revolving around females and drink. The old adage of 'work hard and play hard' applied to us specifically, as we worked our fair share of overtime on a daily basis, and socialised in the local area on most nights. I began to really appreciate having two wholly different social scenes to avail of, one in the north-west and the other in County Down. Life in the 'arsehole of nowhere' was not nearly as bad as I had first thought.

During my two years working in Magilligan, I experienced many disruptions in the blocks, ranging from prisoners wrecking the toilets, kitchen and dining hall areas, to a siege, where a number of Loyalists took a screw hostage, along with a Catholic prisoner, for several days. I remember this incident clearly, as the officer taken hostage was someone who I knew socially, and whose family I had become close to when I started going out with his sister-in-law. As usual, the Loyalists had been complaining about the harsh regime at the jail and what they perceived as forced integration. As local Free Presbyterian Minister Wesley McDowell attended to his flock in H1 on Sunday 5 April 1987, the twenty-nine inmates grabbed him and a Catholic inmate along with the officer and barricaded themselves in B-wing. They had been preparing for some time for the siege and had stockpiled foodstuffs and water. They demanded the NIO look further into segregation at the jail and what they described as 'oppressive conditions'. They lasted for four days, and thankfully all three hostages were released in good physical condition. Up until then, I had considered that the jail was relatively trouble-free and working relationships between the prison authorities and the various factions were at an acceptable level to both parties. The siege was a reality check, and we all took a step back and re-evaluated our roles in our jobs. I never met with the officer in question again, as he was too traumatised to return to work at that stage, but I still think about his ordeal, and the effect it would have had on him. I doubt I would have coped as well as he did.

Magilligan offered me a good grounding in the skills needed to survive as a screw, skills that were transferable to any situation, either inside or outside prison. The cons themselves always left jail with something which they could, and often would, apply on the street, something which generally could not be learned elsewhere. Similarly, my judgement and appraisal of certain situations is now clearly different, as I developed and honed keen instincts and attitude. It was like a schooling in life and survival. What I took to the job originally when I trained at Millisle was compounded when I worked in the blocks at Magilligan, and I know that I have applied many of the lessons I managed to absorb as a prison officer to situations in my day to day life outside of the job.

I spent just over two years in Magilligan, a time I would describe as eventful and humourless. The people with whom I worked, or 'Sandmen' as they were more commonly known, were undoubtedly colourful and opinionated. They were also selfless and warm, and far removed from the brash, reticent 'McCoeys', as the Belfast screws were affectionately christened. Whilst I could appreciate the practicalities of moving to the Crum and working close to home, I felt as if I was taking a backward step, knowing full well the days of the Crum were numbered, and a move to either the Maze or Maghaberry was likely. I made the move reluctantly, and I knew even before reporting for duty on my first day that I had probably made a mistake.

*   *   *

When I returned to the Crum I was immediately placed on what was known as general duties. This was arguably one of the best posts in the jail, adding variety to your routine on an almost daily basis. The one major gripe every screw had was the obvious boredom which came with the job description. But when on general duties, you could be in visits one day and a 'runner' in the prison hospital the next. As far as I was concerned, there was no real downside to GDs. You never had the opportunity to become very familiar with any of the inmates, as you were virtually nomadic, and in many cases the old saying 'familiarity breeds contempt' most certainly applied on the wings. Personality clashes between permanent wing staff and inmates were frequent enough, and they were running into each other on a daily basis. There were occasions, however, where the reputations of some inmates could not be ignored, and you made sure that you were aware of the disruptive elements when visiting any particular wing. It was always better to be informed and prepared than ignorant and vulnerable. I had enough service under my belt to realise that, although there may have been conflict, the permanent staff in the wings were less likely to be a target for prisoners' frustrations, as it would have been virtually the equivalent of biting the hand that fed them.

Even after all the time I had spent in Magilligan, I still had the fascination for identifying the cons with a prominent history, but at first, I saw names on cell cards in passing, recognising only a few. One of the first inmates whose name I did recognise immediately, however, was David Blair.

Blair had been eighteen in 1974, when he and an accomplice, Marshall Colin Graham, shot and killed a young Catholic man by the name of Michael Browne after an eleventh night bonfire celebration in my home town of Bangor. Even though I was only twelve at the time, I remember the incident vividly, partly because it happened only a few hundred yards from my parents' house, but more so because I knew Michael to see and talk to, and had sometimes played with Michael's younger brother, Brendan, who had also been in my class at primary school. The Troubles seemed to take on a totally different meaning for me from that point on. The town of Bangor had virtually escaped the brunt of the early years of conflict, and my circle of friends and I were oblivious to any differences in culture or tradition which would supposedly define us as being opposites on different sides of a political fence. Our youth up until that point was unremarkable, and there was never anything other than encouragement from all our parents to mix with each other, regardless of religion. I saw a tangible change in attitude from the point of Michael's murder onwards. There seemed to have been a line drawn in the sand between the two communities. Everything changed. Throughout the latter part of 1974, I began to become more aware, and read more and more headlines about sectarian murders carried out in my area. Arms and ammunition finds were frequent, and it was clear, even to a twelve-year-old boy, that there no longer seemed to be a comfort zone around me or my community.

Whilst writing this book, I read a newspaper feature on Dublin poet and artist Charlie Whisker, in which he recalls the exact same incident, to which he was an unfortunate witness. He described that July night in detail, and how it had a profound effect on him, providing the catalyst for his subsequent decision to relocate to London and then Dublin. Whisker had witnessed the fatal shots, the gunmen running away, and had stayed to comfort Michael as he slipped away into unconsciousness and death. The impact was more profound when I again heard Whisker recount the events in his own words on a Radio 4 *Home Truths* programme. It was interesting to hear if he, as a significant witness, still feared for his own safety, bearing in mind the fact that at the time of the programme the killers had been released. He was clear in the understanding that they were likely to have been victims themselves of the Troubles, manipulated and used, and that they too had paid a high price for their actions.

Of course only Blair and Graham will ever know the truth about the details of the murder, regardless of admissions during police interviews that they had been forced by other parties into carrying out the shooting. However, during their sentencing to life imprisonment by Justice Basil Kelly on 6 December 1974, it was reported that one of the two shouted 'Up the UVF' from the dock. Hardly the remorse of a victim of circumstance; more of a desperate coward's attempt to ingratiate himself with his inevitable future cellmates.

I first saw David Blair on the twos in D-wing, where he was serving the latter years of his life sentence. I remember him as short and stocky, with a weightlifter's physique, sallow complexion and fairly handsome features. He did not appear to be the archetypal murdering gunman, no matter how hard I tried to make him fit the bill. As I stood on the opposite side of the landing looking across at him, he was deep in conversation with another inmate. I was like a rabbit caught in the headlights, staring at the man who undoubtedly had the most effect on my formative opinions on Ulster politics and sectarian division within those politics.

Michael Browne's murder will never be foremost in everyone's recollections of definitive markers or milestones during the years of conflict in Northern Ireland. But to his family and friends, and those who, until then, had remained virtually untouched by the random cruelty and vicious spectre of sectarianism, it will always be definitive.

At that moment, I despised David Blair. Not as a human being, but for being the someone who had changed me, the someone whose actions took away an innocence and replaced it with a deep fear and resentment. As I stood there watching him, I knew he would not have known me, or recognised me from having lived in the same community as he had. The passage of time had changed me from schoolboy to adult, one who wore a uniform and blended with the other gate-keepers in his world. But I desperately wanted him to know that I knew him, and what he had done, as if to remind him that, for some, he would always be a murderer and a gunman, whether he was time served or not.

When I spoke with older members of staff, some with decades of experience, I was assured that they too had experienced similar thoughts and emotions towards perpetrators of atrocities who had ended up on their landings. Their professionalism prevailed, however; and I was continually reminded that the courts had punished these individuals, and our own job was one of containment only, and not persecution.

Looking back now, Charlie Whisker had more reason to hate Blair and his accomplice than I had. He had been tortured by the events of that evening for some time after, and had suffered veiled threats and intimidation. Yet he was mature enough to reason after all that, that there were all kinds of victims of the Troubles.

It was actually seeing Blair in the flesh that fuelled my interest in the inmates with whom I was working. Bizarre as it may seem,

I believe we are all drawn by the more extreme aspects of human behaviour, none more so than homicide. The challenging part of this fascination was how to remove the person from the crime and try to see beyond the extreme act. Bearing in mind the mindlessness, or brutality, of the various murders which some of these men had committed, it was not an easy thing to do.

*   *   *

As a place to work, in respect of conditions and authorities, the Crum would have been anything but my first choice. But I had made my bed and resigned myself to lie in it for the foreseeable future, even though I knew I would not be happy to remain there.

Over time, however, I would develop a deep respect for the place, born out of a fascination for its macabre history and the non-partisan folklore which thrived within its walls. Of the people I worked with, some remain friends today, and others I will always pass on the street without a backward glance. I count myself lucky that although I have never been one to settle at anything for long, and have in turn paid the price both financially and on occasion emotionally, my life has been all the richer for having experienced some things which others can only read about. In turn, I hope that this book will give the reader an insight not only into the history of Crumlin Road Prison, but also into some of the more well-known visitors who had occasion to remain within its confines at Her Majesty's pleasure. Those who have chosen to contribute will share their unique thoughts and memories, fond or otherwise, on a singularly important chapter in their lives; an indelible mark having been left as a result of just or arguably unjust incarceration.

Chapter 2
Yesterday and Today

To stand in the forecourt of the Crum in modern times and look around, one can still feel the energy coursing through the blocks and stones, drawing you inside for a closer look. Little wonder then that the prospect of the Crum becoming a major tourist attraction is currently being discussed, with a view to assisting with the regeneration of that part of North Belfast. The history of the prison envelopes both political and social aspects of life in Northern Ireland, with prison life having been described as a microcosm of events on the outside. Because of our continual preoccupation with the current conflicts in the North, I felt it was essential to look back to when the building was first constructed and why, and to explore the many events and people caught up in its lifespan. The Crum has been, and will always be, of major historical importance, much more so than the Maze, perhaps, regardless of events like the much documented hunger strike of the early 1980s.

'The Troubles' is a convenient title for the conflict dating back to 1969, but we cannot ignore our less recent past in Northern Ireland, and the troubles that came with it, which in turn had an impact on the prison population in both the North and South. Internment, for instance, was not a phenomenon born out of these last thirty-five years. It was constantly being wagged as the big stick during periods of unrest and possible insurgency, and the Crum held its fair share of internees before, during and after World War Two.

The IRA's campaign for a united and free Ireland had continued, albeit mainly in the Border areas, right up to 1962, when it was abandoned through lack of support. In the forty years leading up to this, from the establishment of the State of Northern Ireland in 1921, virtually every part of the North had experienced murders, intimidation and sectarianism from both sides, and the Crum had housed countless hundreds of offenders caught up in the wake of the perpetuating violence. It would be too convenient to concentrate on the people and events relating to the political storyboard as it unfolded during the turbulent twentieth century, but rather one has to consider the plight of the 'ordinary decent criminals' set in the context of a socially deprived and wholly unstable society during those times, and before.

*   *   *

Belfast as a town in the seventeenth century had been built around its importance as a port, and its merchants thrived on the import and export of goods to England, Scotland and parts of Europe. An unstable period in Irish history it may have been, but Belfast continued to flourish, and as the linen trade rapidly gained momentum, so too did the port, to a point where in the 1770s Belfast was responsible for shipping more than a fifth of all linen exported from Ireland. The increase in the population of Belfast during the early part of the nineteenth century was mainly due to the introduction of manufacturing. Commerce, although wholly important in establishing Belfast as a port, had done little to expand its boundaries and appeal as a town for any unskilled members of the Northern Irish workforce. As the manufacturing industry took a foothold, however, the population of Belfast increased from around 20,000 to 100,000.

The impact the linen industry in particular had is apparent when one considers that in 1750, Belfast was of little or no importance in terms of the general textile industry. But by the outbreak of World War One, it had been transformed into the largest linen producing centre, not just in Ireland, but in the world.

The nature of the work in the mills across the town was such that the workforce was made up not only of men, but also of women and children. Conditions were such that lung diseases were common amongst the workers, and there was little monetary reward for a week's exhausting labour. Even so, there was always someone willing to take up a place in the factories, regardless of the pay or conditions. Poverty in Belfast Town was rife, but still they came to avail of whatever employment was open to them, and by 1901 the population had grown to around 350,000 people, marking it as the twelfth largest city in the United Kingdom.

The shipyard provided jobs for around 9,000 people as Belfast was shepherded into the twentieth century, and the city began to spread and envelope suburban areas both north and south of the Lagan. Within the greater Belfast area, and more particularly West Belfast, the Catholic and Protestant population was already being defined by the Falls and Shankill Roads. The housing in these areas were the poorest in the city, with the Catholic Falls Road being the worst, comprising run-down terraced accommodation, with only 50 per cent of households having the luxury of a gas supply.

With such a rapid growth in population, and with the infrastructure subsequently struggling to keep pace, living conditions like those recorded bred contempt, insecurity and division. Crime was on the increase and, for some, it became the only option they could find to help put food on the table.

Looking back through the available records, it is apparent that the laws of the land over the past 150 years have softened to a degree, and arguably the concept of incarceration today appears less formidable. I suspect the mere idea of a month or more in jail in the 1850s onwards was somewhat scarier than it is today.

The prison system in Victorian times, more specifically around the 1860s, was slightly ambiguous. There were two types of prison, local and convict prisons. Convict prisons held only sentenced prisoners who had been given a fairly substantial term to serve. The local prison was the oldest type, and this normally consisted of either a gaol or a house of correction.

The gaol was a place where people who had been convicted were detained whilst awaiting their trial, or who had been convicted but were awaiting punishment. The sentences could have included capital punishment, but were normally corporal floggings and the like. The average stay of a person in a gaol was therefore short, but as it was also used to house people who were due for transportation to either the Americas or Australia, they did have some longer stay customers.

The house of correction was, as the name suggests, a place of detention where methods were put into place to correct the offenders' behaviour. The majority of the offenders would have been petty criminals, and their respective sentences would have been two years or less. These austere places were christened 'Bridewells' after the very first house of correction at Bridewell Palace in London was introduced in 1556, and it became compulsory to establish similar houses of correction throughout the rest of the isles.

These two very different establishments were formally amalgamated in 1865 through the introduction of the Prison Act, and became known as the local prison. The existence of government-controlled prisons like the Crumlin Road relegated the local jails to purely being holding facilities. Institutions like the Crumlin Road formalised the prison system, providing a singular establishment to house any category of prisoner caught up in the criminal justice system.

Conditions in Victorian prisons were often cold, unhygienic and very oppressive. Prisoners were allocated numbers to de-personalise the experience and disconnect them from their offending background. They were kept separated at all times, even when exercising, and had little if any opportunity to speak to each other. Another extreme was to make them wear masks in the presence of other prisoners, the idea being to reinforce the concept of isolation, and in some ways to maintain their anonymity. The confinement to individual cells was believed to encourage the inmates to reflect on their offending behaviour and thus repent. The authorities wanted to be the only influence upon these people whilst they remained in jail, and separation would reduce any risk of negative influences from fellow inmates. Of course, this method of control has lasted throughout much of the twentieth century, and is still used in penal systems around the world as a more severe punishment for breaking prison rules or general disruption, although it is more commonly known as 'solitary confinement'. This concept of keeping inmates apart continued up until recent times, with prison rule number 121 in 1954 stating: 'In order to prevent untried prisoners from being morally contaminated by each other, or endeavouring to defeat the ends of justice, they shall be kept separate, and shall not be permitted to communicate together.'

This rule would have been specific to prisoners awaiting trial or on remand. It seems inconceivable today to use such terms as 'moral contamination', but the train of thought that some inmates leave prison as more accomplished thieves or burglars is far from new. Many criminals will admit to honing their particular talents during a spell in jail, having availed of one particular master class or another, i.e. safe-breaking, deceptions etc.

Inmates in Victorian times were forced to commit to regular attendance at church services held within the confines of the prison, and they could also avail of the guidance of prison chaplains at agreed times. The belief that spiritual guidance and extreme discipline went a long way to breaking the criminal spirit was flawed, to say the least. Just as they do today, many of the people incarcerated during those times returned to prison as re-offenders, regardless of the knowledge of what lay ahead of them in jail.

The reasoning that crime did pay sometimes prevailed, and career criminals are common in any era of the prison's history. One such inmate whose records I came across was a Dublin-born man who went by several aliases, one of which was James Joseph Carroll. Carroll was fifty-five years old when he was sentenced to five years penal servitude on 8 March 1946 for two counts of burglary larceny and one count of attempted larceny. It wasn't his first brush with the law. He had used the alias of J.J. Fenton during his forty-five years as a consistent offender, and had subjected his poor wife Agnes to being continually left on her own while he served his time in various institutions. His criminal record was of epic proportion, and started in 1904 when, at the age of thirteen, he was sentenced to five years in reformatory school for burglary. From there the downward spiral took him through a further twenty convictions and sentences which, if served in full, would account for forty-two years of his life. He had not confined his offending to Ireland either, and in 1938 he served a substantial sentence in Dartmoor Prison for larceny and burglary, in the jurisdiction of the Liverpool courts.

Carroll appears in his descriptive prison forms to be a man about 5 foot 3 inches in height, with a sallow complexion and blue eyes. His build is described as stout, and his face rounded. When you look at his official prison photographs, he looks to be quite a dapper individual, with a rakish choice in suits. Interestingly enough, his prison records show him to have been a model prisoner who behaved in an exemplary manner throughout his various stays. Unfortunately, prisoner 435c, as was his most recent number, could never seem to resign himself to a life devoid of crime and was destined to return to jail a short time after every release.

I realised when I saw the photographs of Carroll that the way in which he had been posed was very different from earlier records. In earlier times, it had been the norm to sit the new inmate in a chair with both his hands splayed out across his chest, in order to record any missing digits. To the side would be a mirror, shaped at the bottom right corner to close around the subject's shoulder, which, when the photograph was taken, would show a full face image and a good side profile from which to further identify him. This progressed to a mirror placed at the rear to give a front and back view, and then eventually to a full body pose, as in Carroll's case. I suspect from Carroll's record that he saw all such variations first-hand.

Well-known Loyalist figure Gusty Spence tells the story of another prolific offender whom he encountered during his long period in jail, which began in 1966. He recounts how 'Bunky' Hanna had been the typical 'lag', completely institutionalised as a result of a lifetime of crime. At one point, he told me, he sat down with Hanna and counted up just how many years he had spent in prison, while at the same time counting up the monies he had accumulated as a result of his days as a cat burglar. In all, Hanna had taken the equivalent of around thirteen hundred pounds. For the crimes he committed in securing this paltry sum of money, he had served thirty years and six months. It wasn't difficult to work out how painful that would have sounded to Hanna.

In his particular case, the system had won. Apparently he had also served what Spence described as the 'hardest time' of all when he and at least two others, 'Swing' Taggart and a man called Gibson, who Spence remembers as being an accomplished pickpocket, were held in jail on what was known as preventative detention. Such was their re-offending when released from jail that the authorities had considered it wise to detain them to actually prevent them committing further crimes.

Hanna was the perfect criminal, in the eyes of the police at least! He had developed an MO (modus operandi) that was so distinctive, it would have pointed the finger of suspicion at him just as soon as the police began their investigation. After risking his neck to climb into a property, he would immediately light a candle to guide his way. When police attended and found candle wax at the crime scene, it wasn't long before they were knocking at Bunky's door.

* * *

It appears that engaging prisoners in work duties was thought to play a major part in the rehabilitation of the offender, although the work was generally long and arduous, and could do little other than breed resentment. The stereotypical view of prisoners on 'hard labour' breaking rocks with pick axes is taken straight from Victorian prison life, and is well documented as just one of many work duties they had to undertake, come rain, hail or shine. Another laborious task was oakum picking, which involved the separation of strands from ropes, and making mats. Often prisoners would work alone in their cells for the duration of the day, which in turn made few opportunities for human contact. In the earlier Victorian establishments, warders were known to have been rewarded with a bonus directly related to the cumulative efforts of the inmates. The obvious repercussions were for the warder to become overzealous in enforcing the work ethic when there was the promise of financial remuneration.

In 1922, there appear to have been active woodyards, stone yards, shoemaking workshops and tailoring shops in Crumlin Road. The woodyard survived throughout the years, and I myself remember being detailed as woodyard party escort, a perfect post for a long hot summer day, but brutal in the winter.

Even when I was around, in the middle of the 1980s, inmates were still working in the shoe shops and metal shops at Magilligan, and attending crafts workshops in the Crum. They could earn very small amounts of money for their labours, which they spent in the tuck shop on sweets and tobacco etc. On speaking to ex-inmates, there were differing opinions on the subject of working in the jail. Many considered the work demeaning, likening it to slave labour, whilst others considered it a perfect opportunity to pass the time with a little reward for their efforts at the end. The difference was that there was never a choice nor a reward for inmates in Victorian times.

In the prisons of Northern Ireland in later years, the problems which could arise out of providing tools and machinery to inmates was sometimes plain to see, especially when they took the opportunity to express their more 'creative' sides, particularly in the metal shops. The famous zip gun was a regular product of the inmates' production line, and turned up frequently during searches of the workshop or prisoners' cells. Metal cylinders were welded to basic trigger and firing pin mechanisms, and in turn these were smuggled back into the blocks, or hidden in the workshops to be used when ammunition was brought in through other channels. Some inmates were actually shot and wounded with bullets fired from these crude but effective contraptions. On 30 January 1987, Leslie Rodham, an inmate in Magilligan, was found in the metal workshops with an injury to his side. It was only after his admission to hospital that it was discovered he had been shot, and a .22 round was removed from his person.

* * *

I had never thought much about the design of the jail other than in a practical sense, a place of secure containment, and was intrigued by what I found when I researched the transition from bridewells to prisons.

An inquisition, or investigation, into the proposed purchasing of lands for the construction of a new 'Bridewell' or 'House of correction', was undertaken in July 1841 in the town of Belfast. The lands proposed, which were owned in part by a Mrs McCluney and one Thomas Scott, were described as being situated close to the town, fronting on to the Crumlin Road. The wording suggests that Belfast was a good deal smaller in the mid-1800s, with development not having fully reached that far countrywards.

Belfast was fast growing, however, with an almost daily increase in its population due to the flourishing linen, cotton, rope and canvas industries. There were already bridewells in Antrim, Ballymena and Ballymoney, as well as the existing gaol in Carrickfergus. However, in 1835, with over 200 people having been charged with crimes and committed to prison, and a further 106 being committed under Civil Bill decrees, the need for a larger, more suitable establishment was clear.

The architect commissioned to design the jail was Sir Charles Lanyon, a name synonymous with more celebrated structures in Belfast and Northern Ireland. A railway and civil engineer, Lanyon hailed from Eastbourne in Sussex. He spent the early part of the 1830s in Dublin before taking up a post as a County Surveyor in Antrim. He played a major part in the construction of the Larne to Portrush Coast Road, the Belfast to Ballymena railway line and the Belfast to Bangor line. To most people, he is known for landmarks such as the Custom House, Queen's College, the Queen's Bridge and the Ormeau Bridge. His architectural accomplishments were many, yet the jail and court-house, regardless of their obvious purpose, must stand amongst those shoulder to shoulder.

A good architect designs a building with its ultimate purpose as its key factor. The style is almost always purely decorative or aesthetic, but the building is always functional. Lanyon's buildings were no different, and ranged from the Victorian gothic building at Queen's University to the extravagant Italian Renaissance style of the Custom House. Here, however, with the jail, he managed to convey with his design and use of materials an austere and forbidding institution that must have struck the fear of God into its early inhabitants.

Lanyon based its design originally around Pentonville Jail in London, which was completed in 1842, a year before building work commenced on Crumlin Road. The architect of Pentonville, Colonel Joshua Jebb, had taken the concept of Jeremy Bentham's 'panopticon', consisting of a central hall with five radiating wings, and designed what was considered to be the model for a further fifty-four similar builds within the next six years. It was no mere whim to build to Bentham's concept. Bentham, who is frequently referred to as a Utilitarian philosopher and theorist of British legal reform in the early 1800s, proposed his 'panopticon' as the perfect round the clock surveillance machine. He claimed that he could perpetuate a state of discipline in the prisoner by inducing mental uncertainty. The mental uncertainty came from the idea of placing the prisoner in a position where he believed he was constantly under surveillance by his keepers, who stood in the central hall.

With prison numbers rising rapidly in the early 1800s, partly due to the ending of capital punishment for many lesser crimes, the need for a much more definitive prison system was clear, and this new concept of custodial care was embraced. The alternative to the panopticon or radial design came later, in the form of the telephone pole design, which had wings extending off a central corridor. The prime example of the telephone pole design is Wormwood Scrubs, which wasn't completed until 1874.

The Crum was designed with only four wings, each a ray of sun as it were, emanating from a 'circle' area, from which the officers could control movement and activities in each wing.

It is difficult to imagine exactly how much change has occurred over the past 150 years. When you walk around the outside of A-wing, you can clearly see the contrasting blocks and bricks which show the later extension of the wing, adding both length and height. This work was carried out sometime around 1890, and was undertaken as a direct result of the increase in the prison population. The addition of the prison infirmary at the rear of B-wing was completed in and around the same time. As it appeared to me in 1985, with the inclusion of an obscured entrance to A-wing and semi-opaque plastic on the various grills, it would have been impossible to know just what view circle officers were afforded when it first opened. Any changes made would have been purely in response to operational needs. The famous football field, site of many an escape attempt, which lay city side of D-wing, has been swallowed up into the grounds of the Mater Hospital. But it is a testament to Lanyon that very few changes were made over the years to the conceptual design, and that the wings as defined remained just as functional up until the jail's closure in 1996.

Details of small proposed changes, however, are recorded in letters from the prison Governors to the Ministry of Finance on a fairly regular basis. These changes usually arose from suggestions made by officers on duty. One such proposal, for instance, was made in November 1929, when a small wooden shelter with an internal radiator was requested for the officer on night guard duty in the circle area beside the glass door, to afford a view of both A- and C-wings. At that time, the whole jail at night-time was patrolled by two staff. One member of staff was continually on patrol in the wings, and he reported back to the other member in the circle area. The outcome of this proposal I am unsure of, as a myriad of minutes and correspondence passes between the two offices with no apparent resolution. The only shelter I remember in the circle area was the office used daily by the chief officers, which was much more of a command post than a shelter for night guard staff.

At its best, the Crum had around 640 cells for use at any one time, and with the ethos of prison reformers in the Victorian era being an adherence to solitary confinement, it was likely that each cell would have housed only one inmate. These cells had wooden doors originally, with purposeful but poor quality locks and keepers. Lighting was by way of gas lamps, with little if any exterior lighting in the yard areas. These fixtures and fittings continued well into the twentieth century.

In fact it was not until a report on aspects of security at the Crumlin Road in the 1920s was compiled by Captain Morgan, a member of the Board of Visitors, that certain recommendations were made. He specifically referred to cell doors, which he describes as being currently covered in sheet iron, having a gap between the door edge and the doorpost. He also states that the doorpost should have an iron receiver (keeper), rather than rely on a wooden one. He further reports that the iron sheeting should extend around the back of the doorpost, and the locks be upgraded to include an indicator as to whether they are locked or open. Reference is made to the possible availability of five-lever locks from a company in England, which are described as being impossible to pick. His report also states that standard lighting be installed in the yards as it would be presently impossible to observe anyone in those areas at times of darkness. Many of his suggestions refer to staff and their duties during particular shifts, especially night guard, and he suggests that a revamp of officers' responsibilities be undertaken. All of the recommendations he makes are based on common sense observations, and he even provides a figure of about £400 for the budget required to implement the changes, suggesting that the trades department within the prison could and would carry out the structural changes. It is clear when reading through the report that it was compiled in response to a breach of security in some way, yet there are no clear records of an escape or incident immediately prior to the date of its receipt.

The jail had seen upset during 1918, when A-wing republican inmates had wrecked virtually everything in sight, trailing guard rails down from both the twos and the threes. When you see the extent of the damage, it is hard to believe that it was done without prisoners ending up beneath the rubble. The repairs would have had to be swift, as there were few places to transfer prisoners to.

The wear and tear issues at the prison were numerous. Keeping up with the general day to day maintenance of such a vast site was a major task in itself and kept the trades officers on a fairly busy schedule. But as a result of continued occupation and relentless use, the jail had to have a rolling programme for larger scale works, purely to keep the cells inhabitable. As with many other Government establishments, any expenditure was scrutinised to within an inch of its life. In July 1933, inmates had to strip the plaster in 74 cells in B2 and B3 wards, in preparation for an outside contractor to come in and re-finish them. There were numerous letters and other correspondence passing between the departments involved and the prison authorities, and eventually the contractors themselves. A definite dragging of heels, and kicking and screaming seemed to be the order of the day when any such work was being considered, particularly where large sums of money were to be paid out. Eventually, because of rising inmate numbers, there was no alternative but to commence the work as soon as possible, and the tender was approved.

Records in the latter part of the nineteenth century show how the courts dealt with crimes which today would not necessarily have resulted in a custodial sentence for a first or even second offence.

In March of 1898, one John McMullan was convicted at Belfast of breaking and entering a private dwelling, and taking therein one coat, one vest, one pair of trousers, and a pair of boots all worth over five shillings. He was duly sentenced to six calendar months imprisonment with hard labour. Sentences like this were not confined to men either.

On 1 January 1891, Mary Breckenridge (née McBaren) was convicted of the street theft of one bag, one handkerchief and a quantity of beef under five shillings in value. She received one calendar month with hard labour for her sentence. It is not clear where Mary was incarcerated, but it was more than likely the Crumlin Road. The courts didn't seem to become any more lenient as the years progressed. In 1934 a young man called Christopher O'Keefe received a fourteen-day jail sentence for begging. In today's terms, there would be no correlation between these offences and the length of time these men and women spent in prison for having committed them. Having been to various sittings of the Magistrates Court at Laganside and elsewhere, and having kept abreast of reports in the local press, I have noticed that it is not uncommon for serial burglars to build up an impressive record of offences and arrests before the Magistrate finally sends them to prison. The court system now places less emphasis on immediate custodial sentences as the only method of dealing with offenders. This is due to dwindling jail space and inadequate staff resources. There are now all sorts of alternative case disposal methods, like community service, probation orders, suspended sentences and monetary fines. The cost of keeping someone in jail is also a severe drain on the public purse, and the courts themselves must take this into consideration when weighing up the facts of the case.

Even back in the early 1930s, the number crunchers were able to produce the figure of £67–7–0 as the cost of keeping just one inmate from the beginning of 1930 to the end of 1931. When the figures for the year beginning 1931 and ending 1932 were published, there was much rejoicing as the cost had fallen to around £61–9–0. When you consider how hundreds if not thousands of people living in Belfast at the time had to survive on a mere fraction of that, the comparison makes for depressing reading.

Again the 1930s was a time of division and unrest in Northern Ireland, and as the years went by, the numbers committed to prison grew and grew. In 1930, for instance, the number of people committed to jail reached 2,283, rising to 2,356 in 1931 and again to 2,622 in 1932. Admittedly there were all types of inmates included in those figures. Some were there on remand or awaiting trial, whilst others may have been a mixture of long-term and short-term stays. It was plain to see, though, that any consistent further increases could make the system unworkable. The Judiciary still favoured custodial sentences, however, and would continue to do so for some time after.

There is a definite train of thought today in favour of returning to a more stringent form of sentencing. Jail time today is not hard time, and I suspect there are many who would be less willing to live a life of crime if we were to return to a Victorian prison regime, and a similar zero-tolerance judicial system. The attitude of the Northern Ireland Office today is one which encourages the inmates to retain strong family links, with regular visits and close contact where appropriate. In stark contrast, the Ministry of Home Affairs received a letter from the Governor of the Crumlin Road Prison back in March 1930, in answer to the proposed introduction of a new prison rule which would have allowed inmates and their visitors to 'embrace'. In that letter his views were clear and determined when he stated, 'I think that a Prison is the last place to encourage wholesale kissing.' His reaction to the proposed rule was not only based on his moral disapproval, but on the issue of security as well. How times have changed. If we are to believe certain reports in dubious Sunday tabloids, inmates and their visitors have been allowed to go beyond the point of just embracing each other, and have at times availed of private rooms in which they have engaged in sexual intercourse. Over the years I have no doubt that there have been incidents of appeasement towards certain inmates, with security always being compromised as a result. In today's preoccupation with the issue of human rights, we can lose track of the idea of what prison is all about. There has to be a clear line drawn between what is an entitlement and what is concessionary. There is no fear of 'porridge' any more, because there is no porridge.

* * *

Life in the early days of the Crum was harsh, both inside and outside the jail, and people were often driven to steal to provide their next meal. The risks, however, were extremely high. There were those unfortunates for whom even a short sentence would have meant a death sentence, as amidst the poverty and strife in which they existed, health problems prevailed. Poor diet and a struggling health system meant that the poor or lower classes who were willing but not able to secure employment suffered from all kinds of ailments. They were often imprisoned in the Crum as it was in Victorian times, suffering from serious mental or physical illnesses, destined to die within the walls. Whilst there was little consideration given by the court for their conditions when passing a custodial sentence, the prison authorities had adopted a duty of care as such, and would have administered basic medicines and regular health checks. These would have been far from adequate to address the nature of many of the complaints, and fatalities were frequent. In contrast, it was also a place where life itself perpetuated, and mothers bore babies. Whether it was a joyous occasion or not, records of the births would have had to be kept, with any details of parentage noted in accordance with the law. The registration of both births and deaths in the jail duly took place, with earliest records starting in October 1867.

The unfortunate person to take the number one slot in the register of deaths relating to what was known then as the 'County Antrim Gaol' back on 16 October 1867, was a woman by the name of Mary J. Long. Mary was a thirty-year-old housekeeper, and was recorded as being married. There were eight columns in the register, covering the prisoner's number, date and place of death, sex, condition (whether married, bachelor or widow), age, profession and the details of inquest. The entry covering the inquest details was at first a date only, with I assume the inquest documentation being held elsewhere. In Mary's case, the word 'lunatic' has been added into the column. Following on from Mary came James Murphy, another thirty-year-old from the 'labouring class', again described as 'lunatic'. It is a term which is repeated on several occasions throughout the journal, and one can only imagine that these were people who were either criminally insane on entry to prison, or had suffered insanity as a consequence of incarceration. It immediately builds up a sorrowful and disturbing picture for the reader, regardless of the beauty and elegance of the broad sweeping penmanship. Some degree of care and attention has been taken with these registers, as would have been expected for an official document. I suspect that there would have been someone delegated to make the various entries, their skills as a legible writer going a long way towards them being chosen for the post. Also taking a place amongst the many listed were employees who had died in various circumstances in the prison. One in particular, Charles Knight, a married man who is described as a Warder of Antrim Gaol, passed away just six days before Christmas in 1871.

It is fascinating to read the descriptions of the professions of those who appear in both registers, with every conceivable industry of the day being covered. The earlier entries in and around the late 1800s have amongst them farriers, sailors, dealers and steam loom weavers. Controversially, of the women who are listed, there are quite a few whose profession has been described as prostitute. It has always been known as the oldest profession in the world, but I don't believe that there was any hint at legitimacy inferred by the authorities. Rather, the crime for which they were imprisoned summed up how they scraped a living together. What is also apparent in the deaths register is the frequency of entries in the early days. There are years where there are half a dozen or more entries, but without details of the inquest findings it is impossible to know if there was an epidemic of any kind which would have explained any rise in the figures. What I did notice was the fact that the average age of the persons named in the death register was around the low to middle thirties, with the remainder being either infants or juveniles. There was one extremely puzzling entry on the very first page of recorded deaths, and it had occurred in the early months of 1870. A young man of just fifteen years by the name of Bernard Young appears as the sixth person to have died in the care of Antrim Gaol. He is described as being a machine boy, and had probably been employed in the local mills in the town. The details of his demise stand out amongst the rest, as it is stated that he 'perished in a violent snow storm on the Wicklow mountains'. I have struggled to understand just why his death has been recorded here, unless he was in the process of being transferred to a gaol in the Republic of Ireland, with the authorities here still having custody of his person until the transfer was complete. Whatever the reason, it is bizarre to say the least.

As the century turns, and conditions in the jail improve to a degree, the register of deaths itself undergoes a slight change. The results of the various inquests, if any were directed by the Coroner, are listed in the end column. The results of these inquests show that a huge amount of people actually died from natural causes, and had often been moved from the prison confines to local hospitals in their last days to avail of proper care and attention. There were details of heart attacks, cerebral meningitis, general effects of alcoholism and in one case 'prolonged subturation of shoulder joint'. Whilst reading through the list, I recognised the name of Edmond Wylie, a young man whose inquest file I had come across in public records relating to suicides at the prison. He had hanged himself whilst in a state of acute mental depression on 20 January 1925, and there beside his entry was that of another young man by the name of Daniel McCormick, who at twenty-seven years had hanged himself just over a year after Wylie.

The incidents of suicide are all too frequent in the jail, with men rather than women appearing to choose to end their lives in this way. Hanging appears to be the most popular method, due in no small way to the fact that the options were few and far between. The cell bars on the windows provided good purchase for bed sheets, and back in 1916 one Jason Stephenson was able to use a towel and a gas bracket with which to achieve his aim.

Of course, the records of those who were executed at Belfast are of interest to most people. In truth, they are no more than any normal entry, other than the word 'executed' having been written across the columns.

As the years progress further, the register again takes on further importance in that the Coroner himself makes the entry after an inquest. In most cases, the prison authorities are given credit for giving the best care and attention possible to the deceased whilst they were in their charge. The times of accountability had arrived, and any issues of negligence could have been disastrous for the State.

The idea that many babies were born into such a hopeless and desperate situation is often harder to accept than the fatalities that happened at the prison. Where there were women, it followed that there would at some stage be children. It is not a subject I feel comfortable about dealing with. It stands to reason that of all the children who were conceived or born at the jail, there remains a distinct possibility that their descendants are alive and well today. It must be a shock to trace your family tree back to when your great-grandmother or grandfather was listed amongst the births register in a Belfast jail. I am not suggesting that there should be any shame attached, rather, that I do not wish to provide information for others to speculate upon. For that reason I will not include surnames here.

The first birth to be recorded at the prison was a little girl called Kate. She was born on 14 November 1867 to her mother Eliza Jane, and her father Robert, who was a shoemaker. The mother's married name and maiden name are both listed in the register. There are obvious issues in relation to the fathers of the children listed, with some only 'reputed' and not confirmed. There are also several cases where the details of the father's address and occupation are even less clear, as the encounters appear to be of a casual nature.

In all, it appears that at first there were at least two children born each year at the jail. Unfortunately some of their little names were to reappear in the register of deaths as infant fatalities, often not baptized before interment. Although I was able to view only scraps of the register, I can see how such documents would provide great research material for genealogists, and may provide answers to some questions which may not be available in the Public Records Office. Whilst compiling information for this book, the same phrase was mentioned on several occasions to me, that the prison was in some ways a microcosm of the society of the day on the outside.

The details held in both registers must indeed mirror social conditions in Belfast throughout the time they were in existence, and provide us with valuable information about the industrial town, as it developed into the vibrant, sophisticated city that it is today.

*   *   *

The breakdown of prisoner types in the jail would have varied considerably depending on what particular era of the prison's history you were to look at. The repetitive use of internment brought many detainees to the jail right through the early to the latter part of the 1900s, and they were often housed right alongside the ODCs, or ordinary decent criminals. When the British Government feared insurgency, they immediately reverted to internment, effectively imprisonment without trial. It may have seemed a quick fix solution, and one where they believed the intelligence they had amassed was of a quality which provided them with the names and addresses of the most active of Republicans. However, that was unfortunately not the case. The sweeps of the various Republican communities by soldiers often ended with innocent men being lifted and imprisoned. It was a shambles, and, in its indiscriminate approach, proved to be a much-needed shot in the arm for recruitment into the IRA. Young men who previously had little to do with the Republican movement saw their fathers, brothers and uncles being carted off to God knows where without trial or, in most cases, questioning.

The detainees also provided the prison officers with an additional headache in relation to security, as these inmates were often treated more favourably than those who were sentenced or on remand. Dessie O'Hagan of the Workers Party told me that when he was interned in the Crum in 1971, there was a policy of total freedom of movement on the wing, and the detainees could wear their own clothes. He found conditions extremely relaxed in comparison to a previous visit in the late 1950s. It was a flawed system which provided plenty of opportunities for internees to plan and execute escapes, and run the staff ragged with continual demands for their lawful entitlements. It was also the catalyst for a total revamp of the prison system in the North.

Without internment, and the Troubles, and every other peculiarity to the politics and conflict in our history over the last eighty years or so, our prisons would have grown certainly, but only relatively so. Without this unique set of circumstances which we have been unfortunate to inherit from previous generations, the Maze or 'Long Kesh' would almost certainly not have existed. It would be a certainty, though, that the Crum would still have come to the end of its lifespan around the same time as it eventually did. It had served its purpose, and for all its faults, and there were many, it survived for many more years than the Maze ever would.

Chapter 3
Swift Retribution

The executions aside, there were several people over the years who died in various circumstances within the confines of the jail. Tragedy, death and despair are etched into the bricks and mortar of the landings and cells of all the wings, and cannot be confined to any specific area. All manner of unfortunate events took place throughout the jail, from D-wing punishment cells and the tunnel beneath the Crumlin Road linking the jail with the court-house, to the woodyard and the prison hospital. It was not only the cons who were the victims in these matters; both inmates and officers alike can be found listed on the register of deaths at the Crum, and included among those is John McCarthy, someone I knew as a work colleague and a friend.

I suppose when I sat down and thought about it, the Crum was a place where I never felt particularly at ease during the course of a night duty. Even though there were hundreds of men locked in their cells to keep you company throughout the wee small hours, you were always alone on the landings, marking your progress at pegging clocks. The clocks were designed to record your patrol times and make sure you were adhering to those patrols. Any pegging at the clocks was recorded automatically in the control room, with whom you were also required to check in by radio transmission on a regular basis. The way most screws worked the night shift was to break it up amongst themselves, usually so all three of those working would have an opportunity to sleep at some stage. One man would remain on the landings, taking responsibility for a particular period during the night, whilst his two colleagues could read or sleep in the class office, knowing that the pegging was taken care of until their turn came around. I was never particular as to which shift I took and always found it impossible to get any real sleep when on my break. But the middle of the night from around 3 a.m. to 5 a.m. was my least favourite. During those hours, my body was at its lowest in terms of heat and energy, and I found it difficult to stay awake, constantly drifting in and out of consciousness. I had to get up from my seat, set strategically at the stairwell gate on the threes, and walk about in an effort to kick-start my circulation. I was always in fear of sleeping through an hourly peg at the clock, and would adhere meticulously to the fifteen or thirty minute checks on the suicide alerts as required.

When alone in the dead of night, it was easy to dwell on the darker aspects of the jail, and often, when tired and low, your imagination could run riot and present you with all sorts of sights and sounds. Of course this could often be helped along by some idiot with a permanent penchant for practical jokes. One such colleague I will refer to by his first name only—Nigel. Nigel had a grotesque smile etched almost daily on his face and a devious little twinkle in his eye, which belied his deeply warped notion of normality. On one particular night guard, when I had again drawn the short straw for the middle shift, taking me into those hours which I detested, I positioned my soft seat as usual at the second stairwell on the third landing, which coincidentally afforded me a good view of the circle grill. It was customary to do this so you could see the advance of any senior officers from the circle area to check on your hourly reports, and sign off on the night duty book. If by chance you failed to see him coming, the noise of the chains at the grill door were often enough to wake you from your doze.

I must point out that at some stage during the late 1980s, possibly 1986, the Prison Service made a change to the standard issue of uniform; a change which was wholly unpopular with the rank and file. Whereas we would have been distinctive in appearance from our senior and principal officers by wearing blue shirts, whilst they wore white, all shirts were duly changed to

white. It thus became almost impossible to determine at a glance
who were the chiefs, and who were the Indians.

On this particular night, I neither heard nor saw anything that
drew my attention to any comings or goings in the wing. That is
until I became aware of movement around the first stairwell gate,
level with me on the threes. I stood up from my chair and peered
into the gloom left by the shadows from the few overhead lights
which were left on in the early hours, and the more I looked, the
more I knew there was something hiding there. I glanced at my
watch, thinking that I had come to the end of my part of the shift
and one of the others had come to relieve me, but I had at least
an hour left to go. There was nothing left to do but investigate. I
congratulate myself on being one of those people who always ask
the same question when watching a 'slasher' movie—why oh why
is that girl even thinking about walking up the stairs? She should
open the door and run like fuck. It's all about common sense. So,
bearing that in mind, instead of walking directly down the
landing to the next stairwell, I walked down the stairs onto the
twos and made my way slowly towards the bottom of the
offending stairwell so I could look up. As I did, I became more
and more convinced that there was a figure standing in the
shadows looking down at me. The hairs on the back of my neck
were standing up and I could hear my heart beating like a bass
drum in my chest. When I reached the bottom of the stairwell
leading up to the threes, I summoned up what little courage I had
left and started to climb the steps. Before I reached the third step,
a figure in black, with shocking white hair and the hideous face
of an old man, turned the corner of the landing to peer down at
me. I nearly lost control of my bowels. The only reason I didn't
take flight there and then was, as the apparition presented
himself, almost simultaneously I heard laughter coming from
below me on the ones. When I looked back up towards the
stairwell, Nigel was peeling off his latex Halloween mask and
turning his long black officer's trenchcoat around from back to
front. He was killing himself laughing, and the two pricks who
were working alongside me on the wing that night were rolling
about the floor in fits. It had been a tasteless conspiracy which I

took with all the grace I could muster whilst making my way somewhat shakily down the stairs to get a cup of strong tea.

Although I have Nigel to thank for keeping me on my toes for days if not weeks after, I still had a distinctly uncomfortable feeling when nights came around again. I remember an even more absurd moment, again when perched at my vantage point on the threes during the wee small hours. On this occasion I had drifted into a short sleep, when I suddenly awoke, aware of the feeling that something or someone was watching me. I looked around me to my right and left, and below to the next landing, but I couldn't see anything obvious. As I stood up, though, my eye was drawn to the floor only a few feet from where I had been sitting. There, arranged in a semi-circular attack formation, were three small mice. They were absolutely motionless, and looked menacingly at the crumbs spread around the legs of my chair, which had fallen from the doorstep sandwich I had consumed some time earlier. At the time, all I could think about was the theme tune to *Jaws*, half expecting to be rushed by the little bandits at any moment. Crazy as it may seem, the three furry opportunists had a distinctly supernatural quality about them, and just for a split second I imagined that I was caught up in some type of Mexican stand-off, one where I was sure I would not be the last one standing. The mind, when tired, can play some seriously weird tricks.

Despite the obvious canteen humour of the screws, which was undoubtedly a coping mechanism, the reality of day to day events in the jail would often take its toll, as incidents of suicide or self-harm were prevalent. When there was an episode where someone managed to take their own life—and there were many both successful and failed attempts—they affected everyone, and not only in the emotional sense. The sight that may have greeted you when unlocking a door in the morning could be one which would stay with you for the rest of your days. Furthermore, if that person had been flagged as a possible suicide risk and the necessary checks had not been carried out, then a certain amount of blame had to be apportioned and shared equally amongst any staff on duty at the time of the death. Imagine then just how uncomfortable it would have been for a prisoner who was doubled up with someone else, someone who was hell bent on killing themselves. This I do remember happening during one of the first night shifts I worked on my return to Crumlin Road from Magilligan. Sometime during the early hours, I was awoken from my sleep by a colleague who had been responsible for the first watch period up to around 1 a.m. He shook me awake and told me that he had responded to a cell alarm on the twos, where an inmate was attempting to hold up his unconscious cell mate, who had a ligature around his neck that had tightened to a point where he couldn't remove it either from his neck or from where it had been secured around one of the cell's window bars. I shot straight out to the circle area where I met with the night duty principal officer, and we both sprinted with the cell keys he had retrieved from the control room to the second landing, where we opened the cell door. There in front of us was the young prisoner standing with his back to us, supporting the body of his much larger cell mate with all the strength he could muster. The PO and myself took an arm each of the slumped body, and a third officer was able to free the young man from the noose. Although he was still unconscious, he made a full recovery some hours later when he had been removed by ambulance to the Royal Victoria Hospital. The whole incident was a bit of an ordeal for us, but for his cell mate, who had acted with great speed and presence of mind, it was traumatic to the point where he experienced a bit of a breakdown and had to be removed to the prison hospital for treatment for shock.

The subject of suicide will always be an emotive one, and even throughout the years, the prison authorities seem to have approached the matter sympathetically and with suitable empathy for the families and loved ones of those who were left behind. Immediately after an incident of suicide had occurred in jail, an investigation was launched, and the Coroner was given every assistance for an inquest. One such tragedy I read about in records from the prison concerned a young man by the name of Ed Wylie who took his own life back in 1925. Wylie was only twenty-one years old, and hailed from 125 McTier Street in

Belfast, where he had lived with his bed-ridden father. Whatever his circumstances were, Wylie had been sentenced to five years penal servitude for committing robbery with violence. Ed Wylie had been on remand since 13 May 1924, and had his trial heard before the court only one week later on the twentieth. He was convicted on 25 July of that year and took up his place in population at the Crumlin Road. According to the prison's Presbyterian chaplain, Wylie had some concerns that although he had written letters to his father whilst in jail, they had not been answered. His guilt was overwhelming, and he had feared that as the only carer for his dad, he had driven him further into hardship, and had failed him. On the night of 19 January 1925, Ed Wylie knotted the bed sheets from his bed and hanged himself from the cell window. His body was found by the night guard, Warder Rice, and both he and his partner that evening, Warder Fraser, supplied details of their last visitations to Wylie's cell. Warder Fraser reported in his statement:

> I beg to report that I visited the convict's cell regularly during the evening. I turned out the gas about 8.25 p.m., he was then in bed. I visited his cell afterwards and by the aid of a torch lamp, I could see him in bed. The last time I saw him would be about 9.20 p.m. He was then in bed.

The document was signed J. Fraser Wdr. The image which this incident conjured up for me was one of total despair and sadness, more so because I believe that in those earlier years there may not have been structures in place to deal with poverty and illness in the communities, and families could only rely on other family members to provide support and subsistence. When the only breadwinner was removed from the equation, life was very much held in the balance. Competition for food and shelter in times such as these, the period of post World War One regeneration, would have been fierce. The Belfast we know today may still have people living near to, or below the bread line, but at least there are methods and means of identifying and addressing such social issues. Arguably, the sense of community has become more important over the years, and as trust has developed in those communities, issues such as the care of the elderly or infirm have been identified and actioned by ordinary people in those communities, neighbours no less. I don't believe, however, that the communities I refer to are in any way defined by race or religion. In fact, I would argue that the strongest bonds are those within areas where the people have gelled as neighbours without having to pin their 'colours' to any mast as such. Ed Wylie may have done something outside of the law, but his situation may have dictated his actions. Had he been faced with a similar dilemma today, and having all the support, financial or otherwise, to avail of, the outcome would most definitely have been different.

There are many reported cases of young prisoners, in particular, resorting to suicide after only a few days' confinement in the Crum. It is hard to imagine the depth of anguish and pain these people were feeling when they could find no other answer to the situation they found themselves in. Perhaps it was the thought of the sentence itself, or remorse for whatever crime they had committed.

*   *   *

Within the normal shift pattern of an officer, the one duty which I found to be the most anti-social in terms of loss of profitable time was an evening duty. After you had completed a night guard, you would have had a full day off, and then returned the following day at midday until late evening. In respect of the things you could achieve in the hours before work and the hours thereafter, it was a dead loss. I particularly hated it on a Sunday, when activity in the jail was at a bare minimum, and the day seemed to drag by, making it an almost constant struggle to stay awake.

When you were detailed a night duty in a particular wing, you invariably carried out your evening duty in that same wing on your return. As a general duties screw, I was glad to be continually moved from wing to wing, post to post, sampling the best and the worst parts of the job as I went. But at one point, I became aware that a pattern had developed, and I was being detailed most of my duties in C-wing. After having worked in C-wing on a night guard during a less than memorable Friday summer's night, I returned to carry out my shift as one of the evening duty officers on the following Sunday, and settled myself in for the long haul. This was to be a different duty altogether, however, and was to introduce me to an aspect of the prison's past which further fuelled my growing fascination.

I cannot remember the name of the senior officer who brought my attention to the fact that one of the duties an evening duty officer in C-wing was meant to carry out, but rarely adhered to, was checking the condemned cell and the drop cell. I thought he was joking at first, but when he went to retrieve the keys for the grill which led off the wing and down into that area, and returned shortly with a bunch of what looked like antiquated keys and a flash-light, I realised he was serious. I had always been aware that there was a large rectangular section of different coloured tiles on the floor of C-wing. I had been told that at one time this had in fact been a stone staircase leading down into the area where the executions took place. It was a constant reminder of what lay below, and had been covered over sometime after capital punishment had been withdrawn.

The steps down to the drop cell lay around the corner of 'C' wing, through an old door, at the edge of the yards. God knows how many times I had passed it by and never once gave it a second glance. But on that day, as soon as the so turned the key gingerly in the lock and pushed it open, I could sense that what I was about to see would be totally captivating. As we made our way down the old stone steps, I felt the hairs on the back of my neck rise, and was aware of a slight drop in temperature, punctuated by the unmistakeable odour of damp and decay. I have no idea exactly how long it had been since anyone had last visited this place. It may have been months, but could just as likely have been years. At first I suspected the torch was a prop, and that I was about to be subjected to one of the many piss-taking exercises frequently carried out by bored screws. It quickly became apparent, though, that there were very few lights in use, and this would indeed be one of our only sources of illumination. This I can say only added a surreal aspect to the experience, and I admit to having felt slightly uncomfortable at this stage. Unfortunately I was beyond the point where I could just turn around and walk back up to the wing; not because of any loss of face, but because I felt utterly compelled to continue on, as if I had no choice. Like many people, I was naturally nosy, a healthy trait I would argue, and I was genuinely curious as to what I might find there, drawn to it like a moth to the flame.

As we drew nearer and nearer to the area of the drop cell, I felt as though I was viewing all that was unfolding in front of me through the eyes of another person. I had that 'out of body' type feeling, which I would normally associate with a drunken encounter, or after having two strong pulls from my flatmate's spliff (not I may add a frequent experience).

I have never been one to accept that science can explain away all manner of strange events or phenomena, while I balance that view with a healthy cynicism of certain psychic practices. With that in mind, I can provide no explanation, scientific or otherwise, for the effects this place had on me. I feel no shame in admitting that never before or anytime since, have I experienced such an overpowering sense of dread and negativity as when I walked into the drop cell, bathed in the glow of yellow-tinged torchlight. The atmosphere was oppressive and stifling and I could feel myself becoming physically sick with fear. The weight of the despair upon my person was tangible, as if someone was pressing down on my head and shoulders, causing me real pain and discomfort. I tried to convince myself that I was being totally irrational, but couldn't for the life of me shake it off. There was very little to see in the cell, itself, no furniture or fixtures which would have identified it as anything other than an ordinary cell. That is until you cast your eyes upwards and there in the ceiling were the two halves of the trapdoor. It was a very ordinary looking piece of apparatus, but my mind wouldn't switch off, and I had to put my hand up to my mouth to avoid vomiting. I can only describe the feeling as one of sheer terror, totally uncontrollable terror. So distressing was it that I felt close to running away, in a fight or flight type of reaction. The next part of the SO's commentary I missed almost completely, and instead focused solely on getting back up into the wing as quickly as possible. I would estimate that, in all, I was down there for about ten minutes, but frankly it felt like an hour. The SO showed me the other rooms which were down there, each of which was empty and in a bad state of repair, and he enthused about the little stone tunnel which we had come through to stand in the little landing area outside the drop cell. He also pointed out a rusting grilled door, behind which I could see the original stone staircase leading back up into the wing. Back in C-wing again, we moved across to the last three or four cell doors, which lay behind a green meshed enclosure. It was then it dawned on me that what we were looking at was the condemned cell, and we had been using it as a store room for blankets and suchlike. I also realised that the hangman's cell must have been a couple of doors down towards the end of the wing. All the time I had been working there, I had been in and out of the double cell with no idea of what purpose it had originally served. Here, the condemned man had lived out his last days and nights, with two warders on rotation for permanent company. The walk to his death would have been only a few steps away, but for him it probably felt like the longest walk he was ever to take.

When we finally concluded the checks, and returned to our normal duties, I thought that I had gone ten rounds with Barry McGuigan, and I had to sit down in the class office to compose myself. Almost twenty minutes later, and after a strong cup of coffee, I slowly began to come around, and consider the events in a balanced and calculating fashion. For me, a level-headed, totally rational and fairly sceptical young man, I was deeply disturbed at what had taken place, and was confused as to why I had reacted to this place in such a profoundly negative way. There were no obvious explanations, other than the fact that I had felt some connection with the residual energy left behind by those who had lost their lives in this place some years before. At that time, I knew very scant details about the executions at Belfast, but I was aware that those people who had died in this dark and dreary place had done so in an abrupt and violent manner. The tragedy of their demise was further compounded by the refusal of the State to allow their remains to leave the confines of the prison, forever condemning them to remain prisoners, even in death, losing out on a 'proper' Christian burial on consecrated soil. If I had believed in the paranormal, in particular ghosts and such, I would have immediately equated the strange and uneasy feelings that had come over me with an encounter with one or more of those tortured souls; for I am sure if they existed anywhere, they existed there.

Years later, during the time I was compiling information for this book in fact, I turned on the television and tuned in to a programme on BBC Northern Ireland called *Inside Out*, which concentrated on local events and issues. The presenter on this occasion, Joe Lindsay, was partaking in an organised tour of Crumlin Road Jail in an attempt to highlight the prison as a possible tourist attraction for the future. He was accompanied by a film crew and members of NIPRA, or Northern Ireland Paranormal Research Association. His spooky tour took him through certain wings in the prison, with him commenting as he went. Eventually he ended up in the hanging cell, alluding to the people who had been executed there over the years, and focusing on the darker side of the prison's past. The feature on the jail was brief but atmospheric, and at one stage during an unrehearsed link, the presenter reacted quite oddly when he felt that he had been physically pushed by something or someone, when it was clear to all that at the time he was at least ten feet from the nearest person.

Around the same time as the television programme was broadcast, a radio production from the BBC was aired, presented by Gerry Anderson and entitled 'Gerry's Ghost Hunt'. Gerry Anderson, well known in the North for his witty morning radio show on BBC Radio Ulster, hosted an investigation into ghostly happenings at four locations around the Province: Richill Castle, the Grand Opera House in Belfast, the old workhouse in Derry, and the Crumlin Road Prison. Gerry was also accompanied by

Warren Coates, one of the founders of NIPRA, along with some of his colleagues, and on this occasion a psychologist by the name of Bob Curren, who I believe took his role as devil's advocate to any suggestions of paranormal phenomena quite seriously indeed. The idea for the programme had been discussed for some time, around two years in fact, and had first been linked with another presenter, but fell to Anderson to carry it forward. Whether it was the fact that good radio programmes, I believe, can create a much better atmosphere than visual entertainment ever can, or whether it was almost impossible for the listener not to be aware of and drawn into the palpable tension emanating from those taking part in the experiment, I am not sure. What I am sure of, however, is that there were things which occurred on the show that were not easy to explain away, and all who took part had an experience which they would never forget. I found it fascinating in itself just listening to what was an edited version of a twelve-hour visit to the jail compressed into nearly thirty minutes.

After hearing the programme, I tracked down and spoke with Warren Coates from NIPRA, and asked him about the function of the organisation to which he devotes more hours than his wife cares to mention. He explained that although they have been formed for over fifteen years, he and his members remain dedicated to investigating reports of paranormal activity in any situation, whether it be domestic or otherwise. He explained to me that he had formed a good rapport with Gerry Anderson over some years through his radio show, and had jumped at the chance to take part in the programme, stating that he had always wanted to visit the Crum (purely from a professional point of view I may add). Warren's story of the visit to the jail follows the plot of the programme quite closely, but he states quite categorically that when approached to do the show, he and his colleagues insisted that they were given no background, anecdotal or otherwise, into incidents at the jail, nor did they research the jail's history to obtain records or reports from which they could profit.

What transpired during the visit was remarkable and on occasions chilling. During the first part of the broadcast, Gerry speaks with security employees at the prison and is told of little incidents which they themselves have witnessed, such as the sound of whistling coming from inside one of the wings. The scene is then set, and the tour of the jail begins in earnest. I must take my hat off to Gerry for even contemplating the stunt which he agreed to in the latter part of the visit, when he remained alone in the drop cell, without any source of light, in the dead of night, for a matter of about five minutes. From his commentary, it was clear that he was less than comfortable, but he held firm for longer than I would have been capable, and I respect the small sacrifice he made for the sake of broadcasting.

Warren gave me an insight into the parts of the programme which were not broadcast, due in no small way to the escalation in the disturbing aspects of the language and behaviour of one particular spirit manifesting itself through Warren himself. Warren explained to me that he can sometimes channel an entity which is then able to answer questions and respond in speech through him. I remember this part from the programme particularly well, where the sound and voice coming from Warren is said to belong to an entity who identifies himself as a character called 'Paddy Q'. This happens as a few of the group sit down to take part in a séance in D-wing, to invite any spirits there present to come forward and identify themselves. The character of 'Paddy Q' is what Warren describes as violent and disruptive, and in his own words, 'pure evil'.

When the group moved into the jail at first, Warren was immediately aware that they were being watched, and by a spirit who had in fact been a prison warder, and not an inmate. This presence continued with them for some time throughout the visit, and Warren describes the man as old and grey, and names him as 'Bob'. It appears that Bob's role was not as an aggressor, but as a protector, curious as to their reason for being there, but guiding them in a sense, and ensuring safe passage wherever they went. Warren told me that at the time, he had described Bob to the others as a short, balding gentleman who appeared to have died of a heart attack either in or near the tunnel running under the Crumlin Road. When the producer of the programme made some enquiries after the programme had been aired, it seems that there were some details relating to just such an occurrence. There were, however, more aggressive elements in respect of the spirits engaging Warren and the others as they continued from area to area, and these caused some concern for the visitors, experienced or otherwise, at various stages. It wasn't only Warren and his team who professed to being able to see things as they presented themselves, but rather most of the others, Gerry included, witnessed things which were hard to explain away. One incident which can be heard in the broadcast was where someone pointed out a heat shimmer at the entrance to a cell in D-wing I believe. The shimmer was seen by most of the people present, and bearing in mind the jail has lain vacant and in disrepair for some years, the likelihood of an explainable heat source being responsible is slim, lending credence to the much more intriguing explanation of an apparition of sorts. We are all fascinated by the things we cannot easily reason away, and the programme achieved exactly what it intended to do: provide us with just enough of a glimpse at inexplicable events to spark our curiosity. Anderson gave a light-hearted yet balanced account of his time at the jail, and in all fairness never once was drawn towards either corner of thought. I caught up with Gerry Anderson at the BBC in Belfast, just after one of his Friday broadcasts, and he explained just how he had formed this relationship with Warren Coates and NIPRA.

> It was a funny thing, because I had been talking with people from NIPRA, speaking on the phone with Warren, on a number of occasions about various things they were doing. They obviously wanted people to get involved in the things they were doing, taking part in different investigations etc. I noticed that whenever we were talking on the radio, there was an enormous reaction to it. Literally hundreds of people would ring up and want to tell their own story, which in itself is very unusual because you normally get small amounts of people ringing up to talk to you on air about features you're discussing. You can tell sometimes when something is very sensitive or of interest, when the lights on the phones just go like that . . .

Gerry spreads his hands out at this point to emphasise the overload of calls on the switchboard.

> It's almost like a surge, you know, when the national grid lights up when the adverts appear and everybody makes a cup of tea. Everyone just phones at the one time. It's not long before you realise you are on to something. Most of the people wanted to talk about things that happened to them, and had been kind of embarrassed about it. But once the subject came up, and they thought that someone in the media had a kind of interest in it, they all wanted to come forward to tell their stories. Things they had seen, things they had experienced, they all wanted to share this. I then met with the production team and discussed the idea of teaming up with the guys from NIPRA, and going with them to the four different venues which you know were the Crum, Richill Castle, the workhouse in Derry, and the Grand Opera House, and to see exactly what they did. The first one we went to was Richill Castle, and it was terrifying, terrifying. It was a genuine seventeenth-century building, and some of the rooms had never been touched, virtually since then.

Gerry went on to describe how this had been his first encounter with anything remotely paranormal, and seemed genuinely disturbed by his experience. He then brought us to the point where they began a séance, and he witnessed Warren begin to channel as he did in the Crum.

> That was the first time I saw Warren channelling, which is when a spirit takes over his body, using it as a conduit. And he was basically in a trance. The thing that I thought was very impressive was that when the thing happens to him, and he was sitting beside me, he lets out this almost kind of death rattle, you know, and he just kind of goes aaarrrrrrgh . . . like that. Now anybody, and you can try doing that, and it's a very forceful thing, a very loud thing, and he did that for like a minute. And I tried it, and I couldn't do it for

more than ten seconds. It sounded so unreal. It wasn't a guy trying to fool me, I knew that right away. Nobody could do this. This is not a thing you can do as normal, you can't do this. This is not a guy thinking, I'm just going to do this to scare him. This is something else. I sensed right away this was different.

His account of events at Richill and the other three locations were riveting, and I could see that he was genuinely impressed by Warren and his team, and noticeably touched in some way by the various experiences he had during all of the visits. I then asked Gerry if he had started out, before recording the programme, as a sceptic, and he was clear in the fact that he sat fair and squarely on the fence. He did state that he had embarked on the series with an open mind, and admitted to never having seen anything, or taken any great interest in ghost stories or the like. Gerry then admits that after talking with NIPRA, and taking part in the phone-ins during his programme, he began to think that maybe there was something in it after all.

The scariest place was Crumlin Road, for different reasons. First of all, it's a very, very imposing place. It is very cold, both physically cold, and cold in many other ways. The wings were frightening, and also the wee tunnel connecting the jail to the court-house, and we went down there without any lights. What we would do was, we would encourage anything that might have been there to come forward. All we had down there were various noises, and we wouldn't regard them as very significant. The drop cell was very scary, and again D-wing was very scary, very scary indeed. What we did see in D-wing was a shimmer. We were standing there with all the lights out, and we saw a shimmer on one of the doors. A shimmering kind of effect. I had seen it once before in the Opera House, but this was very special. It was a piece of energy, there was no other explanation. Whatever that was there, we all saw it. And then later, we went down into the drop cell. I had a microphone on, and would remain there for some time. Of course you know that the body of the person would drop into that room, die there, and then would be laid out there for some time. People died there in that room. So Warren said to me (before remaining on my own in the room), 'Are you sure you'll be alright?' and I could see something in his eyes, and he said again, 'But do you think you will be alright?' I said yes, but I knew there was something annoying him. Anyway, Warren and the rest of them went away, closed the door, and I could feel this . . . there was something in the room, and it was very, very scary. There were no lights in the room, none at all, and I could feel the person moving about, and I lost my bottle and got out of there. And when I joined the rest of them, I said to Warren there was someone in there, and he said he knew. I asked him why he hadn't told me, and he said he didn't want to. He said that he had seen a woman and a young child in the corner of the room, and that's where I had got the feeling from.

It is clear from talking to Gerry Anderson that there was nothing enhanced during the editing of the programme for the sake of the audience, and it was very much a raw experiment, which makes great listening. He was adamant that research was never carried out prior to the visits to any of the locations, and he took great pains to point out that both themselves and NIPRA strictly adhered to this. In some ways talking with Gerry made me feel slightly more comfortable about my own experience, as I felt that someone else was not dismissing the fact that there is a force of some sort present in that particular space which manifests itself in different ways to different people.

It will be a personal decision for most of us whether we choose to believe in the spirit world and the existence of restless souls who are destined to roam the earth perpetually as ghosts, or whether we believe that physics and the power of suggestion can account for all kinds of phenomena. If we do indeed believe in some small way, is it such a stretch to equate particular locations with extreme paranormal activity? The Crum has all the credentials to be one of the most haunted buildings in Northern

Ireland, and must therefore be a natural draw for ghost-hunters and thrill-seekers alike, a fact which I am sure will not be lost on the people who hold the responsibility for utilising the jail as a tourist attraction.

My own experiences in the drop room, and those of the people who took part in both programmes, gave me the push I needed to investigate the many executions at the jail, and I found myself embarking on a journey of research which would help me to put some meat on the bones of the events which led to these people ending their days in such a violent and abrupt manner.

On a personal note, I believe that of all the ways to execute someone, hanging remains one of the most barbaric in terms of the method, and I find it morally repugnant that the post-war Government throughout the progressive 1950s and 1960s could not have addressed the issue, and found a more humane way to carry out the death sentence. When one considers the alternative methods employed in various parts of the United States where the death penalty still exists, it is easy to see that there has been some degree of thought on the subject, and this begs the question as to why the 'civilised' British did not fall into step. Surely the fact that you intend to take someone's life is the punishment, and the method should be quick and efficient. Maybe we were simply caught up in the vengeance of it all, wanting to inflict suffering as well as death on the condemned; two bites of the cherry as it were, with a good old-fashioned hanging fitting the bill. Regardless of my objections to hanging as a method, I still believe that capital punishment for certain crimes would, or at least could be a deterrent, considering the fact that the perpetrators of these vile crimes place so little value on other people's lives in today's throw-away society. But I do think we would have to consider the alternative methods open to us, and remove the bloodlust from the equation.

*   *   *

There were in fact seventeen men executed in the Crum since it opened its doors in 1854. All of those were hanged, five from various scaffold type gallows erected within the walls of the prison general; the rest would have availed of the hangman's noose in the setting of the executions room. All of the remains of the seventeen men were interred in an area frequently described as the 'lime pit', which I remember as being just beyond the prison hospital at the rear of both B- and A-wings. The bodies were considered to have been the property of the State, and would have been quietly conveyed to an unmarked grave after execution, to remain there in perpetual incarceration. However, the body of one man executed, Tom Williams, was to be removed from its resting place within the jail some fifty years after his execution in 1942, after a lengthy battle by Republicans to free a comrade from (in their words) remaining a continual 'political hostage'. This is poignant, as it appears that Williams was arguably the only political prisoner to be executed in the Crum, even though the history of Northern Ireland has been littered with murders of so-called legitimate targets. Some people will argue that Williams' actions were those of a combatant during a time of occupation, and try to remove him from association with the other 'ordinary decent criminals'. Granted, the company Williams remained buried beside for so many years were a mixture of violent or disturbed human beings, who for one reason or another lost control along with their ability to reason, ultimately reverting to the act of homicide. To others, murder will always be murder, regardless of how you dress it up; and Tom Williams did take a life, whilst of sound mind and fully aware of the consequences of his actions. We will all have opinions as to who, if any, were worse or better. There has since been another body removed from the confines of the jail, but under different circumstances. Michael Pratley is now laid to rest on consecrated ground, and the circumstances of his execution and re-interment will be covered in due course.

The first unfortunate to be hanged at the Crum was a soldier by the name of Robert O'Neill, who murdered a colleague, Corporal Robert Brown, at his barracks in North Queen Street. He shot Brown in cold blood, and after trial, was found guilty of murder and sentenced to death by hanging to be carried out originally on 5 May 1854. The execution was delayed because of an appeal, and only after the circumstances were considered, was it carried forward to 21 June 1854. The promise of an execution for that particular Wednesday had the locals gathering on the Crumlin Road in an almost carnival mood, from the previous Sunday right through until the appointed day. The local press remained so highbrow and morally aloof as to describe the gathering as being comprised of the lower classes, a wholly unfortunate rabble who could not see past the spectacle to the tragic outcome of one human being's life, who had himself become drawn into a terrible cycle of events with dire consequences. In fact the majority of the revellers to line the Crumlin Road on the morning of the execution were females. They, like the others who had bothered to rise early enough in order to try and catch a glimpse of the scaffold, were restricted to observing the spectacle from the pavement outside. The *Newsletter* at the time reported that 'The more respectable portion of the public who may desire to witness the affecting scene or those whose duty may compel them to be present will be admitted to the inner area of the prison.' At eleven o'clock that morning, the sentence was carried out and the prison Governor, Mr Forbes, had the black flag raised above the jail.

The same scaffold was used again for the execution in 1863 of Daniel Ward. It is possible that although the gap between these two executions was nine years, the scaffold remained as a semi-permanent structure, in anticipation of further events. Whatever the case, it would have been a grim reminder to the rest of the residents of the Crum as to the State's predilection for capital punishment. Ward was convicted of the murder of an acquaintance, Charles Wilgar, at Shaw's Bridge, and subsequently faced the hangman on an April morning. The murder became known as 'The Ballylesson Murder' and drew considerable press and public interest at the time, so it was no surprise that the crowds reappeared for his execution. The evidence against Ward was considerable, notwithstanding the fact that the murder weapon was recovered almost immediately at the scene, but witness statements provided evidence of the movements of both parties prior to the act itself. Both Ward and Wilgar had left a friend's house together that evening, 10 May 1863, at half past six. A broken watch found in Wilgar's pocket had been stopped with the force of an impact, and from this it was deduced that he had been murdered just before seven-fifteen. Ward was seen to leave the area of the murder some time around seven-thirty, and when arrested the next day at his home, had, as police described, 'some money about him' for which he could not account. Not what you would call a perfect murder. Amongst the upper classes, there were those who called for the sentence to be passed in the privacy of the jail itself, so as to remove the spectacle aspect. The irreverence shown by the people gathered at the jail was, I suspect, hard for them to accept, as indeed they may have been tainted by any association whatsoever.

John Daly was next to forfeit his life almost thirteen years later to the day, on 26 April 1876. With this obvious gap between executions, the question of capital punishment was debated at length in the press, though frankly there would have been little hope of the sentence being commuted to life imprisonment because of public opinion. Daly had developed domestic problems at home, with regular arguments with his wife Mary Ann. Both were drinkers, and the marriage was a mixed one, with Daly a Catholic and Mary Ann a Protestant. At the end of his tether one evening, he had thrown her out of his house, only to find her and her alcoholic aunt Margaret Whitley there the next day. After a stand-up row, Daly beat Margaret Whitley to death. There would have been little doubt about Daly's guilt, and not much in the way of an argument offered up in his defence. I suspect that a man being portrayed as a woman beater, or worse, a woman killer, would have carried much the same stigma as it does today. Of course certain documented domestic matters are given consideration today in the courts, and can lend some weight in respect of mitigating circumstances. Domestic violence and continual mental and physical abuse can and frequently do happen to males as well as females. Things were much more black and white in the latter part of the nineteenth century. You were either guilty or you weren't. Mary Ann's mother had described her daughter at the time of the trial as being the 'unfortunate wife', but in truth, I suspect they were both as unfortunate as each other, having equally contributed to the escalation of violence which ended in such tragedy.

Daly was hanged in another location at the Crum, out towards the site of the new prison hospital, and I presume a new scaffold had been erected for the job.

It was another thirteen years before the next execution in the Crum, and again it was for a man who had killed a female, his partner no less. Arthur McKeown beat his partner, Mary Jane Phillips, to death, after a domestic incident in August 1888, an incident which was given the title of 'the Robert Street Murder'. He was executed just five months later in January 1889. When you realise just how short the period between the incident itself and McKeown's execution was, it gives you a good indication as to how efficient or possibly flawed the then legal system was. In today's criminal justice system, the mechanics of the legal bureaucracy from time of arrest, through any incarceration to eventual trial, not to mention sentencing, are long and somewhat protracted. The appeals system, in full use today, does not appear to have been readily available to the convicted of the time, and retribution was swift to say the least.

Again the crowds turned out for the promise of a hanging, and District Inspector McArdle of the RIC watched over his forty-strong contingent of officers from within the hall of the court-house across the road, ready to quell any boisterousness or worse. Shortly before the appointed hour of eight o'clock in the morning, the prison Governor, Mr Coulter, came to the front gate to escort five members of the press inside to witness the events. The press members were taken along to the end of the east wing, or D-wing as it was dubbed, where stood erected the scaffold for the hanging. The scaffold had been built up to the level of the corridor at the end of the wing, providing a short and uninterrupted walk for the condemned man and his escorts, and was much praised by the hangman himself, a man given the title of 'the Bradford Celebrity', James Berry. Berry's ten-year-old son was playing around the bottom of the gallows whilst his father adjusted the rope on the iron cross-beam in readiness for his task. The press made a point of describing Berry as an amiable man, with anything but a severe countenance, but nevertheless strong and very capable. He was candid when interviewed, and almost jovial when he admitted to having 'pushed off' more than one hundred human beings so far during his career. He then showed them the rope of the day, and informed them that he had used it on at least three previous occasions, taking pains to point out several strands of silk thread interwoven through the many coils. He was a man who did not seem to struggle with his conscience in any great way, and took satisfaction in a job well done, a perfectionist. The last few moments for McKeown were, like those who were to come after and those who had come before, almost choreographed. The executioner came forward to meet him as he left the condemned cell and completed the pinioning of his arms, and he was led to the scaffold and positioned above the drop. Here he had his legs strapped, and when the noose was finally placed around his neck and adjusted, a white cap was placed over his head, and the deed was done without pause. It was described by one press member as a 'sickening spectacle'.

In August 1894, John Gilmore, only twenty-one years of age, was hanged at the same scaffold as McKeown, for the murder of Lyle Gardner, an elderly farmer who lived close to Gilmore's own family holding outside Ballymoney. Gilmore was said to have struck up a relationship with Gardner's daughter, and had gotten her pregnant. The baby had arrived in early April of that year, and Gardner had talked about taking some action against Gilmore, possibly for monies in respect of the child and its keep. Relations were difficult to say the least, and on 30 April, an argument had ensued in the yard area of Gardner's house between him and Gilmore. After a time Gilmore skulked off, and made his way into Ballymoney, where he purchased a single-barrel fowling gun, some powder and shot, and returned later to Gardner's home. He was seen by some of the family just moments before he fired his weapon through the kitchen window and shot Lyle Gardner in the shoulder as he undressed at the fire. Gardner died from his wounds later that night. Police arrested Gilmore the next day, and after a brief search found the weapon secreted in bushes near his house. He had only bought enough powder to secure one shot, and that was all it had taken. At five o'clock on the morning of 17 August 1894, the then Governor of Belfast Jail, Governor Murphy, entered the condemned cell and spoke with Gilmore. He was said to have slept relatively well, and was already dressed and washed. There would be no press at his execution, and after breakfasting on tea and toast, he was led to the scaffold and hanged at the appointed hour of eight in the morning. His parting statement was that he was sorry for committing the offence, he admitted the justice of his sentence and hoped that God would have mercy on his soul.

* * *

The Crum greeted the new century with the optimism, or possibly the pessimism, of events to come, by the installation in 1900 of a permanent means of execution in C-wing. I suspect the ad hoc arrangement for the erection of scaffolds for any impending hangings would have been contentious in relation to the matter of expense, and the Ministry of Finance held very tight purse-strings. If business for the hangman's noose were to be brisk, a permanent solution to the problem would have been favourable. It was also the first step in taking the execution out of the public view for ever. No doubt the crowds would still attend to soak up any atmosphere, and be first to see the notice appear pinned to the front of the prison, but it was nevertheless less of a sideshow.

First to avail of this contraption in 1901 was William Woods, a peddler of wares in the Antrim area. Woods was no stranger to the law, having previously served a substantial prison sentence for the manslaughter of a woman in 1890. Manslaughter was, I consider, a total let-off as far as Woods was concerned, as he had in fact tied Mary Irwin, a drinking partner, to a cartwheel and hacked her to death with a scythe. His accepted defence was that he had been provoked on numerous occasions by Irwin, and the jury in their wisdom had spared him from the gallows. He was released from prison in 1899, and unfortunately had taken to staying with Bridget McGivern at her small cabin in Eagry when his business took him that way. During one particular stay on 25 September 1900, he attacked and cut the throat of Bridget McGivern as she lay beside him in bed, and upon doing so, handed himself in to local police in Bushmills village, making a full and frank confession. Woods was believed to be suffering from a state of mental illness, and was most likely drunk when he attacked Bridget at her own home, leaving her young son to make the gruesome discovery the next morning. In fact, he had locked the young lad and his sibling in the cabin with their mother's body, which was still warm when police arrived. She had been cut from ear to ear. Woods had a long record of violence, with no less than thirty-two convictions for assault on police and at one time a magistrate. Although his actions may have been due in no small part to his condition, a guilty verdict for murder was returned, and the death sentence was imposed. His mental state was evident when, after sentence was passed, he replied to the court, 'Oh, it's not as bad as a bad marriage.' The eleventh of January 1901 was the date of his hanging, and reports from a witness described how a quantity of blood had escaped his nose as his neck dislocated, with a slight bulging of his face and his left eye being left partially open. Woods had died violently, but no less violently than his victims. In his case particularly, the punishment did indeed fit the crime. It would be a further eight years, 19 August 1909 to be exact, before the hangman was to return and carry out his next job.

Richard Justin died at the hands of the executioner for the horrible crime of beating to death his own child Annie Thompson. He had a history of physically abusing her, and at some point he went beyond the pale, and inflicted such terrible injuries on her that she was unable to recover. On 12 March 1909, Justin beat little Annie with an iron bar to a point where the coroner found the case one of the most disturbing he had ever seen. Justin's defence counsel, Mr T.J. Campbell, had his work cut out for him, and found little to argue against several witness statements from neighbours who had heard the abuse taking place over a matter of months before her death. When he was hanged on that day in 1909, it was fitting he was within half a mile of the place in the New Lodge where Annie lost her life.

The pattern which seems to emerge in imposing death sentences at Belfast appears to be in relation to the murders of women or children. There are no statistics available, however, to measure just how differently these particular crimes were dealt with as opposed to those involving male victims. Society today is, I suspect, just as condemning of those who prey on the weak or defenceless as it would have been back in the Victorian or Edwardian era. However, without the death sentence being available, the punishments meted out by the courts today seem disproportionate to a point of being totally inadequate. Women and children have always been, and will forever be, considered as particularly vulnerable; and when the modus operandi is violent to the extreme, the impact is multiplied.

It was inevitable then that in 1922, the death sentence was carried out on Simon McGeown, an ex-soldier, for the murder of a seven-year-old girl by the name of Maggie Fullerton. McGeown had forced the youngster to accompany him to Shaftsbury Estate, and after killing her, had dumped her body on the grounds. The all too familiar story of child abduction and molestation, which today, in our less than moralistic society, is sickeningly frightening to read about and deal with, must have been extremely hard to comprehend in a time when faith and religious identity were of the utmost importance. I can't imagine many tears being spent on McGeown's passing.

* * *

I am not sure why the Republicans did not fight to secure the release of the remains of the next person hanged at the Crum, as they did for Thomas Williams. Michael Pratley was believed to have been involved in a notorious murder in 1922 of a prominent Belfast Unionist, and if true, would have clearly been associated with the Irish Republican Army, who had supposedly carried out the act in what they described as 'a reprisal for the many atrocities against Catholics in the North'. Perhaps Republicans were reluctant to include Pratley because he was convicted of, and hanged for, a totally different murder altogether, a murder which began as a robbery and went horribly wrong. Had his involvement in the robbery not singled him out as a criminal, and had he been convicted of and hanged for a political murder, I suspect he may have been eligible for consideration as a Republican hero, with his remains fought for just as vigorously as Williams' were. Pratley's warrant of conviction and sentencing lies bundled in the Public Record Office, within the statements and papers relating to the murder of a prominent Unionist MP in 1922, yet he was hanged for a murder he was to commit some two years later.

The reports of the death of W.J. Twaddell in the local media of the time read like an excerpt from a spy novel, with a breathtaking running gun battle between police and enemies of the State. The reality of the last few minutes of the West Belfast MP's life was tragic, and the way in which he was murdered was particularly cowardly to say the least. He was shot in the back as he walked along Lower Garfield Street to open his well-established draper's shop late in May of that year. One witness to the incident was Marshall Coulter, a caretaker from the YMCA building in Wellington Place.

Coulter recalled falling in step just behind Mr Twaddell as he strode up Lower Garfield Street that morning, and as they approached an entry which led to the rear of a public house called The White Cross, five men stepped out into the street. Coulter saw the first man shoot the draper in the back with a revolver, and then a second man came forward, also carrying a revolver, and shot Twaddell several times in the back as he lay on the ground. The group of men then hurried away towards Royal Avenue, with one of the gunmen walking backwards to deter any followers. Mr Coulter did follow, and was shot at himself close to the 'picture house corner', but not before taking time to look closely at the men and their features. He apparently continued following the men up until the point when he witnessed a police officer (District Inspector Ryall) taking a shot at the retreating men.

Ryall himself reports having taken two shots at the gunmen on Upper Garfield Street, and it was he who later identified Michael Pratley as being one of the gunmen. Ryall also stated that had it not been for his gun jamming, he may have got a few more shots off as the men disappeared into the Smithfield area. Pratley was distinctive in the fact that he had a 'kick out' with his left foot, and both Ryall and another witness had been drawn to this particular characteristic. That abnormality was in fact due to Pratley having a wooden leg. Pratley, however, wasn't identified at the time, and in fact, had he not been caught red-handed some two years later for the murder of Nelson Leech, he may never have been considered a suspect. Leech was a wages clerk and general book-keeper for a firm by the name of Purdy and Millards, and would have been engaged every Friday in the making up of employees' pay packets. Whilst doing just this on 7 March 1924, three armed and masked men burst into the office, and attempted to rob the premises. Nelson Leech went to raise the alarm, but in the following minutes he was shot and fatally wounded by one of the gang. The shooting was heard by a police constable on duty, Francis Morteshed, who was able to give chase to the robbers, eventually catching up with one of them. He survived an attempt by the man to shoot him when a gun was pointed at him at close range during a struggle but failed to fire correctly. This man was Michael Pratley.

The case against Pratley could not have been more watertight, and his subsequent warrant of conviction and sentence from the court dated 10 April 1924 made grim reading, stating he was, 'To be hanged by the neck until he is dead on Thursday the eighth day of May 1924 pursuant to Warrant to the under Sherriff in that behalf.'

* * *

I am sure that during the many years of expeditious trials and questionable procedures, one or more people convicted and executed for the crime of murder were totally innocent. As the laws of the land have changed, and the burden of evidence has tipped to weigh more favourably towards the accused, we are duty-bound to provide a fair trial, and a conviction based on there being no reasonable doubt as to the guilt of that person. When I read about the circumstances of the murders of Maggie and Sarah McCauley at their farmhouse in Armoy in May 1928, and the later arrest of William Smiley for those murders, I was uncomfortable with the strength of the evidence against him which led to his conviction, and inevitably his execution in August the same year. Smiley had been in the employment of the McCauleys as a farm labourer, which gave him reason to be in and around the house on the day in question. The linchpin of the case against Smiley was that £40 was reported taken from the farmhouse around the time of the murders, and on his arrest, he was in possession of £30 hidden in his boot. Smiley openly admitted to taking money from the house but strongly denied any involvement in the women's murder. The bodies had been discovered by a servant in the household, Kate Murdoch, who in turn informed Smiley, and it was he who then rushed to Armoy to inform local police, and was heard to tell locals along the way of the news he was relaying. When police began to treat him as their main suspect, and interviews took place, Smiley made slight variations to his story but still maintained his innocence.

Of course, this took place some eighty years ago, and information in relation to the evidence put in front of the court is almost impossible to access. But certain questions in relation to forensics, and in particular trace and residue from the murder scene, should surely have been a huge part of the Crown's case against Smiley. A shotgun had been used as the murder weapon and was left lying along with the victims on the fateful afternoon, providing police with several opportunities to obtain vital evidence to link the weapon with the killer. The case as reported seems to have weighed heavily on circumstantial evidence alone, and regardless of Smiley's continual denials, he was hanged on 8 August 1928. On that day the sun shone brilliantly, and Governor Long handed Smiley over on the demand of the Sheriff just before eight in the morning. It was reported that Smiley had found his saviour in Christ some weeks earlier, and had gone to his end with the trace of a smile on his lips.

We know only too well that in our current criminal justice system, Smiley, amongst several others mentioned, would have had a fighting chance, and may very well have escaped conviction, regardless of innocence or guilt. Our trust in this system to deliver retribution on our behalf defines our society as being civilised, yet at times we can all react emotively to particular crimes and the seeming powerlessness of the court to exact the revenge we so desperately desire. Revenge may appear to be too strong a word, but I think, deep down, we would all like to adopt the 'eye for an eye' attitude, and I don't believe it makes us any less civilised. The most abhorrent crimes, in my eyes, are those which have children as victims, and whether it was right or wrong, or for that matter unprofessional, when I occasionally encountered some inmates whom I knew to be sex offenders, more specifically paedophiles, I had an overwhelming desire to see them come to harm. Many of them had a smugness which I could not understand, as if they were proudly wearing their label, unashamed and remorseless. I didn't want their time in jail to be easy. I wanted them to be uncomfortable. I wanted them to suffer abuse and physical harm from other inmates, and, hand on heart, I believe I may have turned my back if someone had instigated an attack on any of them. Since becoming a parent, instinct has naturally made me more vigilant as to the existence of sex offenders living amongst us in our communities, and even less forgiving of crimes perpetrated against children. I cannot turn a valve and shut off this emotion, but I can and have learned to deal with such incidents I come into contact with, in a balanced and professional manner.

* * *

Samuel Cushnan was the next man to be dispatched at the hands of the hangman, on 8 April 1930 to be exact. Cushnan's case was one of pure greed, and he had laid quite elaborate plans to commit an act so dastardly, there would be few people shedding a tear at his passing. Cushnan was a farm labourer and worked in the area outside of Toomebridge, which was very rural and remote. He had actually known and worshipped at the same parish church as his intended victim, James McCann, a postman. McCann had a regular postal run in the direction of Crosskeys, and it was well known that he would cycle to the area on a Thursday to deliver around £60 worth of pension cheques, in time for them to be cashed on Friday by the recipients. Cushnan had already decided to ambush McCann by way of inviting him to stop off for a drink from a poteen bottle during his journey, just around an entrance to a farm known as Harris's Lane. When McCann took Cushnan up on the offer, and took a long pull from the bottle, Cushnan reached into the hedgerow and took out a single-barrelled shotgun and shot him. His planned escape was to be by bicycle, but he found he would have to pass some workers in a top field, so he took to a ditch to make his way to a field where he had planned to carry on topping potatoes as was usual. On his way, though, and in his urgency, he snagged his coat on a bush close to the murder scene, and was also witnessed hurrying to his alibi destination by a local woman, Mrs Robinson, and her niece. She engaged Cushnan in conversation, saying, 'What's the hurry, Sammy?' but was given a less than satisfactory response from him. She also noted that his boots appeared wet, even though the morning was particularly dry, probably due to him negotiating several drains along his way.

The piece of material at the murder scene was tested forensically, and matched to the coat he had been wearing at the time. Advances in the science had actually enabled investigators to establish what Antrim loom had produced the bolt of cloth from which the jacket had been cut, and further enquiries had established the distribution of the jackets to local retailers. Evidence against the accused was substantial, including the stock of a shotgun, possibly the murder weapon, found at his home. There were other bits and pieces recovered close to the scene of the crime, and all pointed towards Cushnan as the murderer. Local press reported on the day of the execution that a small crowd had gathered, kneeling in the mud outside the gates, and had offered prayers on his behalf. Major Long passed the prisoner over to the Sheriff, and Cushnan took his final twelve steps in this life, and shook hands with the hangman.

The execution of Cushnan was the first of four to be carried out in the 1930s, in consecutive years no less. In 1931, Thomas Dornan, a turfcutter from boglands near Ballymena, was hanged for the double murder of two sisters, Bella and Maggie Aiken. Bella had been having a relationship with Dornan, a married man, and had fallen pregnant by him, which would have been scorned at the time. She had given birth to the child, and Dornan had entered into an agreement with a local solicitor as to the amount of monies he would be willing to pay in respect of the child. He had agreed to pay six shillings weekly to Bella, and had in fact paid her £18–12 shillings up to the day of the murder. We are not quite sure what sparked his murderous rage, but he turned up to look over the area where the two sisters were working along with some others, before casually strolling away. He returned later with a shotgun and chased the women across the bog, firing until they were dead. He had in fact shot one of the sisters six times, and the other four, a sight which was witnessed in disbelief by James Aiken, the brother of the two girls. There was no need for a lengthy trial as the incident had been witnessed by several of the other turfcutters working alongside them, and Dornan's guilt was clear. His own defence counsel in the form of Wm. Lowry KC and Jas. McSparran BL, had little to offer in negation, and did not even call the accused to give evidence. He was sentenced to death and hanged on 31 July 1931, less than two months after the murders.

The next hanging at Belfast was unique in the sense that the man convicted and sentenced was not a citizen of the North of Ireland, but was in fact an American. Even more intriguing was the fact that his victim was also from foreign soil, a Turk no less. Eddie Cullens was described as a film operator from New York, and together with two Turkish men, Achmet Musa and Assim Redvan, formed a bona fide business agreement to show to the world a man considered to be the oldest living human being at

156 years, Zara Agha. The four had travelled to England and were to become associated with the Bertram Mills Travelling Circus, in which they were billed as a human interest sideshow. It was clear that all was not well in the three-way partnership, and it seems Cullens had laid plans to get rid of Musa at least once before. Perhaps it was through greed, but whatever the reason, he wanted to lure his victim to a place where he believed he could leave him behind without his identity being discovered. The pair set off to visit Northern Ireland, staying at Ryans Hotel at Donegall Quay on their arrival.

Cullens was ever the ladies' man, and soon took up with a young woman and her friend, taking them on day trips in an automobile to Bangor. On one such day, a Sunday, Cullens had a flat tyre, and with no garage open to mend it, he reverted to using the spare wheel. As he removed a cloth from the driver's door pocket, a blue and white ladies' bathing cap fell out onto the roadside, and one of the young women asked why he had needed it. Cullens told her that he bathed daily, and never wished to get his hair wet. The cap was to become just one of the little details which would lead to Cullens' downfall. The body of Musa was found in a ditch at the side of a road near Seskin, Carrickfergus, on 4 September 1931 with a single gunshot wound to the head. He was totally naked save for this distinctive blue and white bathing cap on his head. Both Cullens and Musa had been integrating socially on their visit to the North not only with the young women, but with Mr Ryan and his wife, who were privy to details of their business and personal relationship. In fact, when Cullens was eventually caught up with, for he was no longer in the North at the time police had begun their investigation, he would try and use Ryan himself as an alibi. It was not long, however, before the police turned their attention towards his residence in Leeds, and it was there that the murder weapon was recovered.

The case against Cullens was virtually open and shut in that it took the jury less than half an hour to unanimously return a guilty verdict and convict him of the murder of his partner. The original date for his execution was 29 December 1931, but his appeal was entered and heard on 1 January of the new year. The defence team for Cullens consisted of William Lowry KC and Bernard Fox, and, despite their most diligent efforts, the appeal was fruitless and Cullens was to be hanged just twelve days later. A member of the Jewish faith, Cullens was administered to by Rabbi Shachter over the last few weeks of his life. He never admitted to the murder, and managed to convince the Rabbi of his total innocence, to a point where Shachter was reported to say to the press on leaving the jail after the execution, 'He went to the scaffold with the deep conviction that his hands were clean and clear of the blood of this man.' It seems that Cullens was forever the conman, right up to the last.

*   *   *

The case of the murder of Minnie Reid, a young woman living in the town of Portadown, was one which my mother was able to recall some detail of, though I must stress not from her own living memory, as she would have me state quite clearly that she was a child of the 1940s, not the 1930s. My mother and father were both brought up in Portadown, and she clearly recalled childhood car journeys with her father during which, when passing Derryane, an area out along the old Dungannon Road, he would point out to her the spot where Minnie's body was found slain in the bushes. This fascination he showed would have been typical of people in close-knit communities, in particular rural or market towns of that era, where such an event would live on in people's memories for a considerable length of time. Minnie's murder was not a crime of passion, but one it seems where a philanderer had become cornered by making the fatal mistake of getting one of his girlfriends pregnant, whilst agreeing to marry the other. The philanderer in question was Harold Courtney, a 22-year-old lorry driver from the Dungannon area, who it was believed savagely attacked and murdered a heavily pregnant Minnie when he lured her out to Verners Corner. Her partly exposed body was found by children playing in the area around a week after she was murdered, a sight which would have been gruesome because of the defensive wounds to her hands, and her throat having been cut. The ground around the body, however, showed no signs of a struggle, leading the investigating officer to conclude that she had known her killer.

At first, Courtney denied having had any contact with Minnie for some time, and said that the only reason he could not account for his movements at the time of her death was the fact that he travelled about with his job and couldn't remember where he was. In fact, Courtney had contacted Minnie days before, and asked her to meet him out by a public house called Verners Inn, just a short walk from Vernersbridge train halt. He himself had hired a car in Dungannon from Robert Ardres, a hackney owner, and had driven there to meet up with Minnie that evening. A witness, Olive Symington, remembered seeing the dark blue car on the night of the murder at a place close to the scene itself, and actually picked the car from an identification parade consisting of several other vehicles. When the evidence looked to be overwhelming, Courtney began to change his story, saying that he had driven out to Derryane to see her, but had not actually met her. There was some medical evidence submitted at the trial which suggested that the wounds on Minnie Reid's body were consistent with those inflicted in suicide incidents. However, attention was drawn to the blood-stained cut-throat razor, which had been found exactly 13ft 7 inches from her body during a fingertip search of the crime scene, and consequently, after five long days, and fifty witnesses, Courtney was convicted. He was hanged on the morning of 7 April 1933. Large crowds gathered outside the gates of the jail, including members of his close family. A sombre mood was maintained, and his departure from this world was described as dignified.

*   *   *

The legacy of World War Two in terms of the North of Ireland was the loss of many young men and women who died alongside their allies to defend the free world from Hitler's tyranny. There were some, however, who took the opportunity to profit from the situation in continuing their own war against an occupying force, a force which was already heavily committed in other parts of the world, ably assisted by volunteers from north and south of the border. The IRA did not let up in their lengthy campaign against the forces of the Crown, and benefited from the shortfall in manpower in the local constabulary and the Army garrisons. On 5 April 1942, a small group of men armed with handguns met up in the Kashmir area of Belfast, intent on attacking a police patrol. All were IRA members, and amongst them was Thomas Williams, a ranking officer, who was himself just nineteen years of age. Along with Williams were Joseph Cahill, Harry Cordner, James Perry, John Oliver and Patrick Simpson, the eldest of the men being only twenty-one. Williams and his group, on seeing a police car approach them, opened fire, hitting the car several times. The police were able to give chase to the gang, and pursued them into Cawnpore Street, where they were seen to enter a house. It was not long before the police officers surrounded the house, and Constable Patrick Murphy took it upon himself to approach the back door of the property. The exact events of the next few minutes are not entirely clear, as there was shooting from all areas of the kitchen or 'scullery'. Williams claimed to have shot the constable, as did Cahill and indeed Perry, and no less than five bullets were removed from the dead police officer.

The case made legal history in Ireland at least, when all six men were convicted of the murder, and all sentenced to death, to be hanged on the morning of 18 August of that year. The IRA were less than popular at the time of the trial, and did not have the support that they professed to have during the later times of conflict, in particular the 1970s and the 1980s. However, what did not sit well with moderate-minded nationalists of the day was the fact that a court under the jurisdiction of the Crown was about to hang six Irish Republicans. A legal appeal was launched immediately and, on 21 August, it upheld the verdict of the original court. All appeared to be lost as the revised date for the hangings was set as 2 September, less than two weeks away. The campaign to save the lives of the men began in earnest, and several petitions were drawn up and signed by countless thousands of people, politicians and clergy alike. All but one of the accused were given a reprieve just two days before the set date. Williams was to be the only member of the gang to hang for the murder. It must have been an impossible position for the authorities at the time, who could not be seen to bow down under pressure from the public, and had to adhere to the sentence as decided by the court. Whatever the outcome, there was never going to be a victory for either of the interested parties, and in some ways, the fact that one out of the six comrades was to stand alone to face his nemesis only served to raise public sympathy.

The body of Tom Williams was buried alongside those who had been executed before him, unmarked, in a burial pit at the rear of B-wing. That is where some believe the story began rather than ended.

Joseph Cahill, one of Williams' co-accused, went on to become a veteran figure within the Republican movement, and years later he recalled the conversations he had with his friend and fellow volunteer as they faced the spectre of the hangman together. Cahill was clear that Williams could not bear the thought of his remains lying anywhere other than the Republican plot at Milltown Cemetery, especially not in a prison grave, stating that he would die as a Republican and wished to be buried as one. The campaign for the release of Williams' remains continued for over fifty years, and with mounting pressure on the British Government from Republicans, and in light of the delicate peace which was painstakingly brokered in the middle of the 1990s, the decision to relinquish his body was taken in 1995. Many would have claimed this act to be yet another form of appeasement to the Republicans, and argued against such a blatant reversal in policy. Others saw it as a small yet significant gesture in the British Government's recognition of the armed struggle as a 'war' against an occupying force, and Williams as having been a soldier rather than a terrorist. I believe the Republicans had already decided that the way forward towards a lasting peace, and the only realistic avenue to pursue their dream of a united Ireland, would be through all-inclusive negotiations—the ballot box rather than the Armalite. But like all political parties constantly rutting against their opposites, it was sometimes the small victories which were the sweetest. Of course, the process to identify and remove the right person from the grave would not have been easy, as it was unmarked, and in fact DNA profiling was eventually used to determine which were indeed the remains of Williams. After releasing the body some time later, the wishes of Tom Williams were carried out, and he was re-interred at Milltown.

To my surprise, I was informed recently that the remains of Michael Pratley were also identified, removed and re-interred at the request of members of his family. His identification was less of a problem to the authorities, as the unusual gait with which he walked was down to the fact that he had a wooden leg. I cannot remember the event being covered by the local press, but if it was, it was certainly low-key. This must surely open the floodgates for families of the other fifteen to make similar representations. The task would be one of some enormity, but may be a possibility if the prison were destined to become a tourist site. When the bodies of the executed were being buried by their fellow inmates, there was little attempt at creating distinctive graves. A grave was dug in a general area normally at the rear of A- and B-wings, and the body interred with a coating of ashes laid above it. If and when another grave had to be dug, the layer of ash would alert the grave diggers to the presence of another grave, and the dig would commence somewhere else. Hardly a great plan, but one which was deemed suitable at the time. When I was lucky enough to be invited back for a personal tour of the jail by Jane Campbell from the First Minister's Office, she pointed out two of the markings on the outer wall which had been scratched into the stones by the burial party. The clearest of them were the initials S.McL and the year 1961. This inscription referred to the remains of Samuel McLaughlin, whilst the other initials H.C. and the year 33, marked the date and final resting place of Harold Courtney.

* * *

Over twenty years later, the executioner was to return to the Crum to hang Samuel McLaughlin for the murder of Nellie McLaughlin. McLaughlin was originally from Derby, and during what was said to be a drunken episode, battered his wife to death at the home of her mother in Cloughmills in October 1960. Circumstances are not exactly clear as to their relationship, but substantial petitions from both the Cloughmills area, and his home town of Derby, were testament to the normally good character of McLaughlin, yet proved a vain attempt to gain some sort of reprieve. McLaughlin went to meet his maker on 25 July 1961, with the assistance of hangman Harry Allen and his assistant Rickard.

To be the last at anything reserves you a place in the history books, and for Robert McGladdery, the last man to be hanged in Northern Ireland, and the Crumlin Road Prison for that matter, it is no different. He would have gladly given up his place in history to remain just another life sentence prisoner, and indeed he fought hard to plead his innocence during his trial and subsequent appeal; an appeal which was made up primarily of a sixteen-page autobiography.

McGladdery was only twenty-six years old when he attacked and murdered Pearl Gamble, a young woman who lived close to him at Damolly outside Newry. Pearl, a shop girl, had attended a dance in Newry Town the evening of 28 January 1961, and on her home journey was brutally strangled and then stabbed in a field only yards from the safety of her home. The police investigation soon centred around McGladdery, as he had discarded some blood-stained clothing in a septic tank near the scene. He was described as quite an educated young man, having attended a public elementary school, but had seemed to lose any real direction in his life, having eventually travelled to work in the trendy nightclubs of London as a waiter. On his return to Newry, he became the veritable young man about town, dressing in the latest fashionable clothes and living a playboy's lifestyle on a farm labourer's wages. His image in the community would have made the idea of him being capable of murder absurd, but he appears to have been an accomplished liar, living out a Walter Mitty existence. He only redeemed himself a short time before he was executed, making a full and frank admission of guilt for Pearl's murder, an admission which must have further broken the heart of his widowed mother, who had travelled to Belfast to be near her son in his last moments.

The two men who had escaped the noose during 1961, George Bratty and Patrick Gallagher, must have felt the rush of wind as the body of McGladdery fell through the trapdoor to end an era of supreme punishment at the Crumlin Road. There would be further death sentences passed, but never carried out. The dubious honour of last man executed belonged to McGladdery.

* * *

When one talks about the executions over the years, the focus is quite rightly on the condemned; but how could we forget the part played by the executioners themselves, and the notoriety they received from what was effectively a position of celebrity murderer. In context, the laws of the State in the hands of a judicial court and a jury consisting of peers of the accused decided the fate of the accused. The hangman was the person employed to carry out the sentence of the court by executing that person. By all accounts, they were handsomely paid for their work, albeit on a payment per execution basis, with no retaining fee; yet all carried forward a sense of duty and pride in the expertise they showed whilst delivering the retribution of the law of the land.

As a hangman, they were expected to calculate the length of drop required for the height and weight of the person, and have some formulae in place for the final coup de grace, to enable swift and efficient dispatch. It is said, particularly in the case of the Pierrepoint family, where the career of hangman became a family tradition, that there existed a fierce sense of competition in relation to recorded times for completion of the job. It is hard for any reasonable person to imagine how they could begin to remove themselves from such a barbaric act, showing little if any emotion or remorse. It is not akin to soldiering where one may be required to take the life of another during conflict or war. Even then, combatants have frequently struggled with their conscience and sought some kind of comfort or justification for the supreme act against their fellow man. The executioners, however, seemed totally and utterly oblivious to any such emotion, a wholly different breed of individual.

The first executions at Belfast of Robert O'Neill and Daniel Ward were reported to be carried out by an inmate within the jail; a man who had also executed at least one person in an establishment in the South of Ireland. There is no definitive record of his identity, but the name of Smyth has been suggested.

John Daly's execution in 1876 was carried out by William Marwood, a tradesman from Lincolnshire, who took to using a free-running noose as an alternative to a fixed knot as favoured by his predecessors. Marwood did carry out other executions in both the North and South of Ireland, but was soon to be replaced by the prolific James Berry, who was the epitome of the professional hangman. Both Berry and John Ellis hanged one each at Belfast, but their services were used frequently throughout the rest of the Isles, notching up over 120 executions between them. Following on in their tradition were William Willis of Manchester, and Harry Allen, who had the auspicious reputation as the last hangman to carry out his trade in Northern Ireland. In fact, it was he who hanged both McGladdery and McLaughlin just five months apart in 1961.

One name which remains synonymous with executions anywhere in Britain or Ireland is undoubtedly Pierrepoint, and I remember as a child, my father telling me how the tradition of executioner had been passed along the family line, much the same as any other business would have been in those times. Their business was not one of butcher or furniture maker, however; the Pierrepoints traded in death, and so successfully that at the end of their reign as such, they had collectively notched up more than 800 executions amongst them.

The Pierrepoints hailed from Clayton in Yorkshire, and it was Henry Pierrepoint who, after reading about the success and celebrity that the position of executioner had brought to James

Berry, took it upon himself to correspond with the Home Secretary in an attempt to enter the career which he believed would offer him opportunities to travel and broaden his horizons. His persistence eventually paid off, and in 1901 he was appointed as an assistant to James Billington, and then succeeded as principal executioner. It was Henry who compiled diaries of his many executions, recording details of the condemned person's height, weight, age and name, a tradition which was carried on by his own son many years later. Henry, like all the hangmen, was making history virtually every time he carried out an execution. His name was just as important as those criminals he had the task of sending to their death, and he received a mention in the press when the act was being recorded for the masses to read about. Henry's brother Thomas had not sought out the position of executioner as willingly as his brother had, but must have recognised the job as being both lucrative and obtainable, especially when Henry began coaching him from an outbuilding at the rear of his own home, honing his skills as it were. Thomas succumbed to his brother's suggestion, and himself applied through the Home Office for the appointment. When trained, officially, he embarked on a career in the family business for a period of over forty years, and only retired at the age of seventy-six. He had hanged at least 300 people in Britain and Ireland, and in his latter years had drawn Henry's son Albert into the position of his assistant, to further carry on the family tradition.

Albert was to become the most prolific hangman in the history of executions in Britain, and had the deaths of over 400 people to atone for when he eventually shed his own mortal coil in 1992. Albert became the Chief Executioner in 1940, at the tender age of just thirty-three years, and plied his trade as no other had before him or would again. Albert was obsessed with cutting the time of the executions down to the bare minimum, competing with his late father's achievements and those of his uncle. His method of delivering men to their maker was not significantly different to anyone else's, but the little changes he did make made it possible for him to actually record a time of seven seconds from first step from the condemned cell to time of

death for an execution at Strangeways in 1951. To say he was a
perfectionist would be an insult to anyone who deems life to be
precious, regardless of whose life we are discussing. Albert was
the grim reaper to all who met him on a professional footing. He
was the angel of death, the man who appeared to have no com-
passion or sensitivity, an automaton of State-imposed murder. It
beggars belief then that during the period he was carrying out
his duties as executioner for the British Isles, he also managed to
run a pub just outside Manchester, a pub which, legend has it,
had relics from his chosen vocation mounted around the bar in
a macabre display for locals to peruse whilst they sipped at their
beer. I can't for the life of me understand why anyone would
have felt comfortable in such surroundings. Human nature
being what it is, however, our obsession with the darker side of
life compels at least some of us to want to stand and stare, and
what a showcase he must have had at the aptly named pub the
Poor Struggler. Albert Pierrepoint may have portrayed himself as
the media-shy professional, carrying out a loathsome yet
essential job, but I do not believe that he could have been in any
way a compassionate and caring individual, and suggest that his
character may have been predisposed to the act to which he
appeared to be so well-suited.

I do not believe that times have changed so dramatically that
as human beings, our individual conscience has only developed
in the last twenty or thirty years, a conscience which has
identified us as a species who struggle with the taking of life in
any form. It was always there. The modern approach to capital
punishment in the United States has, in some cases, methods set
in place where more than one hand may be responsible for the
final act of execution. The people collectively taking part are
never aware just exactly who it is who delivers the final element
in the process. They have identified the trauma and self-
recrimination felt by one human being when they believe they
have taken someone's life, albeit as part of a 'lawful' act.

When you begin to challenge the idea that the hangman was
professional and dispassionate, a man to whom we owed a debt
of gratitude for having rid our society of a dangerous individual,

you may, like me, find it hard to distinguish exactly who the baddies actually were.

On Tuesday 19 September 2006, having walked around the parts of Crumlin Road which were still accessible with my informed guide Jane Campbell, she took me completely by surprise when she offered to show me one of the two original executioner's boxes. I had no idea that they existed. I had assumed that the various pieces of equipment used by the hangmen were particular to them, and that they would have retained such items, carrying them onwards to their next engagement. That was not the case. The Northern Ireland Prison Service, who have been, and still are, compiling items for their own museum at Millisle, have retained what are known as the number 1 and the number 2 boxes. The number 2 box is believed to contain the noose which was used to hang McGladdery, and had possibly been used on several others. Jane was quick to mention that there was another noose on display at the Ulster Folk and Transport Museum, and that there had been some claims over the years that it had been used at Crumlin Road. I have since done a little digging, and found that there is little provenance in relation to that particular noose, and what there is remains purely word of mouth.

The number 2 box was stored on the floor of a room just off the main corridor of the administration block. It was in amongst tables and chairs and various scraps of paper. It stood out amongst the rest of the contents of the room because of its appearance. It looked similar to a treasure chest, a brown wooden box with two hasp and staple locks, one with a padlock firmly attached. On the outside it said no. 2. When Jane opened the lock and we lifted the lid, my eyes shifted over the items inside in utter disbelief. On top of everything was the noose itself, and lying close beside it was a cream-coloured cloth hood. There were other bits and pieces, which I wanted to root through and look at, but I first had to read the small label which was carefully placed on the inside of the lid. In black ink, it appeared that the contents of the box were listed, a gruesome inventory of everything an executioner would need for a successful send-off. The items were listed as follows:

ROPES	2
BLOCK AND FALL	1
STRAPS	2
SANDBAG	1
MEASURING ROD	1
PIECE OF CHALK	1
PACK, THREAD	1
COPPER WIRE	1 piece
CAP	1
TOTAL	11

Who would have made such a box up I am not sure, but they were obviously acquainted with the tools of the hangman's trade. The contents were all intact, right down to a piece of chalk in a little compartment at the left side of the box. I lifted the noose and was surprised at its construction. The rope itself was free to run through a permanent metal ring at the top of the loop which would be placed over the victim's head. The actual noose, which would have closed around the throat, was not just rope, but had been sheathed in tan-coloured leather and stitched permanently in place. It appeared slick and lethal, and would have created a smooth and instantaneous tightening around the neck. I almost expected to feel some kind of energy from the bits and pieces I lifted up, especially the hood, but I was disappointed. It was all so ordinary. Nevertheless, I couldn't bring myself to place the hood over my head, which would be an experiment I would love someone from NIPRA to take part in.

When I began researching the executions at the jail, I became immersed in each story as it unfolded in front of me. I felt a degree of sympathy for how the condemned men's lives had brought them to such a sorry end, and could visualise the utter panic and despair at the time of their deaths. I knew that someday I would have the opportunity to revisit the scene of the executions, but I never thought I would have access to the very tools which may have ended their lives.

For some reason I thought that such items would have been stored in a more secure environment than this room. I would have imagined them behind a glass case in a museum, with the public able to look but not touch. Yet here they were. If the prison, or at least part of it, were ever to be open to the public, I could see the box and its contents being one of the attractions people would like to see most. I suspect that in such circumstances, they would indeed be housed in a different fashion, and treated with the reverence which I believe they deserve.

Chapter 4

Cons and Screws

My fascination with the Crumlin Road Jail was not restricted to its past, although admittedly I found it hard to ignore its history when the very architecture was blatant and uncompromising. The inmates themselves serve as markers on an imaginary timeline within the jail, and none more so than those who were, and remain, instantly recognisable figures in Northern Ireland's political arena.

The conflict in Northern Ireland has spawned many activists on both sides, some of whom were able to make the transition from soldier or volunteer to bona fide politician. It is no surprise then that the Crum has at various times opened its doors to people with whom we are now more familiar as they appear dressed in suits and ties on national and international television. The 'respectable' faces of Ulster politics have, in many cases, a notable background and, it must be said, have acquired their insight into the future of dialogue rather than terrorism from having experienced the futility of conflict and the misery of wasted lives in jail.

Although many of them sacrificed part of their youth, willingly or otherwise, to further their cause, some used the time more wisely than others and have ended up making more of a contribution towards reaching a political solution to the age-old problem of the black North.

Making less of a sacrifice, however, were those who courted the press and contrived their own 'dramatic' headlines in an attempt to score points with the grass roots voters. To see a public figure being sent to prison for a minor offence, under circumstances that were relevant to a point of principle, was abhorrent to the general public. It somehow elevated these people to near martyrdom in the eyes of some of their voters, which of course was the original intention after all. The one man capable of creating a propaganda victory out of virtually nothing was Ian Paisley.

I remember Dr Paisley visiting the jail over the Christmas periods, more specifically every Christmas Day. He had formed the habit of delivering boxes of chocolates to Loyalist prisoners on the wings every year, and continued to adhere to this tradition. He would be shown to the visits areas by staff, and he distributed his gifts to whoever wished to receive them; a singularly Protestant Santa, as it were, and surprisingly, just as cheerful. He was pleasant to inmates and staff alike, and wished all he came in contact with a very merry Christmas. I can still recall standing in the gradually disappearing grip of a hangover one Christmas morning at the gate in the forecourt which opened towards the A-wing visits, the collar of my long black overcoat pulled tight around my ears to ward off the chill. I turned towards the main gate as I heard it being unlocked, and saw Mr Paisley approach with another person I didn't recognise, and his officer escort. He greeted me heartily, and I replied with equal enthusiasm, although directing my reply into my gloved hand in a vain attempt to mask the smell of drink from the night before. Of all the people I knew to be in the public eye at the time, I would have said Paisley was the most identifiable to the man in the street. I was slightly in awe of him and, in my naivety, couldn't wait to tell someone of my minor brush with celebrity. Even though I lived on my own at the time, I would always avail of a traditional Christmas dinner at my parents' house. That year was no different, and when I sat down that afternoon amongst the gathering, and blurted out the events of the morning with genuine enthusiasm, my dad, who I had never witnessed express any extreme viewpoint in relation to local politics, went off on a tirade about Paisley and his 'bigoted and sectarian' stance towards Catholics. He bellowed how he would have given him a piece of his mind if he had been there. Even though I knew my dad was always two, if not three, sheets to the wind around the time of Christmas dinner, and was likely to forget all or most of the things which happened during that day, I felt as if I had betrayed him in some way by even acknowledging 'the big man' as he passed me by. It was too late to backtrack, the damage had been done, and I had to struggle through the rest of the meal listening to him rant and rave about the need for more people to denounce any clergy holding positions in politics in Northern Ireland as it only contributed to broadening the gap between the two communities. I had never seen my father so animated as I did that day, and I realised then that although he was generally passive about issues of a political nature, and was anything but a 'good Catholic' in respect of attendance at Mass and the likes, his identity as a Catholic and all that it stood for mattered a great deal to him, and he genuinely despised Paisley and his anti-Rome doctrine. In some ways, it made me feel rather alienated. I hadn't a foot in any particular camp as far as religion was concerned, and if religion was there to define us, then I was out on a limb. It is only now, in middle age, that I realise we are defined by our actions and our morals rather than what God we worship, if any. The violence in Northern Ireland has been less to do with religion and more to do with greed and pure hatred, a hatred which was perpetuated by many politicians.

Needless to say, when Mr Paisley made his trips to the jail, it was deemed prudent to restrict the visits area to Protestant prisoners alone when he chose to empty his big red sack. I considered his Christmas visits as purely selfless acts at first, undeniably partisan, but on consideration, I believed adopted by a man who I suspected was more in touch with what mattered inside prison than most Unionist politicians. The future bro-kering of the 'peace' in Northern Ireland was to be orchestrated in many ways from the inside of prison cells, as much as party offices. It was a great surprise to me, then, that he should return to the prison in 1987, not as a visitor but as an inmate, albeit for a short period of time.

Ian Paisley remains the most controversial political figure in Northern Ireland's recent history. The self-styled doctor emerged

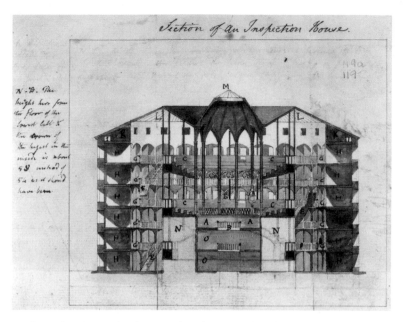

Section of an inspection house taken from Bentham's panoptican drawings.
(Bentham Papers (119a/119), UCL Library Services, Special Collections)

Aerial view of Crumlin Road Jail (c. 1981). The court-house can be seen
directly opposite. (Pacemaker Press International)

Visitors entering the jail through the wicket gate. (Pacemaker Press International)

The circle area with the chief officer's box in situ. (Pacemaker Press International)

Interior view of the condemned cell. The double cell provided fairly comfortable and spacious surroundings for the inmate's last days.

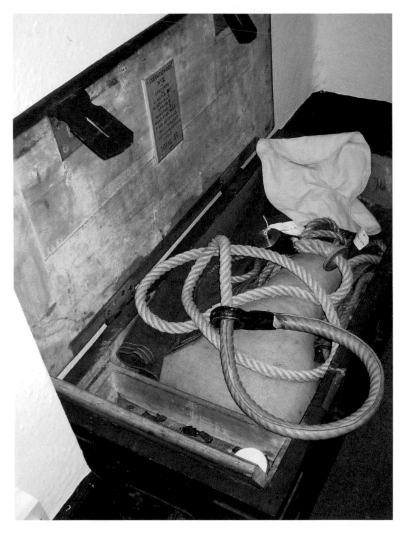

The tools of the trade: execution box no. 2. The noose is probably the actual one used during the last two executions at the jail.

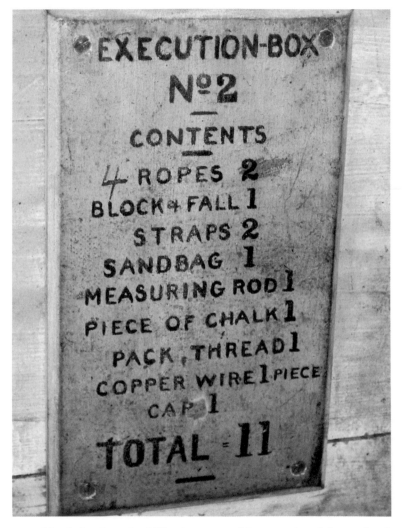

Everything in its place: the chilling inventory of the executioner's box, as listed inside the lid.

The passageway leading from the drop room out towards the rear of C-wing. The corpse of the hanged man would travel this route to the site of his burial.

The last resting place of Harold Courtney is inscribed into the stones of the rear wall of the jail. The inscription was made by one of his fellow inmates, assigned as part of his burial party.

Ian Paisley leaves the jail after his two-day sentence for refusing to pay a fine. (Pacemaker Press International)

Ken Maginnis takes advantage of the media presence and holds up two cheques which he intends to present as repayment for his prison wages. (Pacemaker Press International)

within the 1950s to establish the Free Presbyterian Church of Ulster; his open denouncement of the Catholic Church was apparent with the publishing of his Protestant *Telegraph* and its anti-Catholic content. He always maintained a hardline approach, adopting the 'No Surrender' slogan, one for which he was to be dubbed 'Dr No', along with other nicknames reflecting his almost tyrannical grasp of grass roots Unionism, like 'Big Ian' or the 'Ayatollah'.

It was in March 1969 that Paisley was first jailed for organising an illegal counter-demonstration in Armagh City in protest at a civil rights march taking place there. He, along with several others, was released under a general amnesty for political prisoners. Paisley went on to forge one of the most memorable careers in Ulster politics, asserting himself as leader and founder of the Democratic Unionist Party, and 'defender of the faith'. Always one to court controversy, he cleverly manipulated the press in many situations, from his removal from Parliament during one of Margaret Thatcher's speeches, to rallying the crowd of 500 on a lonely hillside in 1981, waving their firearm certificates and introducing Ulster to the Third Force.

Paisley's return to prison was no less contrived or dramatic than his first visit. A point of principle led him to offer himself up to police for arrest, rather than pay an imposed fine, which would then have reverted to a money warrant.

Money warrants are not what can be described as practical to enforce by any stretch of the imagination. When a fine is imposed by the court, a date for full payment is listed. If monies are not received by this date, a warrant is issued which gives the police power to demand immediate payment of those monies, or if payment is refused or denied, they can arrest and remove to jail the person named on the warrant. Either way the warrant is executed. The amount of monies owed can relate to either one week or two weeks in jail etc. on a sliding scale of some sort, which to this day I have not been able to work out. When one considers the amount of money it takes to keep a person incarcerated for one week, balanced against the monies owed on a fine, which can start from as little as £50, I believe the system is somewhat flawed. Many ordinary decent criminals, who are well schooled in the ways of the system, will rather 'do the time than pay the fine'.

Dr Paisley had, I believe, some commitments in the early part of the week in which he was brought to jail. He had manipulated the police into arresting him in the middle of the week, knowing full well that with the normal 50 per cent remission applied to every sentenced prisoner in Northern Ireland, he would be time served on the Friday, as they did not release on Saturdays. The point of principle was weakened further by his restriction from the general prison population and a confinement to the base reception area, due to the logistics of booking him on and off a wing. His partner in crime throughout this charade was the Reverend William McCrae.

When I saw both Willie McCrae and Ian Paisley appear at the door of a search box I was in, I nearly fell off my chair. Prisoners who were time served and about to leave the jail were randomly picked out for a strip search, to ensure they were not smuggling any items out. It was common knowledge that some Republican prisoners had smuggled communications or 'comms' both in and out of the Maze during the hunger strikes, and this practice was not restricted to Republicans alone. Many items which would have been of a sensitive nature in terms of security were taken out by inmates from both factions, and their ingenuity in secreting these items on their persons was legendary. The communications were usually written on small pieces of paper, cigarette papers on many occasions, and folded down to the smallest size possible. In turn, these little pieces of paper were hidden in various orifices of the body. I remember reading about one Republican prisoner who had placed several 'comms' under his foreskin, and obviously had successfully managed to pass through the routine searches on his way out.

I was fairly sure that I would find nothing on either Paisley or McCrae, but I had to follow procedure. There were no exceptions to the rules, and I genuinely believe neither men expected any.

When performing a strip search, the inmate is asked to remove his top half first, whilst leaving his bottom half on. The request is then reversed, with the top half remaining on whilst the bottom is removed. The inmate is therefore not subjected to the embarrassment of being fully naked at any time, thus sparing the blushes of both he and his searcher.

So here I was staring at Ian Paisley, an immediately recognisable figure throughout the modern world, asking him to remove the top half of his clothing so I could search through it. When I asked for his bottom half, I must confess to taking little interest, if any, when he removed his trousers. I just couldn't bring myself to make the search as thoroughly as I normally would.

For years after, when I recalled the incident, I was continually quizzed as to the accuracy of his 'Big Ian' title, even though it had clearly not derived from any inference as to that particular physical attribute.

It was altogether a totally bizarre experience, and to Dr Paisley's credit, he did what was required of him with a cheery smile and a farewell. I also assisted in Reverend McCrae's search, and he again was chipper and upbeat, but then again, it was the start of the weekend, and they would both shortly be emerging from jail to a hero's welcome, having 'suffered' for their principles.

The concept of creating uproar through public figures being seen to be sent to prison whilst defending issues on points of principle was one which was being used with great effect. One person who openly admitted to pushing the authorities into an untenable position, and revelling in the after-effects of that, was Ken Maginnis, now of course Lord Maginnis. The ex-primary school teacher, B Special and UDR officer managed to create a scenario which was to provide him with numerous opportunities to score valuable points of protest against the inception of the 1985 Anglo-Irish Agreement.

I clearly remember seeing Ken Maginnis standing at the threshold of his cell in D-wing in Crumlin Road, peering out at all the activity around him. I thought when I had watched him being interviewed on television over the years, that he cut a distinguished figure, with a shock of greying hair and moustache, and a distinctly military bearing. In contrast, looking at him then in jail, my reaction was similar to someone seeing a soap star or film actor in real life; surprised at how small they appeared when not on the screen. In all fairness, put into the context of those surroundings, anyone would diminish in stature. When I spoke with him some twenty years later, in a coffee shop in Belfast, the man had regained all and more of his larger than life image. His voice resonated around the almost empty seating area, as he steered me towards a time in his life during which he had clearly more energy and dynamism for local politics. He openly admitted to having an awful memory for names, dates and times, but as we talked, he began to recount the full story of his brief imprisonment, and how he had managed to score points for his media crusade at every opportunity along the way.

When I asked him what had triggered his lapse into the 'darker' side, he leaned back in his chair and stated:

> It was 1985 and the Anglo-Irish Agreement, and again, it was one of these things as far as Unionists were concerned, we didn't want to be outrageous, and weren't going to support any violence against the Agreement. There were a lot of people who would have been advocating that. And I think it was Harold McCusker sort of said, 'Look, wait till I tell you, the Republicans did all they wanted in their civil disobedience, and it paid big dividends. We should embark on a civil disobedience campaign.' Well, we were all young and hearty, and we thought this was a good idea.

Both of us had a titter at his point, me especially, as it reminded me of a group of little boys conspiring to commit some heinous act from the retreat of the tree house den. It was obviously a more serious state of affairs than that, and after a moment or two he continued:

> I remember the meeting in Parliament, of our eleven Ulster Unionists, that was the day after it was announced at Hillsborough, and we were all sitting around and Harold was saying, 'Oh we all should look back at Northern Ireland

at the people who elected us, and lead them on this campaign of civil disobedience.' And Enoch [Powell] was sitting there looking quite forlorn, because he was the one who had told us, 'No, Parliament would never tolerate this power.' Parliament did tolerate it, it was sold, and we were an afterthought. Enoch was adamant that he would be sitting where he was elected to be, on as he put it, 'My corner of the green bench'.

Mr Maginnis went on to explain how he personally removed himself from a fairly prominent position on the Defence Select Committee, and others, like the Reverend Martin Smith, made similar gestures. With their roles having been reduced in Westminster, they then spent most of their time in Northern Ireland, but still kept up a boycott of Ministers, which obviously made it exceedingly hard to carry out any constituency work. Something as dramatic as being imprisoned was then considered as the ultimate route for any real progress. He admits: 'It was all terribly naive however. Nobody would have cared if I was imprisoned for forty years! But it made as much impact as . . . well let's say very little impact. Well, what would I do? I wouldn't pay my car tax, and I wouldn't pay my television licence.'

In an attempt to draw attention to his blatant law-breaking, he took it upon himself to write to the various authorities to tell them what he was doing. He still didn't get an immediate response. Eventually a representative from the Television Licensing Authority arrived at the door of his home one evening with an RUC officer in tow. As she stood on his doorstep, she brought his attention to a letter they had received stating that he had not paid his license. This came as no surprise as he was looking down at his own signature on the said letter. The woman went on to explain to Mr Maginnis that she had to enter his home to confirm that he had indeed a television. It was then that he asked if they had a warrant, to which came the answer that they had. Regardless of this fact, he refused them entry and barred the door. Of course, the police constable would have been within the law in breaking down the door to gain entry, but I assume that the matter was hardly deemed important enough for such disproportionate action, and they duly went away.

Not content with this minor victory, and convinced he had escalated his offending behaviour to obstructing a police constable in the execution of his duty, he wrote to the Chief Constable. In his letter he also drew attention to his car tax not having been paid, and even gave a specific time when his car would be parked on a public road outside his Enniskillen office. The circumstances could obviously not be ignored by the Chief Constable, and after the issuing of a ticket on his car windscreen by a bemused local peeler, a court appearance was imminent. When Ken Maginnis refused outright to pay the £100 fine imposed, he left the RM Robert Porter in a somewhat embarrassing position to say the least. An appeal was made in chambers to encourage payment of the fine, but to no avail. The court imposed a seven-day term in prison to commence immediately. The plan had worked so far.

When he was taken to the police station, awaiting further transport to be arranged to Crumlin Road, he was allowed to use the phone. Of course, after calling his wife to arrange for some pyjamas and a towel to be brought before his departure, he took the opportunity to make a second call to Party headquarters. The nature of this call was to arrange some form of demonstration at the Crum when he would eventually arrive from Enniskillen. He also asked them to be sure some members of the press were there to record the events.

He describes his arrival at the front gate of the jail as a 'pantomime', with the car pulling up to a stop just on the road. A prison officer came out of the pedestrian gate to check the occupants of the car and, when satisfied, returned inside the jail to open the vehicle gate. The supporters were verbal to say the least, and just before the police car could enter the jail, one of the supporters looked down at the windscreen of the police car and noticed that there was no tax disc displayed. Of course this became an immediate issue for the television and press cameras to focus on, and all attention turned to the windscreen. Ironic as it seemed, here was a man committed to prison for not paying his car tax, being delivered by police who themselves were remiss in displaying their tax disc. It couldn't get any better. The next morning Chief Constable Jack Hermon had to explain the gaff to newspapers and television alike, adding further fuel to the situation.

I probed Ken Maginnis for his thoughts when faced with being confined to a cell for the next few days, bearing in mind that this confinement was of his own design. He admits to feeling uncomfortable when being booked in at the reception area, and he had the distinct impression that the screws on duty were showing contempt for his position as a public figure. Granted, he expected to be treated no differently than anyone else but had made no provision for his notoriety creating an overly adverse reaction from staff, and he described the encounter as not being terribly reassuring. He describes being 'made to strip off and shower' and adds that, in retrospect, he should not have complied with the request if he were to follow to the letter what he had begun and intended to carry on. After being booked in, he was doubled up with another inmate for the night in base reception, and moved to the wing the following day. Not one to suffer from claustrophobia, he was comfortable to a point, but admitted to being concerned about having no control over his exit from the cell should something like a fire occur.

Although his incarceration had achieved a victory of some magnitude, he continued with his campaign of civil disobedience whilst in jail, by refusing to accept prison food. As if to make a point, he pats his ample stomach and says that at the time, he considered it would not do him any harm not to eat for the week, and he only availed of fluids. On his second day, he was approached by an officer and asked if he would like to work. When he replied that he would, he was taken along to the gym and introduced to the officer who looked after the inmates and apparatus when in use, who went by the name of Tom King. He recalls being slightly suspicious of the introduction, as this man shared his name with the then Secretary of State, an irony not lost on either of them. Tom King asked him if he liked reading newspapers and if he did the crosswords, and when he answered in the affirmative, he was shown to a store room where the mats were kept, and told to relax and keep out of the way. This was to be his employment for the next two days.

Not only did he manage to put in a few hours away from his cell, but he was later approached and asked to go to the class office to receive his 'pay'. Although he did not want to take payment under any circumstances, he was convinced by the class officer that he could convert the pay into cigarettes, and even if he didn't smoke, there were always plenty who did. Eventually he did go and collect his payment, in some ways to accommodate the officer, and duly distributed the cigarettes during association time that evening. He had accumulated about £1.36 for his two days work, a figure he remembered well, as he was to use it to further exploit his position on release.

Whilst he remained in the Crum, he was forced to attend at Cookstown Court to answer the charge of obstructing a police officer during the course of his duty. This referred back to his refusal to let the Television Licensing Authority representative and her police chaperone into his house to inspect his television some weeks earlier, a matter which I suspect was being dealt with expeditiously to avoid giving Mr Maginnis the opportunity to exploit this situation also. He did, however, manage to create more publicity at court, when he was able to raise his hand and display the fact that he was handcuffed, which was purely procedural, but effective all the same. He conducted his own defence during this hearing, and was given a discharge which left him to serve what was left of his original sentence only.

Although he openly found some relief from the boredom of his cell by working in the prison gym during his stay, he realised he was placed in a somewhat difficult position by actually being paid for his work. He knew that on his release he would be asked all sorts of questions by the press, including if he had worked in the jail, and if he had been paid for his labour out of the Anglo-Irish purse. Of course he wished to continue his campaign of civil disobedience through to its end, being as true to the objective as possible, and he realised just how he could turn even this small detail to his advantage. When the time of his release came, and he was being given all his property back, including his personal cheque-book, he immediately started writing out two cheques from his bank account. The first he made out for 68 pence and payable to Tom King, the Secretary of State for Northern Ireland, and the next for the same total made payable to Peter Barry, Minister for Foreign Affairs in the Republic of Ireland. The two cheques would total the £1.36 he had been paid for his labour in the prison, and when he was asked the question which he had anticipated by the press as he stepped out onto the Crumlin Road, he held both cheques aloft, one in each hand, and replied, 'I was forced to take the Anglo-Irish pay, but as you can see I have paid it back.' Later, Ken Maginnis followed up the promise to repay the monies, and duly posted the cheques to the payees. Needless to say, neither cheque was ever cashed.

I enjoyed talking to Ken Maginnis, or should I say listening to him, for he has a certain presence and a charisma with which he controls the flow of conversation. I could tell that he was enjoying the opportunity to reflect on this time in his life when he was more active in politics, even though he explained to me that his current role in the Ulster Unionist Party gave him little time for anything else. A few weeks after our meeting I saw both him and Gerry Kelly from Sinn Féin being interviewed in one of the yards at the now empty Maze Prison, or Long Kesh for those who remember it from the time of the compounds. It was the 25th anniversary of the hunger strike at the jail, in which ten IRA men fasted to their deaths in protest at the lack of political prisoner status. Both men stood side by side to give their opinions as to how they saw what effects, if any, the deaths had on future events in the North, and if this one act of human sacrifice could be considered a turning point in Ulster's politics. They were two very differing opinions, as you would expect, with Maginnis happily bandying the words 'murderers' and 'killers' quite freely in his description of the IRA and their activities at the time. The Sinn Féin representative stood almost toe to toe with Maginnis, and of course challenged his every word, but in a calm and balanced fashion as you would expect from a politician. I have the utmost respect for anyone who stands up for what they believe in and is not afraid to call a spade a spade, and I could tell from the tone and inclination in his voice that Ken Maginnis was anything but intimidated by Kelly. I trust that Gerry Kelly, and others like him, who have openly engaged in acts of terrorism, would rather be debating with someone who is not afraid to speak their mind, and will constantly remind them that the process which we are all facing will have to be open and honest, with all the cards on the table, however unpleasant or compromising they may be.

In some ways, inmates like Lord Maginnis could have been described as celebrity prisoners. In Northern Ireland, where our daily diet of news and current affairs was dominated by local politics, such faces as his were constantly on our television screens. However, the word 'celebrity' was used in a wholly different sense by some screws to describe the infamous 'red book' prisoners in D-wing. These particular celebrities had earned their A-list status in a very different manner altogether.

*   *   *

I was seldom on the threes in D-wing, but when I was, I could tell that the atmosphere was different. There was a strict adherence to security, a no-nonsense approach. It was clear that the possibility of escape was always more believable when you were surrounded by men who had at one time made it their business to break out and return to an active role in terrorist activities on the outside. The many red book prisoners who lived on the landings were used to the continual disruption they faced, simply because they had an extremely high security risk attached to them. They were regularly moved cells to interrupt any possible plans for escape. Their every movement was recorded in the book which accompanied them wherever they went, as well as having a permanent escort officer. They were continually under scrutiny, day and night, and had their mail censored rigorously both in and out. Even during their association periods and mealtimes, their behaviour was monitored closely by the staff on duty. For those screws who were not familiar with the names and faces, the observation posts had within them photo montages of all the major risk prisoners, and it paid to familiarise yourself with them.

One face which was easily recognisable to most at the time was veteran Republican Martin Meehan. Meehan stood out amongst the rest as a small but powerful figure whose expression never seemed to change that much, whatever the circumstances. It was his solid barrel chest and thick legs and arms which you noticed first. He wore a thin, finely trimmed beard, and at times looked scholarly, yet there was always a hard edge to his eyes. I found that he had a presence which almost compelled you to watch him. I knew even then that he was a key figure within the ranks of the Republican prisoners, but I had no idea just how much of a seasoned prisoner he was. When we met in 2006, and I had a chance to hear his story, or at least a scaled down version of it, I could see just how important the Crumlin Road Prison was to him. It was part of him in a sense. Not that he would ever remember the place fondly, but he could not deny that a large part of his adult life was spent inside it. His own ideas and philosophies on life were partly shaped from time spent in jail, and even his love of theatre and the arts grew and were nurtured from within this harsh environment.

I had agreed to meet Meehan in the Governor's Room at the Linen Hall Library, and as I waited for his arrival, images of the man in his prime flooded back to me, and a degree of apprehension set in.

In my favour, though, was the knowledge that Meehan had embraced the peace process in its entirety, becoming a very vocal advocate of dialogue as the only productive route towards solving the Northern Ireland issue. When he eventually did arrive, I sensed that even after all these years he had not lost any of his determination.

Obviously he looked older and was slightly more portly, with his precision-trimmed beard whitened by time, but he carried himself with dignity and pride. And when he shook my hand he gripped me with a strength which belied his aging façade. As we settled down to business, he removed his leather beret and overcoat and leaned in towards me with what appeared to be enthusiasm.

I did not want to mislead Martin Meehan, or for that matter anyone whom I proposed to speak to about the jail, and immediately told him that I remembered him from the Crum, as I myself had served there as a prison officer. I then told him that I would understood fully if he did not wish to speak to me. He took a moment or two to consider this before he agreed to continue, and I got the impression that there was nothing or no one he would not now have trouble engaging, old enemy or not.

I knew that Martin Meehan was one of the few people who had managed to escape from the Crum, and I looked forward to hearing the story straight from the horse's mouth, as it were. But his insight into prison life as a 'high risk' Republican prisoner was just as captivating, and I decided to probe him on those issues first.

Meehan successfully crossed over the Border into the Irish Republic just days after his escape, and he explains that the decision to return to 'the war' was one he made without hesitation. He immediately retook his place as a volunteer and operated along the South Armagh border, remembering one memorable gun battle.

> When we were on the Border, we were involved in a major gun battle at Drumgooly. There was twenty thousand rounds fired by the Brits. Twenty thousand rounds in four hours. It was even on the ten o'clock news that night. The only thing killed during the gun battle was a prize pig, a farmer's prize pig. In fact the South Armagh men came up on my birthday some years back, and presented me with a wee piglet, saying that this was a descendant of 'Percy' the pig, and a piece of corrugated tin which had about 140 bullet holes in it. That was an indication of just how many bullets the squaddies, the Scots Dragoon Guards, fired. They said they actually ran out of ammunition and had to send back to Forkhill for more. Then of course we were all arrested and remanded in Mountjoy Prison. We were there

for several weeks and then we were acquitted. During that time, Bloody Sunday had happened. So I came back up North just after Stormont fell, and direct rule came in. On the first anniversary of internment, I was arrested in Ardoyne. An elderly man, resident in the house I ran into to escape arrest, was shot at through a window, was hit in the chest and later died. I was subsequently found, arrested and charged with escaping from lawful custody. I was again remanded to Crumlin Road Prison. By this stage we had gained our political status, and Billy McKee was the OC. There were almost two hundred political prisoners there at that stage, and I ended up the oc of the remand prisoners in C-wing. The detainees had all been moved to Long Kesh.

We had the run of the wings, more or less, and we had things like our education classes. There was no hassle what-soever. We had our training officer, our education officer, a quartermaster and the OC. Billy McKee would have been the man in charge overall. He had been on hunger strike fighting for political status, and was a very highly respected Republican; people looked up to him. There were also prisoners coming on to remand, and you had the intelligence officer there in the wing to debrief them. And obviously if there had been information disclosed to Special Branch or police, that information would have been sent out to our people to say, look, this fella has broken under interrogation. He may have disclosed this or that, and he may have mentioned this name or the other, and the individuals concerned would have had to get off-side. So as soon as they came in, the intelligence guys would have taken them aside for the debrief. Now some people didn't tell the truth, and in turn compromised people on the outside. It was extremely important to us that they told the truth to us immediately after being interrogated in Castlereagh, or Holywood Barracks or wherever it may be.

Throughout the Troubles it was common knowledge to the security services that the IRA ran a tight ship with regards to internal security. Many believed the 'war' could only ever be won through the gathering and use of intelligence, and virtually all the paramilitary organisations had to look within their ranks for both informants and weak links. The many active service units within the IRA relied on the fact that they worked in small teams, with their identities known only to the other members within that unit, and possibly members of their Army Council. The protection of key players and sympathisers was paramount in retaining a well-oiled network of terrorism, and loose words cost them dearly. The IRA 'intelligence' officers within the jail were well versed in the methods and tactics the security forces used in extracting information from a detained person, and would have been able to tell when someone had broken under interrogation.

I was curious as to whether the early Republican prisoners had used 'conditioning' to further their aims within the jail, and asked Martin Meehan if and how it was used.

> There was no hard line in relation to that, and I cannot remember anyone trying to get under the guard of any screws. There was an understanding of sorts back then. I don't think we were that advanced in them days. It was sort of do your time, and get your freedom back, and then get back out to the war.

Meehan was keen to tell me more about the Republican structure within the jail, and not dwell on side issues. I let him continue.

> Now there was also an escape officer in the jail, and he was there to motivate prisoners to escape by any means. There were different methods discussed, like tunnels, and I suppose we did try to manoeuvre people into positions where they could exploit the security, or should I say lack of security, in the prison. But Billy McKee in them days would have kept a tight rein on things. He didn't take chances and let any hair-brained idea gain momentum. He was very protective of the prisoners. Younger people like myself may have said 'take a chance'. A success was another blow to the 'establishment', that we were able to get out of their prisons.

Martin Meehan's arrest at that time proved to be controversial, as he explained. Another prisoner by the name of Tony Friel, an Armagh schoolteacher, had approached him and told him that he believed that he should contest his charge, and that if he did he could win. It seems that when Meehan had first been arrested in Ardoyne, and placed in the Crum, he could have saved himself an escape. According to Friel, Meehan had been arrested illegally by a British Army soldier, who under the Special Powers Act invoked at the time had seemingly no power to arrest a civilian. Meehan was given clearance to take his case to court and to represent himself. He recalls the court contest well, although, as all Republicans would have done at the time, he refused to recognise the court. However, he reserved the right to cross-examine, as he put it, 'all purgers and liars'. The trial lasted three days, and Justice McGonigle agreed that Meehan would have had every right to escape from custody as not only was his initial arrest unlawful, but his detentions in Holywood and then Belfast prison were also unlawful. Meehan was awarded £800 for his troubles. The loophole in the law could have proved critical to several other detainees in the early days of the Troubles, as they too had been arrested in similar circumstances. Within forty-eight hours of Meehan's acquittal, the legislation was swiftly amended in Westminster, and it was done so retrospectively. The case was well covered by the press in early 1973.

Meehan began to chuckle when he recalled the whole fiasco, and particularly the aspect of being awarded £800 for escaping from prison. The story would have been sweeter if, on acquittal, he had then been free to go, but unfortunately for him, he had already been charged with and convicted of membership of the IRA some months previously. He was therefore destined to remain in prison to fulfil that sentence of three years, and was time served in October 1974. But his freedom was short-lived, and just three weeks later he was back in again.

Meehan's profile as a known IRA active member was so high that it was inevitable he would end up as a detainee in Long Kesh. In 1975 there was a phased release of detainees from Long Kesh, but Meehan was last to go. He had been identified as the OC of those men remaining and, as such, was the forty-seventh prisoner out of forty-seven to walk out the gates.

The next few years saw Meehan out of jail, right up to late 1979, when he was arrested and accused of kidnapping. He denies vehemently any involvement in this incident, but, as he put it, it was 'par for the course', as he was an active volunteer at that time. There is an honesty in his words that is quite disarming, and makes you question just how many people were arrested on dubious grounds during the less accountable days of the Troubles. Meehan seems to take little issue with it, however, accepting that his detention was an occupational hazard. It was 1980, and he was convicted and duly sentenced to twelve years in prison. He professed his innocence vigorously, embarking on a hunger strike to further highlight his position. It wasn't until 1985, though, that he again walked free, having completed half of his original sentence. His time on remand awaiting trial had accounted for a year of his sentence, including the normal 50 per cent remission.

Again his time on the street was short-lived, as he was arrested in July 1986 for the kidnapping of a soldier. He admits: 'July '86, the Brits hit the house and I was arrested. I got fifteen years. I was involved in that alright!'

There is no ambiguity here. Meehan will, it seems, admit to everything he had any involvement in. It certainly makes me wonder as to the reliability of any evidence presented to the court during his trial in 1980. What I notice from our conversation is that he doesn't dwell on any possible injustice. I get the impression that because he has spent so much time in jail during his life, he has had to learn to move on and not let bitterness twist him out of shape. It's almost like a 'win one, lose one' philosophy.

For someone like Meehan, a seasoned campaigner and no stranger to prison life, I was curious as to how he could cope when faced with yet another period behind bars. His answer was a surprise, to say the least:

I had a great interest in drama. I put plays on, concerts and even sing-songs. And then when I went to the H-blocks and was a 'red book', moving cells every couple of weeks, and wing to wing, I couldn't settle. So I began to look at it in a positive way. If they were going to do that, then I would approach the Governor and ask him for a collapsible stage, curtains and some form of amplification. I even asked for drama tutors to come in so we could learn about acting. He was suspicious, of course, and asked if there was an ulterior motive. I said no, that is what I want. Initially he refused. And then gradually he gave in. So we had concerts and sing-songs and such, and that is how I got my time done. When I moved on to a wing for another few weeks, by the end of it I had a play organised. I remember the Governor calling me up to see him one day, and saying that he had an unusual request. He told me that the Loyalist prisoners had asked for a lend of the curtains and all. I said I had no problem, as I didn't own them. I pointed out that he owned them, not me. He still asked me if we had any objections. They were being loaned out over the 'twelfth' and so there was a wee 'hands across the divide' thing going on there, you know!

There were obviously some instances when both factions had to agree on certain matters, but all in all they were happiest when apart. Meehan recalls that the general policy was one of no interaction with Loyalists, and no outward aggression. He still remembers that segregation was well worked between the two sides. When the Loyalists were locked, the Republicans were out and vice versa.

One incident he did mention, which he remains bitter about, was when a prison officer who had the task of censoring inmates' letters, actually handed a Loyalist prisoner one of Meehan's own letters from his wife. The Loyalist prisoner certainly made it clear to everyone on the landing the intimacy of the letter, reading aloud the more personal aspects of its content. He recalls a lot of 'mixing', as he so aptly puts it, by certain screws, and believes that the Republican prisoners were discriminated against at every opportunity. When I asked him how he thought they were treated any differently than their Loyalist counterparts, he asked me if I had come across any Loyalist 'red book' prisoners in my time. I thought back and in truth couldn't remember any. However, that is not to say there weren't any. He went on to say that he believed the introduction of the 'red book' category was there to frustrate and annoy Republican prisoners. He remembers being moved cell continually and believes he was always moved into the dirtiest cells the prison officers could find. He also remembers the cell lights being put on every hour or so during the night, and the flap being banged at the same time, in his opinion to keep them from getting any real sleep. He believed they were being hassled the whole time. When in the early 1990s he was moved to the Maze, he took part in a protest with other red book prisoners, and as a result of an injury he received when being moved from his cell during that protest, he was awarded compensation of £15,000 in open court in 1999.

Meehan was eventually released from prison in 1994 after being time served, and he said that on his return to the Crumlin Road on one occasion as a sightseer, he found it very emotional. His eyes betray him slightly as he recalls all the ex-inmates he knew who have passed away since leaving prison themselves, through ill health or otherwise. His personal memories he describes as 'vibrant', and he makes reference to a particular kind of camaraderie he found with other militant young men and women, and how back then, in the thick of the conflict, he had not wanted to take part in any type of political dialogue. He goes on to tell me, however, just how much he now embraces the road to peace through negotiation and inclusion. His enthusiasm for conflict resolution through engaging both victims of the Troubles and former adversaries alike is infectious. He refers back to the television programme 'Facing the Truth', in which he took part. I had watched this programme myself with great interest. It had made a ground-breaking approach towards reconciliation, by seating victims of the Troubles across the table from the very people who had carried out acts of aggression against them or their communities. Archbishop Desmond Tutu presented himself as the facilitator and mediator over each meeting. His personal experience in dealing with and resolving many aspects of conflict in Africa made him an obvious choice to chair such a programme, and his blend of empathy and warmth came across to the viewer as well as those who took part in the whole experience. Meehan tells me that a few days after it was shown, whilst walking through Belfast with his wife, he was approached by a Protestant couple. The gentleman told him that although he most certainly did not agree with his politics, he felt that what had happened during the programme had made a contribution to moving things forward.

I know that Martin Meehan is a 'hard man', and I may not entirely agree with his ideology, but I do find his story both emotive and thought-provoking. My own personal memories of him up on the threes in D-wing almost twenty years ago are as clear as if it were yesterday. The man I had just sat down with and spoke to is undoubtedly the same man, but a lot less scary than I remember.

* * *

Many who have kept abreast of matters in the North will immediately identify Meehan as an active player, but there are few people who grew up through the recent Troubles who will not recognise the name Gusty Spence. The imprisoned combatants from both sides in the conflict owe him, and a few others, a debt of gratitude in the fact that he helped shape the conditions in which a large number of them served their time in jail. David Ervine was not exaggerating when he told me that Spence had a mind as sharp as a tack, and a detailed memory of places, dates, names and events which took place throughout his seventy-three years. I pestered and badgered him for about four months into sitting down with me for an hour or so. After all, here was a man who had spent nineteen years of his life in both the Crum and then later Long Kesh, the name he prefers to call what others refer to as the Maze.

It is immediately apparent when you walk into Gusty Spence's living room that he has a love for all things military, with numerous regimental badges and emblems adorning all the walls.

Notably, a print depicting the Battle of the Somme takes pride of place amongst the other memorabilia, a line of inscription stating that it had been presented to him some years earlier as a token of respect. In fact, when I arrive, he is sitting glued to the History Channel watching a documentary relating to an infamous battle which took place during World War Two. In sharp contrast to these masculine artefacts, however, is a photograph of his late wife, and a reminder of his devotion to all matters of family. The sense of military service is so strong here that he feels the need to explain to me immediately that he comes from a military background, having served in the Royal Ulster Rifles, and other family members before him having been in various British regiments. He is quick to point out, though, that his family were never particularly politically minded, although his origins in Joseph Street in the Lower Shankill would have suggested otherwise to some. What is clear when he starts talking is the fact that he is a man who realised long ago that there was never any difference between the Protestants in the Shankill and the Catholics in the Falls other than their religion. The problems in Northern Ireland which erupted into bloody conflict from the late 1960s onwards he believes were shared problems stemming from social deprivation and in many ways deep-rooted fear.

When he eventually began to develop an interest in local politics and saw the divisions within Unionism, which in his opinion always existed, he decided to join the UVF. On a poignant note, Gusty had actually been on the brink of joining the police after his stint in the Army, and had gone along with his best friend at the time to talk with the recruiting sergeant. When his friend decided it wasn't for him, Gusty had followed suit, and instead went to work in the post office. I could see why this was an easy decision in 1961, as apparently a postman was being paid around seven shillings and sixpence a week more than a policeman. He recalled details of his introduction to the UVF but, even now, remains slightly guarded about particulars.

So there were four of us ready to be sworn in, myself and three others who shall remain nameless. But we found ourselves in a bar on the outskirts of Pomeroy of all places. And there was a man who was taking the swearing-in ceremony, an ex Lieutenant Colonel in the British Army. From there, things went from bad to worse.

What Spence was relating to me were the circumstances of his arrest and subsequent sentencing to life imprisonment in 1966. He waves away the issue, stating that it has been covered by many on countless occasions, and that he is sure that most people have tired of hearing the story. He did, however, tell me that the circumstances of his trial were somewhat unusual in that he was indicted under the Grand Jury system, which had not been used for over fifty years prior to that. A verdict of 'true bill' was returned against him, and he was duly convicted. Spence admits to being totally confused by the way the case proceeded, and he still denies several of the charges against him. He does state though that he was 'up to his neck and ears' in other things relating to UVF activity.

> So whenever I went into jail [the Crum], the Governor says to me that I would be going to work in the tailor's shop. So I asked 'What's the wages?' He replied, 'Half an ounce of tobacco a week.' So I replied no, that's not for me, I was a trades unionist after all. So the first seven months I spent in solitary confinement. All of it behind the door. But later a deal was worked out where I would go to the tailor's shop, but I wouldn't do any work. And whenever the Governor came around, I would have to pretend I was working. About once every morning he came around, but that was it.

These were the early days of the Troubles, and Gusty Spence recalls that as the jail filled up with prisoners, Official IRA and Provisional IRA as well as Loyalists, they agreed amongst themselves on a 'no conflict' policy. The co-operation was based on the fact that the prison regime itself was strict but not necessarily oppressive. There were 'adversaries' enough without making life any more difficult. He recalls that there was a particular incident where there was some squabbling when someone had passed a remark about a news item on television. As a result of this, it was agreed that no news programmes were to be shown on the telly, and those who did want to hear it could do so on their transistor radios in the cell.

Of course, at the end of the night the Queen was played up loud in the cells, and as it was in those days, the Soldiers' Song would be heard, turned up loud. Nobody paid any attention to that. Things were harmonious enough and we decided that we would go for the 'big thing', which was special category status, or political status; no matter, it was only a play on words. And we turned the jail upside down, and they couldn't handle it, so they brought the soldiers in. Again, they couldn't do anything with us. We would make placards in the laundry, and we would walk around in protest. We had sat down behind closed doors, Billy McKee, the Provisional IRA leader in the jail and myself, and discussed how we would go for the 'big thing'. And it was agreed that we could not be seen to be supporting the IRA, and so we would go for division and segregation, and they would go for political status working outside the prison. It was all planned that way. It was Billy who said to me, 'Now you keep your men out of the way, Gusty, we don't want any getting hurt.' And the jail more or less became unworkable. Prison officers couldn't get into work, and it finished up in a hunger strike. And I went for thirty-five days, and I also had a ten-day and a seven-day. But Prods don't hunger strike, Republicans do. So to cut a long story short, we achieved political status. The plan was: A1 would be all Provos, A2 would be half and half Provos and Officials, according to the numbers, and A3 would be Loyalists. It was a good defence position in case everything went wrong, the top tier being easily defended. The Provos were not altogether happy, as they wouldn't share A2 with the Officials. So there was a degree of doubling up in cells. But you can't have men all together like that without some form of political debate going on, and so the debates started.

We were very sympathetic towards the Officials, because when they said they wanted an 'All Ireland', they wanted justice and a fair share, this and that and the other thing, which was something which we wanted too, apart from the aspect of a united Ireland. So we decided to co-operate, and have some good political debate. You could in effect say that it was the first embryonic expression of political thought, real political thought, with real bread and butter issues, that occurred amongst the Loyalists.

I wasn't surprised at this revelation of co-operation and debate between what most would have considered sworn enemies. I had been told the exact same thing by Dessie O'Hagan of the Workers Party. Gusty Spence had known O'Hagan well and addressed him by his adopted name of 'the Divil', stating that he remained a good friend. Like Dessie O'Hagan, Spence began a rant about the food and living conditions during the early days of the Troubles.

The food was awful, honestly! It was terrible. And one thing I must mention was the hypocrisy of the prison rules as they were. One of the rules, I cannot remember the number, was that they would ensure that the inmate and his family unit were given every opportunity to continue a solid relationship. And then they went and restricted you to twelve letters a year. And you had a visit a month. You saw your family for six hours a year, just six hours a year. It was absolutely scandalous. But anyway, getting back to the food. There was this old officer, who got into the habit of saying, 'It'll do them rightly', and that's how he was known. You got a pound of bread a day, and it was weighed out and every-thing, and what passed for soup was what had remained in the can from the previous day, and they just put water to it. Juveniles were running the kitchens. There was also a bit of meat that you could have read the *Belfast Telegraph* through, and a spoonful of cabbage, and I am not overstating the case here . . . the grit was still in the cabbage, and your two potatoes. That was your main meal. The jail was ready for revolt. Now whenever I went into the Crum there were only thirteen lifers in the whole jail. Almost overnight the population expanded to something like 700 from 460. The prison officers were losing control. Not a bit of wonder as there wasn't enough of them. The place was overcrowded. They were sleeping in the chapel and everywhere, and they even let some of those who were near their release date out early. It was the first time that prisoners were doubled up . . . and it was a complete nonsense. The NIO could see the writing on the wall—people were going to die. So we were moved from Crumlin Road Jail on 12 December 1972, down to Long Kesh.

It is for the part he played in the following years, during his time in the compounds or 'cages' of the Maze Prison, that people will remember him most. He had established leadership over Loyalist prisoners in both the Maze and the Crum, and because of the overall dejection felt by the inmates at the time, he chose to impose a regime similar to that of the Army in an effort to boost morale. The prisoners under his command would rise early in the morning, take physical exercise and then breakfast before ablutions and parade. It was drill, drill and more drill. The 'no conflict' policy which had been agreed upon in the Crum was also adhered to throughout the time of the cages.

Gusty Spence has described how in 1974, he had become 'disenchanted' with the use of violence, and had become a strong advocate, even then, of open and frank exchanges which may in some way contribute to a democratic solution to the conflict. It was the first step towards the politicisation of the UVF, eventually leading to the construction of the Progressive Unionist Party. They would describe themselves as democratic socialists, and, in his own words, 'they prospered'.

It was clear that Gusty Spence had a long story to tell and was only just skirting around the years he spent in Long Kesh. He was keen to return to the subject of the Crum and how profound an effect jail had on him throughout his life.

If I had my way, and it may seem outlandish, but I would make everyone go to jail for two years, and I know that when they would emerge from it, we would be living in an absolutely different society. Whenever you have everything removed from you, all you have is your mind and your body.

He was passionate when he described how the broadening of people's minds would be the key issue in solving any political problem. He slates sectarianism as the biggest canker in Northern Ireland, and he virtually spits the very word out of his mouth like a foreign object which he has been so close to swallowing. One thing I pick up on, though, is that he believes the Provisionals have been very clever at masking their own sectarianism. I am not sure what he means, but possibly that they hide any such notions behind an established, and in some people's belief, credible ideology. It is obvious, though, that Gusty does not fear criticism from any direction, and makes a bold statement when referring to the Official IRA as the least sectarian organisation which had existed in those times.

When I eventually steered the subject back to the Crum, he referred to the thirteen lifers he knew of when first he took up residence in cell 11 on A1.

They were all in for domestic murders, there weren't any serial killers or whatever, and they were all in A-wing. It was the only long-term wing in the jail. You had to be serving two years or over to be in A-wing. And I remember the punishment cells. Not that I was in often, but I do remember being put in a punishment cell one time, and I woke up during the night, and the mice were chewing on my hair. I also remember making a doll's house for the kids in the handicrafts. I always looked after the kids with things like that, and I had made this for my youngest daughter and had left it in the punishment cell overnight to store it. The cells were not used that often, in fairness, but when they were, those inside would have been restricted to bread and water and would have slept 'on the boards'. Everything else was taken out of the cell and you were left on the boards. So I had put the doll's house down, and the wee roof had been made of artificial tiles which had been pasted down. For the Saturday morning visit, I came down to get the doll's house, and there was a million wee bits of these tiles all over the place. The mice had got at it. It was the paste which they were after. The wooden structure was still there, but I had to re-paste the whole roof again. I made sure it never went into the punishment cell again. And never mind the mice, the cockroaches were all over the place.

There was always a pest problem in the Crum, and little visitors were frequent and in many forms. The jail was showing its age even then in the early 1970s, and plans were afoot to create a new, more people-friendly establishment. For Spence, though, the 'cages' came before then. From there he would recognise the need to move away from violence and fear, and into a shared society with real issues being fought over by democratically elected politicians; the type of real issues which mattered to both communities. He was always looking for someone credible to carry that banner, and he believed he found that someone in David Ervine.

*   *   *

When I spoke to PUP representative David Ervine about his time in Crumlin Road Prison, he almost dismissed the seven months he stayed there on remand and awaiting trial. He denied that he could make any major contribution, unlike Gusty Spence, who he described as having made an enormous impact on life in jail for political prisoners, and possessing a memory which was 'massively superior' to his own. I had to agree with David Ervine that speaking with Spence had been a must, but I conveyed to him at the same time that I proposed to tell a story about the jail which was not purely about historical events, but also included anecdotal evidence to portray daily life for the people inside it.

Although his experience of the Crumlin Road was a reasonably short stay in 1974 into 1975, David Ervine remembers the very cell he was confined to, and his recollections of prison life remain vivid today.

Ervine was arrested in 1974 when he was stopped in a car containing a bomb, and he entered the Crum in November of that year on remand. As he went through the procedures of the reception, he recalls being stripped, checked, re-dressed and sent to base reception. The checking, as I remember it, was a rather archaic procedure, in which the inmate was made to strip, and then wear a wraparound loin cloth affair. These loin cloths were no more than small sections of torn white sheets, just enough to go around the person's waist and preserve some dignity at least. Inmates were weighed, their height was then measured and all details were recorded and photographed, with an inventory of scars and tattoos listed on a descriptive form. It was a baptism of fire into prison life, where privacy and normality would be left behind for good. I remember watching men as they came through, standing nervously on the scales in this barrack of a room, confused and disorientated, and jumping at every barked request from the staff in their long brown storemen's coats. Here in reception was where their sentence started, and where the enormity of their personal situation began to sink in.

David Ervine dismisses the issue of any mistreatment by officers at reception but clearly remembers the base area as being, in his own words, 'dull, dark and oppressive'. He recalls being asked by screws as to where he was going, a reference to his preferred destination within the prison. On stating his position as a Loyalist, there was never any other destination for him than the Loyalist remand C-wing. As the base area ran adjacent to the yard used by C-wing inmates, it was common for those exercising in the yards to approach the cell windows, and try to establish the affiliations of those about to join the general population. Ervine recalls an inmate in the cell next to him having a lighted newspaper pushed through the bars of his cell in an attempt to burn him alive.

It was incidents like these that reinforced the obvious need for segregation in the prisons, and may have forced the hand of the authorities to bow to what may have been considered the easy option. With segregation, however, came control through numbers. The collective Loyalist or Republican voice on the wings was stronger and more effective than it would have been had they remained integrated.

On spending his first day and night in base reception, Ervine was moved to C-wing, and took up residence in number 10 on the twos. He was told by others on the wing at the time that someone had been murdered in that cell, poisoned by a fellow inmate, when cyanide had apparently been poured down his throat. The very fact of being on his own in the cell was disconcerting to say the least, but with this added enlightenment, he admits to having been less than comfortable.

Ervine struggled to recall the name of the inmate, suggesting it may have been Collins, but I believe he was referring to Mervyn John Connor. Connor had been an associate of the late Lenny Murphy, so-called leader of the infamous Shankill Butchers. Connor had been complicit in the murder of William Pavis, having driven the motorcycle which had carried Murphy on the day of the murder on 28 September 1972. Pavis was in fact a Protestant who had supplied a shotgun to a Catholic cleric of all people, an act which had highlighted his questionable allegiances and had singled him out for the ultimate punishment. Police arrested Murphy and Connor a short time later when their modus operandi linked them to the murder, and they were duly remanded in the Crum whilst the police case was being constructed. Part of this construction was the alleged coercion of Connor to turn Queen's evidence against Murphy. Murphy would have realised that the singular piece of evidence which may convict him would come from Connor, and that would have sealed his fate. When Connor was eventually discovered dead in the cell, beside him was a hastily scrawled note exonerating Murphy from any involvement in the murder.

I asked Ervine if he had felt any presence in the cell, evil or otherwise, but he said he had not. He did say, however, that he was aware of other inmates having experienced certain apparitions or events, but his only discomfort came from the graffiti above his cell door which made reference to Satan living there.

The consensus on whether it was better to be confined to a single cell or bunked up with others would, I believe, have been a split decision. I witnessed many a tear and tantrum from men who were losing their individual cells to share with one, or sometimes two other cons. Likewise, I saw others who were clearly devastated at losing their multi-occupant lairs to be confined to passing the evenings on their own. The decisions to re-allocate cells were taken mainly by the security staff within the jail, and based on operational needs and occasionally practicality. The class officers on the wings did, however, use cell movements to their own advantage, often as a punishment; some small yet significant victories were won this way.

Eventually, after six months on remand in the Crum, David Ervine was moved to Long Kesh to await his trial. When he was returned for trial at Belfast's Crumlin Road Court in 1975, he was again placed in C-wing in the Crum, but this time in a shared cell. His recollections of this period in the Crum appear to be more upbeat, and his stories are more colourful. Through talking to him on an informal basis, I can imagine that he is a person totally at ease with either himself or in company. He has a naturally gregarious side to him. When I probe him as to the obvious problems with living so closely with other men, he does remind me of a phenomenon which cons and screws alike will immediately remember.

As one can imagine, when three men are locked all night in a cell, and one or more needs to physically pass a motion, then a dilemma has presented itself. Ervine is more candid when he declares that due to a bad stomach or whatever, the need to 'crap' is sometimes on the cards. The thought of using a plastic piss-pot in itself is not the problem, but to leave the offending material floating there for the duration of the night would have been inexcusable and an abhorrent breach of prisoner etiquette. Hence the birth of the 'mystery parcel'. He smiles as he recalls how cons, when caught short, would direct their deposits into a newspaper, and then wrap this into a tight parcel and launch it through the cell window into the night.

I can't help laughing at this point as I remember talking to many a 'doggy man' (dog handler) who had been the near recipient of such a projectile as he carried out his patrol throughout the prison yards on a night shift. I also remember having to pick my footsteps carefully when on yard duty during exercise time to avoid such entities, not forgetting of course to look skyward on occasion, in case of a sudden golden shower.

The fact that humour played a large part in prison was no less due to the natural ability of the Northern Irish to laugh at themselves, than the prison population being made up of men from similar backgrounds and interests; almost like a continuous lads' weekend. The story Ervine told me of a short and ineffective hunger strike on the wing at the time was gloriously self-deprecating and hilarious.

> I remember I was up for trial, and was not under the regime of the UVF in C-wing. They got all upset in the prison about some issue or other . . . and decided to go on hunger strike. There was a guy called Tommy McAllister who was in charge at the time, so he got the boxes out, and gathered everybody's grub in. Of course, the hunger strike lasted about fourteen hours, and instead of getting back what you put in, say it was a tin of salmon, you got back a tin of beans. And nobody could do much about it, but everyone estimated that the springs on Tommy's bed were sitting somewhat higher than normal. At that time I was sharing a cell with two other guys, and one of them was on a special diet. His special diet was set inside the cell anyway, as it would be, and it was a salad with a boiled egg cut in half. I think that was Tucker McKee. I can't remember whether I kicked it accidentally, the tray that is, but I tipped it over, and lo and behold the egg came apart and the yoke was missing. A guy called Bob Welsh had eaten it and put it back together, as if nothing had happened to it.

Although I could not help but laugh, I was constantly reminded of the subtle differences between Republican and Loyalist prisoners in jail. If it had been a hunger strike imposed by a Republican OC on a wing, this type of behaviour would not have been tolerated. The Republican command structure was adhered to at all times, and it would have been unthinkable for a volunteer to undermine his superiors in any way.

From my own experiences whilst working in Magilligan, I remember two Loyalist prisoners who went on hunger strike, beginning on 16 June 1986; the late Francis 'Pig Face' Curry and Joe Nellins. The two had begun the action in protest at the regime in Magilligan, stating that Loyalist prisoners were being forced to share with Republicans in an ever-deteriorating situation. Larne DUP man Jack McKee verbally attacked the NIO at what he described as their 'near casual' attitude to the situation after the two men were visited by relatives. The mothers of both men had spoken with their sons that day, 1 July, and Mrs Curry was concerned at her Francis having visibly lost weight and his rapidly declining eyesight. Mrs Nellins told reporters that her son had lost over a stone and a half since beginning the strike two weeks previously. Other prisoners were to join the strike a week later, and eventually all Loyalist prisoners in the Crum and the Maze as well as Magilligan would show solidarity by taking part in a three-day fast over 12 July. There was very little in the press after the July celebrations, and as I recall the strike ended quite soon after. There were little in the way of concessions in the wings as a result, and I do not think the strike would have been deemed a success by the Loyalist prisoners. Whether it was true or not, their campaign was rumoured to have been undermined when one of the meat pies delivered to Curry had been weighed when taken from the cell, and found to have had the top removed and some meat taken from within. I cannot confirm if this was the case, but the screws would never have let the truth get in the way of a good rumour. Unfortunately Francis Curry is no longer here to furnish us with the definitive answer. He was murdered by UVF gunmen at Malvern Way some time later, during a bitter feud between the UVF and the RHC, or Red Hand Commandos, of which Curry was a leading figure. I did happen to run into Joe

Nellins in East Belfast during the summer of 2006, but frankly I hadn't the heart to ask him.

One lasting memory of the Crum for Ervine was the way the floors in the wings, and more so in the circle area, were spotless, and continually being 'bumpered'. The orderlies from D-wing used large rotating disc type contraptions with heavy cloths on the bottom to buff the highly polished floors. The process seemed to be continual, and it was rare to cross the circle without seeing this in progress. The polished floors, however, could not detract from the fact that the building housed many a creepy crawlie, especially cockroaches, which Ervine could remember being permanently present 'by the yard' in the cells. He was just grateful that the mice, which again were unwelcome guests, never made their way up to the twos.

I have a degree of tolerance for most spiders and small insects, but have always detested cockroaches, more particularly their scuttling movements, which, being almost robotic, make my skin crawl. Burned into my memory, therefore, is when I took part in an organised search of the inmates' kitchens below D-wing in the very early hours of a night guard. Frequently, such searches were made of various areas in the jail at randomly chosen times, but because the kitchens were open to inmates from a very early hour to accommodate the feeding of the whole prison, it was prudent to choose a time when the cons were not there. As myself and a small group of screws designated as searchers descended the stairs and switched on the main kitchen lights, I physically gagged, as I saw the floors visibly moving, almost completely carpeted by cockroaches. With the stark strip lighting high-lighting their vulnerability, they immediately began trooping towards the large steel extractor fans, escaping back into the darkness. Those not quick enough in retreat were sickeningly crunched beneath the boots of the search teams as they continued with their task. I was astounded at the sheer numbers of the creatures, but was informed by some colleagues that the phenomenon was not restricted to the inmates' kitchens alone, and that the officers' canteen was just the same. From that day forward, I brought a packed lunch to work or survived on bags of crisps to keep me alive until I got home after a shift.

The sheer ingenuity of the inmates is a constant topic when someone begins reminiscing, and each person recalls methods employed to move objects, whether it was food or otherwise, between cells during hours of lock-up. David Ervine remembers the use of sheets with items attached being dangled from cell windows, and then swung back and forth until caught by the recipient at his own cell window one or two doors down the landing. The objects could only be moved a short distance, and synchronisation was the key. There were obvious disasters on occasions, and evidence of these lay in the yards, but generally it was a tried and tested system. Of course, hanging items from the cell bars using fishing line or fine twine enabled prisoners to hide things from view inside the cell. As the majority of officers were trained in search techniques, we were always wary of attempts to secret any such things in this fashion and had a few successes when tasked to rummage in a particular cell. There were those cons who went that bit further to conceal their bits and pieces though; even to the point of developing their own plaster type substance from toothpaste mixed with paint colour from the cell walls. They would first scrape off some of the paint from the wall, and grind this into a powder-like substance, which when diluted would give them some colour which could be mixed with toothpaste to make a pliable plaster. When they had created a small hole in the wall where they wished to hide an item, they would place whatever it was inside, and then smooth over the hole with their own brand of filler. The surface looked just like the rest of the cell walls and was very difficult to detect with just a cursory glance. The lazier con, however, would rely on Samantha Fox or Linda Lusardi to hide his makeshift alterations, hoping that the screws' attention would be drawn to the pleasantries of the female form, and that he would be reluctant to remove such a pleasing image to investigate behind it. On a lot of occasions this worked, as random cell searches to some screws were an opportunity to seek out any legitimate porn. Human nature was the enemy of the prison regime, and the cons could rely on the screws to follow a pattern of behaviour which was fairly easily anticipated. If a con were to leave a stash of porn in a cell, he could be sure that the screws would take more interest in it than the object of the search.

The average ordinary decent criminal, or ODC, was well versed in the can and can't do's in jail, and his survival instinct drove him to acquire as much canniness as he could to outwit the system and make life bearable. The major currency, other than blow (cannabis), was of course tobacco. It was cheaper and more efficient for smokers to roll their cigarettes from scratch than to rely on more expensive filtered packets. Those who didn't smoke either used tobacco to trade or consumed chocolate instead. When orderlies were able to acquire filtered fags from a screw, their bargaining power increased, and they could trade them much quicker. The cons traded in many things, but drugs were definitely the prized commodity. The boredom and monotony in a cell was easier to cope with if drugs were introduced, and it was common to see many a wasted con exiting his cell in the morning, heading for his breakfast at breakneck speed. I couldn't blame them, to be honest, as I always found it hard to imagine a single night locked down in a cell, never mind months or years.

Those who couldn't or wouldn't indulge in the illicit drug culture within the jail had to revert to the help of the prison doctor to administer to their needs. The doctor was almost always inundated with complaints of insomnia and acute depression amongst more commonplace problems, all of which, although very differing conditions, could be miraculously cured by the consumption of drugs which became known as 'wac tablets'. The queue to see the hospital officers in the morning as they administered medication was a joy to behold. The living dead would have been an apt description; men lined up like lemmings with panda-type dark rings around their eye sockets, and lifeless sallow skin, jittery and impatient. These were men who, according to other cons, couldn't do their 'wac', another term for jail time. The medication kept them in a continual state of relaxation, and dispelled the panic to some degree. I am sure that the condition remained with them for some time after release, with some becoming dependent on the medication, regardless of how well the dosage and frequency of administration were monitored by the hospital authorities. A lot of these men had addictive traits in their personalities and were arguably more prone to becoming addicts to many things, not only drugs or alcohol. Even the way of life of some petty criminals is due in large part to the addiction of the 'buzz' or high they achieve when engaged in thefts, robberies or burglaries. In turn, the proceeds of their crimes often go towards paying for drugs or alcohol, and thus the cycle continues.

Although the jibes from other more seasoned residents were always there, I believe that all prisoners would have agreed that whatever it took to get them through the next night would have been alright. There was always bravado, but equally there were always wet pillows. I remember one young man coming into prison reception like a lamb with his police escort. He was 'yes sir' this and 'no sir' that, and shook like a leaf as he went through the booking-in process. When he was ready to go to base reception to spend his first night before joining one of the wings, I escorted him across, and stayed around until he was placed in a cell. When I closed the door behind him and his new-found pal, who had already chosen the bottom bunk, I caught the start of their conversation. After ascertaining that he was of the same persuasion as his cell mate, the new prisoner declared that he was in for three months, saying, 'I don't give a fuck, I'll do it standing on my head.'

The more seasoned campaigners would never have come out with such an idiotic statement. Very few would ever admit to doing time easily. There was nothing easy about your freedom being taken away, even if it was only for a week, never mind a month or a year. There was nothing easy about leaving behind family and friends, trying not to dwell on what they were getting up to as you had an early night, every night. All time in prison was hard time.

* * *

It was always a difficult decision for newly arrived remand prisoners as to whether they would integrate with paramilitaries of their own 'persuasion' or avail of prison rule 32. This particular rule, when enforced, allowed the inmate to be locked up for 23 out of the 24 hours, with the one hour left for exercising only. It was considered their choice. They therefore did not have to associate with anyone whom they perceived may be a threat to them within the general population. Several prisoners availed of the rule in often very different circumstances. You may have had an inmate who was arrested for the supply of drugs, whose activities may not have been sanctioned by the paramilitaries in a particular area. His position was precarious to say the least. Another instance, one more common than most, was a male who had been arrested for unlawful carnal knowledge. In a lot of these cases, the circumstances of the person's arrest were investigated by the paramilitaries. They would not automatically consider this person as a sex offender if they believed the female 'victim' had a past history of sexual activity, and that the man had just made an understandable mistake with regards to her age. However, it was safer for the prisoner to ride out the storm until he was given the 'nod' that he could join their gang as it were. It was certainly not a foolproof method of escaping the unique justice meted out by the different factions, as I was to witness one afternoon.

One young man had availed of the rule for a few days when he first arrived on the wings. He had been arrested and remanded for burglary offences which had occurred in North Belfast, and he was a prolific offender to say the least. After a few days, still rather wary of the Loyalists' reaction to his activities, his cell on the ones in B-wing was approached by a prisoner coming back from the prison hospital on his way to C-wing. Brief words were exchanged through the side of the closed door, and minutes later the inmate pressed his cell button and asked to speak to the class officer. He requested he come off the prison rule and be allowed to join the Loyalist faction in C-wing. His whole manner changed the moment he believed that he had been accepted into the fold. He became cocky and brash, strutting along as he dragged his big brown paper bag of belongings from one wing to another just a few hours later. As he entered C-wing, arriving just as the Loyalists were filtering into the yard for their exercise, he dumped his belongings in his new cell and breezed out through the grills into the throng who were sitting around in the sunlight.

Nothing spectacular happened at first, but as the yards were called in by the class officer and the crowds closed in to come back inside, there appeared to be a scuffle. The young man who had gone out with such expectations now came in a bloody mess, with one ear almost completely ripped off and the other hanging by a thread of skin. He was pressing both his hands against the side of his head and screaming for medical assistance. All in all I think he had lasted about forty-five minutes. As usual, nobody witnessed anything of significance, and there were never going to be any complaints from the young man with the injuries. A few days later, word leaked out, as it almost always did, that the young man had inadvertently burgled a house belonging to a ranking Loyalist who was not at home at the time, due to his current incarceration. He had deprived the rest of this man's family of a television set amongst other more personal items, and had to be taught a lesson. The lesson was of course 'never steal from your own'.

Although the choice to mix amongst paramilitary prisoners was one which the individual could make, they had to realise that they would forfeit certain privileges. This did not stop people complaining about the conditions in the prison, and expressing how they felt they were being victimised. On 17 July 1986, a small letter written on prison toilet paper was smuggled out of the Crum. The contents suggested that the paramilitary inmates were getting at least three quarters of an hour for each meal, as well as three hours of exercise daily. The author went on to complain that they had access to a shower each day and could associate for two hours at a time. In comparison to this, he described how he was only able to shower twice a week, had only one hours' exercise a day and had to eat all his meals in his cell. He was allowed to associate with other inmates every other day, and this was at his own discretion.

* * *

The Prods were not unique in administering their own type of justice. The Republicans were damning in respect of many types of breach of etiquette, and would have quickly reeled in the individual for a little guidance. On one matter, however, both opposing factions invariably agreed, and that was in relation to sex offenders, more particularly 'kiddie fiddlers'. They had to be the most reviled of the breed of sexual predators who were always present in prison populations. Religion had no influence on how deep the hatred for these men plunged. Whether they were Catholic, Protestant or Muslim made no difference whatsoever. These individuals were considered the lowest of the low, and not only by the other inmates. Nearly every prison officer I remember despised having to work with and look after paedophiles. These individuals were known to one and all as the 'roots', 'bullroots' or 'rubbers'. It was up to the individual as to how indignant he became when addressed by any of the aforementioned titles, but a negative reaction, indeed a reaction at all, was not recommended. When they arrived on a wing, be it sentenced or otherwise, the class officer would give them a reality check as to how he thought they should proceed and with whom, if anyone, they could safely integrate. It was almost always a case of the roots bonding together. Safety in numbers.

I will never forget my first visit to D-wing dining hall, during a teatime meal, when all the sentenced prisoners from the ones and twos descended to eat their meal. The last group of people to arrive were the sex offenders, around a dozen in total. It was clear that they had waited until all the rest of the ODCs were seated before braving the serving area. When they made their appearance, they were showered with slices of bread which the other prisoners had thrown at them, and were verbally abused remorselessly. This was a daily ritual. Not one of them turned to face the crowd; they made their way over to a nearby table where they ate the meal with heads lowered. Even for me, it was an intimidating experience. There were around a hundred prisoners staring over at them, filled with so much hate and aggression, and they made no bones about showing it. If they had decided to wreck up and pull these individuals limb from limb, I and my colleagues would have made absolutely no difference to the outcome. And there lay the problem.

As a screw, you were not only entrusted with securing the prisoners under your charge and ensuring they received their entitlements under law. You also had a duty of care for those prisoners. The difficulty was that the majority of inmates in the prison population would have gladly taken any opportunity to get two minutes alone with a kiddie fiddler. Quite literally your eyes had to be in the back of your head.

I spoke to a friend recently with whom I had worked in the Crum, but who moved to Hydebank Young Offenders' centre at the start of the 1990s. He had worked in D-wing on the ones at the same time I had been on general duties. After sharing a few laughs and catching up on each others' lives, I reminded him of an incident he had been involved in, and asked him if he could remember the circumstances. He gave me a wry smile and nodded as it came back to him:

Oh yeah, how could I forget that, it nearly cost me my fucking job. There was this little orderly working on the wing, a slippy wee guy, typical Belfast. He would swagger up and down with his mop and metal bucket, smoking a roll-up, and was always ready to kill dead things. I never gave him much thought, and would let out any rubbers who were locked to wash their smalls, or use the toilet. I just never thought they would ever come to harm with this wee shit running around. This day, however, I unlocked this root and let him go down to the ablutions. I knew the orderly was mopping the floor as usual but didn't take any notice until I heard an almighty crash and a yell. I looked down the wing, and saw the orderly coming out of the ablutions with his mop, but no bucket. When I looked inside, the root was on his back like a crab with his head split open and blood everywhere. He had been smacked on the head by the metal mop bucket as he sat having a shit. Those things weigh a brave bit, and he needed a few stitches. The orderly told me that he had no idea what had happened, but there was no

one else about. It was him alright, but because the root
refused to make a complaint, there was fuck all I could do.
The PO didn't quite see it like that, and gave me all this shit
about neglect of duty etc.

I knew that it wasn't as simple as that, and I suspected there may
have been a heated exchange between my old colleague and the
wing PO, as they had never really seen eye to eye. The incident
had almost provided the perfect opportunity for the PO to settle
their differences once and for all.

I know that when it came to searching the cells of sex
offenders, and worse still, strip searching them, nobody was keen
to do it. Personally speaking, I would have preferred to deal with
any other type of prisoner before I went near a root. I was
repulsed by them and found it difficult to even bring myself to
speak to one of them. As a parent myself now, those feelings of
repulsion have been replaced by fear. I often struggle with
decisions about how much or how little freedom I give to my
eldest child, when he asks if he can cycle round to his friend's
house. I can't imagine how I will be when my daughter gets to
that age, and she asks the same question. In some ways, ignorance
is bliss. We all know that these people exist in our communities.
But when you spot someone walking down your main street who
you know had been serving a sentence for molesting a child, the
reality is harder to accept. People walk by them without giving
them a second glance. I know that in a lot of cases we are told
that these men and women do not re-offend and can once again
contribute positively to society in some way. Reluctantly I accept
that in some cases there may be physiological reasons for their
deviant behaviour. Like it or not, there are strong arguments that
these people suffer from an imbalance which makes it impossible
for them to control their sexual urges. The targets of their desires,
however, are among the most vulnerable members of society, and
with good reason the paedophiles number amongst the most
hated because of their particular penchant. I am not sure if I
would prefer to behave like the ostrich and stick my head in the
sand, hoping that my life would never be touched by any of these

people and wishing them to exist anywhere but in the town where I live. What I do know is that my experiences as a screw have left me an incurable cynic and a realist in terms of the shortfalls of human nature, and I am more comfortable being that way.

*   *   *

A prison officer's job was difficult at the best of times. You had to be able to read situations and people accurately, and remain focused and in control at all times. It was always easier to deal with the ordinary cons who, although they would still try and stretch you, were predictable. There were inmates, though, who by their actions and temperament were clearly insane or had severe mental health issues. The prison hospitals were full of deeply disturbed individuals, often those who had been committed to jail for sexual offences. In one instance, there was an elderly male who reminded me of one of the patients from the film *One Flew Over the Cuckoo's Nest*. As you walked past his cell, he would gaze out at you with huge bulging eyes and a maniacal smile stretched across his lips. His medical condition was such that he had a permanent erection, and he was being treated with drugs to try and suppress his sexual urges. He would frequently masturbate in full view of passers by, with no attempt made to spare anyone's blushes. Just looking at him put the wind up me. In fairness, the hospital officers did their jobs as best they could, having been trained only to a certain level. A lot of these people needed round-the-clock psychiatric care, which the Prison Service was unable to supply.

The authorities also insisted on placing certain individuals amongst the general population, people who would have benefited from a direct psychiatric input. A particular episode of incest in the Antrim area had seen several members of the same family being placed in prison awaiting trial. The father figure in the family, along with his eldest teenage son, were committed to the Crum to await the bureaucracy of the courts and found themselves amidst 'ordinary decent criminals'. Word travels fast in jail, and it soon became clear that they were at risk from the other inmates on the wing. Both males were withdrawn and inarticulate, and had a sub-standard level of education, with the teenager displaying all the attributes of a small child. These weren't the observations of a professional. It was plain to all who came in contact with them that they were emotionally and psychologically stunted. Regardless of their obvious shortcomings, they were treated exactly the same as the inmates around them and remained in ordinary population for some time. They did get a hard time at the hands of screws and cons alike, and to some it may be considered justifiable, as the damage to the younger members of the family would be permanent in many ways. Of course they were not a normal family, and the whole investigation threw up all sorts of abhorrent details which beggared belief. But the reality was that these people had lived this type of life for so long as to consider it normal, without any intervention from any aspect of the Social Services. There would never be anything normal about them if the system didn't address the cause first, and attempt to educate and counsel the victims as well as the perpetrators. A spell in jail would never cure these people, assuming there was a cure.

There were also those inmates who displayed all the traits of being unhinged in order to engineer a place in the prison hospital. I remember one idiot who always took a slab of butter to the showers to wash with, and his block of soap to the dining hall with which to butter his bread. He tried his best for a few weeks to draw attention to himself but ultimately got tired of ruining his bacon sandwiches. The rest of the cons on the landing would take the piss out of him but, if nothing else, he provided them with a humorous interlude. I remember Gusty Spence telling me about an inmate he knew well who had engineered his relocation from the Crum to Purdysburn Hospital. Apparently this young man had taken to masturbating onto the floor of his cell and performing other weird and wonderful things in order to bring himself to the notice of staff. His plan worked. The sad thing is, he had immersed himself so deeply in character that he gradually lost any grip on reality that he had. Only recently was

Spence made aware that, almost thirty years later, he was still a resident of Purdysburn.

*   *   *

The need for opposing factions to co-operate on occasion was essential when the smooth running of exercise, showering, feeding and associations were the issues. With that in mind, it was still the case that there was genuine hatred displayed by each side towards the other whenever there was a confrontation. I remember that during association periods in A-wing, usually when the RCs were out and the Prods were locked, the large water boiler which was placed in the area around the stairwells on the threes became a major bone of contention. It was placed there so that those individuals who were locked at the time could be let out, one at a time, to grab hot water for a cup of tea in their cells. Almost every RC who left the association area to either go to his cell or the ablutions for some short task would make a point of rattling the lid of the boiler as he passed. You could guarantee that within seconds the Prods would be pressing their cell alarms, or banging the doors, claiming that the RCs had dropped something into the water in an attempt to try and poison them. We all knew why the Republicans did it. They just couldn't let the opportunity to wind up a Prod go by.

We may have had a laugh at the childish taunts and jibes aimed in both directions, but the incidents on record where factions had clashed with serious consequences were numerous. As well as that, jail may have seemed like a secure environment, but the murder of Billy Wright in the Maze showed everyone just how vulnerable inmates and staff alike were. The Crum was to see the murder of two Loyalist inmates in November 1991, when IRA inmates devised and planted a time bomb in C-wing dining hall. The men who died as a result of the bomb were 27-year-old Robert Skey, a UDA member, and 23-year-old Colin Caldwell, a member of the UVF.

It was a black day for the Northern Ireland Prison Service, and naturally questions were immediately asked as to just how explosives could have been brought into a high-security jail such as the Crum. The answers were being turned up only hours after the event when forensic officers discovered six torn-up condoms in a waste bin in the jail. It was believed that the eight ounces of Semtex which was used for the construction of the bomb had been smuggled in by female visitors, with the condoms used as the carriers for the material. It was a well-known fact that some females visiting the prison smuggled items in their vaginal cavity, and would retrieve them sometime during a visit when there were no prying eyes. It was a practice which was almost impossible to stop, as the searches of visitors were cursory, and may only have been aided by metal scanners. As well as that, all visits in remand wings took place in cubicles, which provided cover for intimate acts and discretions, and patrolling screws had to focus on numerous individuals at once.

Robert Skey died immediately in the blast, and seven others were injured. One of the injured, Colin Caldwell, was believed to have a fractured skull, but at first his injuries were not reported as life-threatening. Caldwell had only been in custody since September, having been remanded on charges of attempted murder, hijacking and possession of firearms. His condition worsened over the next few days, and on 28 November, the same day as the funeral for Robert Skey, he passed away. As was the way in Northern Ireland over the previous two decades, one tragedy was closely followed by another, when a quiet-natured delivery man was shot dead on the Ormeau Road at Candahar Street in retaliation for the bomb at the jail. He was a Catholic by the name of James McCaffrey, forty-eight years of age, and he was to become the 86th victim to die that year at the hands of terrorists. He was simply in the wrong place at the wrong time.

The Republicans had claimed the bomb, and Loyalists had reacted promptly and carried on the tradition of 'tit for tat' murder.

Lord Belstead, the Prisons Minister at the time, dismissed calls for his resignation over the lack of security at the Crum. He made a statement to the press reporting that Lord Colville would be heading an inquiry into the circumstances of the attack, from which recommendations would be made and implemented. Within a week of the inquiry taking place, remand visits in both A- and C-wings were revised, and all cubicles were removed. Open visits were apparently the way forward, and B-wing was to follow suit shortly. The inmates were far from happy, describing the move as a further attempt to integrate the opposing factions. The bomb had supposedly been a display by Republicans in protest at the lack of segregation in the jail, but all that it succeeded in doing was making matters worse. Inmates fought amongst themselves and with prison staff on the wings, and in the visits areas, with visitors to the jail reported as having been caught up in various incidents. As was expected, Lord Belstead was to become the scapegoat, and Dr Brian Mawhinney became the new Security Minister on 9 December of that year.

*   *   *

Whilst serving in Magilligan and the Crum, I came across many individuals whose names were well known for one reason or another. Over time they blended with the many others around them, and I began to place less emphasis on their notoriety. There was always the exception to the rule, of course.

I had always considered myself open-minded in relation to the conflicting politics in Northern Ireland, condemning neither the aspirations of true Republicans for a United Ireland, nor the desire of the Loyalists to retain their British identity. I do, however, condemn the methods used by both sides in supposedly furthering their 'cause'. The rule of thumb during this conflict appeared to be that anyone, civilian or otherwise, was a legitimate target, and all methods of disposing of enemies were considered within the rules.

Reading about these murders in the newspapers, often on a daily basis, and listening to journalists on radio and television reporting from the scene was graphic enough to say the least. But to watch the events unfold in live time, as we all did when Michael Stone went on the rampage in Milltown Cemetery, was almost surreal. It was one of the most bizarre spectacles I have ever witnessed on television, being played over and over again by all the news programmes on every channel. I could only compare it to the footage of the JFK assassination and the subsequent Lee Harvey Oswald murder, where on every appropriate occasion it was wheeled out for fresh appraisal. For the families and loved ones of the three victims it must have been torture to watch the episode unfolding, time and time again, reliving the horror as if it had just taken place. The audacity of the act itself turned Michael Stone into an enigma. The general consensus was that he had acted alone, and his actions were those of a madman. For others, though, particularly Loyalist paramilitaries, he had struck a major blow for their cause and was to be regarded as a hero. Hero or madman, I remember the day's events well, and the circumstances which led to him wreaking havoc in the Republican stronghold.

Virtually all the major Republicans in West Belfast had turned out for the funerals and interment of the 'Gibraltar Three'; Danny McCann, Sean Savage and Mairead Farrell. Their killing by British soldiers was to become a defining moment in Ulster's politics, with the question of a 'shoot to kill' policy being raised and lodged as a continuing area of contention by Sinn Féin. If Stone had to pick a high-profile event at which to carry out his master plan, he couldn't have picked better. Stone had trailed the massive cortèges to Milltown on foot but had supposedly abandoned his assassination attempt at the graveside, and he had to make good his escape as best he could. He did so in a way which was both bizarre and frightening. Here was a man bent on a killing spree, knowing full well that the world's press would be in attendance and any attempt at anonymity would be futile. It was impossible not to watch the events as they unfolded. Stone kept firing his handgun and throwing grenades at the mourners as he fled towards the M1 motorway on foot, seemingly in no particular hurry. He was to end up killing three people on that day, wounding at least sixty others, and becoming a legend in the eyes of many Loyalists. After a brief confinement to the military wing of Musgrave Park Hospital to recover from injuries he received at the time of his arrest, he was remanded to the Crum. His answer to charge at court was well rehearsed, and added fuel to the media frenzy which followed every aspect of this remarkable story. When asked if he had any reply, Stone spoke out:

> That I alone carried out this military operation as a retaliatory strike against Provisional Sinn Féin IRA in response to the slaughter of innocents at La Mon, Darkley, Brighton and Enniskillen. I would state that I am a dedicated freelance Loyalist paramilitary. No surrender.

His infamy carried with it a threat from Republicans to assassinate him at all costs, and created a nightmare for prison authorities in the Crum, who had responsibility for his containment and safety whilst on remand and awaiting trial.

Michael Stone was housed in the very back of D-wing, in an annexe area, totally removed from any other inmates in the jail, including Loyalists. I remember seeing him on the day of his committal, and was aware that he had reasonably severe bruising around his face, lingering injuries from when the crowd eventually caught up with him at the motorway. He had long dark hair and was fairly stocky, but with the look of a man possessed. Whether I based my opinion on his looks or purely on the association with his moment of utter madness I am not quite sure. He did, however, become the most talked about inmate at the time, and we were all curious.

The threat to Stone's life was such that all movement of other prisoners had to be stopped, and all inmates, including orderlies, locked, when he was taken for visits, legal consultations or to the prison hospital. He cut a very lonely figure, being guided through the grills with at least one officer constantly at his side. The screws who worked in the secure unit with Stone were also heavily vetted before being allowed so close to him. From what I can remember, the authorities were reluctant to permit any officers with less than two years service into that area, in fear that they may have been recruited with the sole purpose of getting within striking distance of him.

I first got to work close to him on a night duty. When detailed a night duty, you were required to work from seven-thirty in the morning until lunchtime of that day, and then return at eight o'clock that evening to stay through until eight the next morning. It was my most hated of duties and always knocked my body clock out of kilter. I found it impossible to stay awake throughout the night without continuous cups of coffee and volumes of reading material. At that particular time, I was on general duties and had no permanent post, which meant that I could be detailed any post in the jail and wasn't confined to any particular wing. When I paraded for 'pre-nights', I was sent to D-wing annexe to work alongside the permanent staff looking after Stone.

My lasting memory of that morning was standing with Michael Stone in the small exercise yard beside the annexe. He struck up a brief conversation with me, asking if I had seen just how close he had been to Gerry Adams at the graveside, saying that he had been standing only yards behind him. He then continued by adding that there were children close by, and that he had decided to abort any attempt at killing Adams because of this. Stone was obviously aware that images of his actions at the cemetery had been shown on terrestrial television stations around the world, and he assumed that anyone he came in contact with would know of him by reputation. I don't think it was arrogance on his part, rather he struck me as being singularly focused on the one subject he would always be known for, like a record stuck in the groove. It was as if he had no particular aspirations other than obtaining the recognition for his escapade, and to be able to 'dine out', as it were, on that one definitive incident. He was extremely articulate when recounting his story, and it struck me at the time that maybe by talking about it he was attempting to rationalise it, for his audience at least. I had heard the rumour that he had been asked by another screw a few weeks after he had come in, if he had any regrets. Apparently his answer had been that just a few days prior to his rampage, he had bought the cap which he was seen wearing, and was most annoyed at having lost it when it blew away during his escape.

At the time, I couldn't imagine what the solitary aspect of his confinement was like for him, and any interaction between himself and the screws would probably have been a welcome relief for both. The surreal events that took place in West Belfast on the day of those funerals caused myself and others to look at Stone as an unknown quantity, capable of anything without thought for consequence. With nothing to lose, he remained unpredictable. I found that disconcerting in many ways and can safely say I was unnerved when in his company. Even though we would have had short conversations which bordered on the mundane, I never lost sight of the fact that he was a dangerous and calculating sociopath.

From television and newspaper interviews with Stone since his release under the Good Friday Agreement, he has remained somewhat contradictory as to his having any regrets or remorse for his actions. Stone was one of the many to appear on the recent television programme 'Facing the Truth'. He stood apart from the others, however, as he portrayed all the trappings of a person with serious mental health issues. There was nothing redeeming about him in any sense. Where other perpetrators had in some way given us a reason for their actions, albeit an unacceptable reason in the eyes of their victims' relatives, and had displayed some attributes of humanity in openly admitting to being genuinely remorseful, he did not. I believe he showed nothing other than arrogance and contempt for his fellow man.

Michael Stone still remains a bogeyman in my head. I remember a series of adverts aired in and around the time of the Good Friday Agreement, where people were being reminded about the bad old days, with very graphic images of shootings being played out to the audience. One of those adverts depicted a long-haired, heavy-set male with a machine gun, opening up on people in a pub who had been enjoying a night out. There was a slow-motion shot of him spraying the bar with rounds, wild-eyed and teeth gritted, looking as if he was enjoying every sickening moment. Whether the advertising company chose this particular actor unwittingly I will never know, but when I watched it again and again, I could only think of Michael Stone. It was as if they had picked him as the template for the lead character. Maybe he was the bogeyman for others too, and let's face it, none of us wanted to return to the days when people like him were around.

Who else then would take it upon themselves to remind us of those times other than Stone himself, when on 24 November 2006, the date set for the closest step towards devolution we had witnessed to date, he decided to mount a one-man attack on Stormont. He took us all by surprise when he limped up to the main building armed with an imitation firearm, some explosive devices, a large knife and a garrotte. Before actually entering the revolving doors at the main entrance, he sprayed anti Sinn Féin graffiti in bright red paint on the wall outside, and then made his dramatic entrance. At just over fifty years of age, and suffering from arthritis, the outcome was always going to be the same. He was detained almost immediately by a male and a female civilian security guard, and relieved of his imitation firearm and other weapons. If his state of mind had been questionable before, here was the proof that he had serious mental health issues and was a threat to himself and others. The events of that day caused mayhem for the Assembly and its members, but provided the world's press with a ringside seat yet again at the Michael Stone show.

For anyone who has ever come in contact with Stone, they would probably agree that he was always capable of carrying out such an act, and that it would have always been on such a scale. It would also have been less about the political motivation and more about the person. If I were even more cynical, I would suggest that for those 'art lovers' who purchased one of his paintings since his release from prison, they may just have cause for a small celebration, as they may have seen an increase in their investment.

As far as launching himself into the public eye again, if that indeed was the purpose of the exercise, he succeeded in doing just that. He may unwittingly have reminded us, though, just how fragile the road towards Stormont can be, and how just one crazed individual could upset the apple cart and draw us back into the darkness once again.

I resigned from the Prison Service a short time after having come in contact with Stone. My decision was made after some deliberation, as I knew I was leaving a secure and stable job to launch myself into self-employment. The positives of a new and exciting venture greatly outweighed the negatives, and I had already factored in a reduction in income. I had felt sad leaving behind some colleagues and friends, but just as soon as I had handed in all my uniform and kit, the sense of relief was enormous. It was as if I had finished a prison sentence myself, and in many ways I had.

Chapter 5
Screws and Cons

To say that the Northern Ireland Prison Service was a natural choice of career for me at the age of twenty-two would be a lie. In fact I can't imagine anyone ever aspiring to becoming a prison officer. It is more of a job which you can conveniently turn to, just when you think your options are limited. It just wouldn't be something I can imagine many children at school shouting out when they are asked what they want to be when they grow up. Fireman or policeman, yes. But prison officer, not likely. For me, there were other opportunities for employment, skilled or otherwise, and if nothing else had appealed to me, I could always have applied for the Royal Ulster Constabulary as a regular police officer. With the Troubles still prevalent at that time, it was a secure career, but one not without obvious risks. Even then, members of the Roman Catholic community were actively being encouraged to make application for the police due to under-representation, with the percentages reported as gradually shifting. Unfortunately, a previous experience with the RUC had left me disillusioned with the force in general, and at the time I had found it hard to reconcile any differences I had with it. Like a lot of employable young men in Northern Ireland in the mid-1980s, I found it difficult to look beyond uniform jobs, purely because of the remuneration packages on offer. The average pay far surpassed that of any other jobs which required similar academic qualifications. Those who joined the police, UDR or Prison Service quickly got used to having money in their pockets, and spending that money on houses and cars, and a certain kind of lifestyle.

In truth, the Troubles created a generation of material-minded individuals, a great majority of whom would have openly admitted to loathing their uniformed security jobs, but who were financially hog-tied.

Whilst growing up, I had several interests, most of which centred around the outdoors—hunting, shooting and fishing in particular—and if I had had the opportunity, I would have loved to have taken up a position as a gamekeeper. I have never been that material-minded, which would have been a pre-requisite for any keeper's job, as the pay and prospects were severely limited. I tried to make in-roads into several private game estates in my local area, and further afield, but it was very much a closed shop. The keeper's job was often passed down from one generation to the next, a family tradition as it were.

My friends and family will agree that over the years I never seemed to settle into anything for very long. That is not to say that I stayed unemployed for any length of time; somehow, I always managed to secure some sort of income from somewhere. I would have to say, though, that I was never comfortable with jobs in which I could not express myself, or was not able to make my mark in some small way. The rigidity of some of the working conditions in many of my past jobs, I found difficult to adhere to, and restrictive to say the least. I have always wanted a challenge in my working life, but I had to be realistic at times, especially when money was tight, and there were no obvious opportunities presenting themselves.

I first became aware of the Prison Service as a possible career through a friend who had just left the ranks of the UDR (Ulster Defence Regiment). He told me just how well paid it was, and that he was aware that they were recruiting fairly regularly. I made some enquiries, and kept an eye on the *Belfast Telegraph* job section until I finally saw the advert one Thursday evening. It was there in front of me at exactly the right time. My back wasn't to the wall by any stretch of the imagination, but there was a lull in the momentum which I believed was carrying me forward towards something better. The criteria for entrance into the Service was an exam, followed by an interview and a medical. My whole attitude towards the selection process was one of near apathy, and I never felt any great pressure to succeed in getting placed as a candidate for the Prison Service College. This may have worked to my advantage in the fact that I hadn't suffered from any nerves whatsoever during the interview, and had answered the questions put to me in a relaxed and confident manner. But when I did manage to complete the first part of the process, progressing through to the next stage, I began taking the opportunity seriously, and eventually, on acceptance, I fully applied myself to the training.

Whether it was the camaraderie of my squad during the weeks in Millisle Training College, or just being caught up in other people's enthusiasm, I am not quite sure, but I did begin to look at the broader picture, and was coming around to the possibility of a career as a prison officer. The others in my squad were from all walks of life. Many had come from a military background, but others had been civil servants, mechanics, and there was even an undertaker amongst them. An odd mix to say the least, but all in all, quite sound and reasonable individuals. Each of us brought different life skills from our other jobs, but nothing which would go any way towards preparing us for becoming warders. Even when we were presented with certain realities about the job, and given a no-nonsense, warts and all insight by training staff into what would be expected of us, our fervour was seldom dampened. We had begun to bond as a team. I remember being particularly keen to complete the training so I could get to my posting as quickly as possible and establish myself in the job. Most of the others were the same, and when we eventually came to our passing out parade, we were like kids getting out of school.

This enthusiasm remained with me for a short time. About as much time as it took for the novelty of the job to wear off, in fact. Which, if the truth be known, wasn't very long at all. Certain experiences and observations of the people around me made me realise that I would never be a career screw. No matter how hard I tried to imagine it, I just couldn't see myself in twenty-five years doing the same thankless task, in the same place, having become just as institutionalised as the very people I was locking away each and every night. The biggest eye-opener was the fact that a lot of my work colleagues were genuinely suffering from stress and mental fatigue, and these pressures had a habit of manifesting themselves in various ways which were often self-destructive. No, I realised quite quickly that this was most certainly not a 'job for life', not for me anyway.

I have never professed to being an angel, and will admit that whilst stationed at Magilligan, I engaged in many a night's drink and debauchery in the local hostelries. I had a healthy appetite for socialising, but often sought out a less visited haunt for a quiet pint away from the hustle and bustle. On one beautiful summer's evening, shortly after being posted to the prison, I chose to walk the two and a half miles down from the prison gates to the main Downhill/Limavaddy Road, to sample the wares of the local. Although it bore the name 'the Mallard Bar', it was affectionately known as the 'Dirty Duck'. It was the first time I had ever set foot in the bar. I had been told that the people living in the townlands surrounding the jail were indifferent towards screws, but I was always aware of my personal security, and whilst walking towards this little rural establishment I tried to concoct the perfect cover story in case I was engaged by a local. I needn't have bothered. When I opened the door to the lounge bar, it was like walking into the last chance saloon in Dodge City. If there had been a piano player, I'm sure he would have stopped playing to emphasise my entrance to anyone who may have missed it. Everyone present in the little lounge, around a dozen people in all, swivelled in their respective seats, and eyed me with keen interest. I acknowledged the glances with a feeble 'Evening', and skulked over to the counter, taking a seat beside this frail-looking gentleman in an ill-fitting striped suit and an off-white shirt buttoned up to the throat, with no tie. I ordered a pint of stout, not by choice, but again thinking about fitting in as best I could, when all of a sudden, the little man in the suit turned towards me and said, 'You're a warder aren't ye?' I don't think it was a question, more of a statement. When I replied that I hadn't realised it would have been that obvious, he replied, 'Oh aye, sure there's not a hedge nor a woman in the land you'se haven't been through!' I almost choked on the first pull of my pint. Just as quick as he had spoken to me, he turned away and buried his head in the local newspaper. It was my first lesson as to the unenviable reputation I had to live up to, a reputation that had been cultivated by better men than me.

In the coming months and years, I tried to keep up with some of the more seasoned campaigners on many a night out, but I could honestly describe myself as a lightweight compared to them. I was almost always late for duty in the morning and was unfairly pigeon-holed as one of the 'live-in reprobates' by some senior ranks. But to be fair, I never drank on duty, and chased the women as much as any other single man. I embraced the 'work hard, play hard' ethic as much as I could.

Thankfully, I had taken to include a fitness regime into my day, running the roads in and around the prison, and notching up 50 to 60 miles a week on some occasions. This was self-imposed and helped to relieve the boredom of living and working in such a remote location. It also kept me out of the Officers' Club, which was far too handy, to say the least. I found that exercise relieved any stress I had, or went a long way with helping me to manage it. It was the first thing I turned to after a hard day in the blocks when something had annoyed or upset me, or if I was on edge. When I transferred back to Belfast, I kept up the running and gym work, and was able to cut back on the nights out. I had plenty of things to busy myself with now that I was living in my own home instead of within the confines of a prison. I am a strong believer in separating my social life from any working relationships I may have, although on some occasions it is incredibly difficult not to overlap the two. Shift work, mixed with a stressful job in a male-dominated workforce, creates a situation whereby some find it hard to bond with people outside of those parameters. Throughout my time in the Service I managed to retain a healthy circle of friends from all walks of life who helped to keep me well grounded. Without that constant in my life at the time, I suspect I may have been drawn into a spiral of one drinking binge after another.

The Prison Service as I knew it had no reasonable coping mechanisms set in place for officers who were struggling with stress, and I cannot remember any real emphasis being placed on good mental health. It would not have been rocket science to establish that there was quite a large drinking culture in most of the prisons in the North, both off and on duty, and the Crum was no exception. The problems which arose from officers abusing alcohol were many, ranging from breaches of codes of conduct, to lapses in security in the jail, and right up to committing criminal offences. Thinking back, incidents involving drunken screws occurred almost on a weekly basis, and the authorities must have been aware of what was happening both inside and out. It was certainly common knowledge to any of us working there at the time, and I suppose we were just as guilty for accepting it and turning a blind eye. One of the factors which should have been addressed as being contributory to the drinking culture was the Officers' Club. I've always wondered why in God's name they placed such a temptation in easy grasp of those screws who were known to have a problem. I will always remember the quote by George Bernard Shaw that 'fidelity is lack of opportunity', a sentiment that could so easily be applied to sobriety and alcohol abuse. If the authorities had closed down the club, they would have gone some way towards addressing the problem, in work at least.

The Prison Officers' Club in the Crum was situated at the end of the little row of houses which had once been occupied by officers and their families. It was far from luxurious with regard to fixtures and fittings, and appeared purely functional as a watering hole for the many or the few. Those who did frequent it, particularly in the evening after a day shift, could only be described as the serious drinkers. I could think of no more depressing a place to retire to after a hard day's work than the club. These men had an overt reputation as 'boozers', and no distinction was made in relation to rank.

I can remember several incidents of fights and marital indiscretions originating in the club and then spilling unceremoniously into the yard leading up to the extern gate.

Rumour has it that many a marriage was wrecked, and many a child conceived, on the top of the pool table in those premises. Those unfortunate enough to be detailed at that wicket gate (which opened directly onto the Crumlin Road) at the start of a night shift, had often to request the closure of the club to enable the jail to be locked down for the night, as they would eventually move inside the main building when the outside gates were secured.

One such incident, which I will never forget, was at around 10 p.m. on a week night, when I had been detailed night duty starting at the gate along with another screw, who was of the old school of non-communicators. As I settled into the post, occasionally letting the odd straggler out into the street, I became aware that a car was still parked up towards the area of the club. It wasn't long before I heard the car approach the double gates and stop just before the pedestrian exit. I looked out to see who was driving the car and saw a male who I knew lived in Newtownards (a market town about ten miles away) slumped over the steering wheel. At first I thought he had dropped something into the footwell and had bent down to retrieve it. But when he didn't straighten up after a minute or two, I went over and knocked on his driver's side window. It was another moment before he turned his head towards me and uttered something totally incomprehensible. He was pissed. He had that thousand-yard stare and the vocabulary of a four-year-old.

I kept telling him to leave the car and I would get him a taxi home, but he wouldn't listen and became abusive, telling me to 'open the fucking gate'. Of course I had no power to detain him, and I asked my colleague to help me out and see if he could talk him around. Acting in the spirit of goodwill and fellowship to all men, he told me to open the gate and let him out. He had absolutely no interest in the possible consequences of letting this drunk onto the Belfast streets in what was effectively a mobile killing machine. Neither did he care what would happen to his colleague should he not manage to make it home. I couldn't believe what I was hearing, but eventually I had to do what I was told. I opened the gate and watched with one eye closed as the car limped out onto the Crumlin Road, narrowly missing another car heading countrywards in the process. Luckily enough he did make it home with not so much as a scratch. I suspect the journey was one he had made on more than one occasion in similar conditions, and the car was on autopilot. It was what could have happened that sent a shiver down my spine.

There was also the added peculiarity that a lot of the prison officers serving throughout the years of the Troubles, had taken to carrying PPW's or personal protection weapons. The guns they carried were often pistols like the Walther, or in some cases 38's, and when issued with the weapon, they had to attend a not so rigorous firearms handling course. Put the two elements together, alcohol and firearms, and the cocktail becomes lethal. Further to that add a prison warder, and the cocktail becomes a Molotov.

Reports of the incidents where drunken screws had firearms in their possession in suspicious circumstances were, on many an occasion, never carried further than the Wicket gateat the Crum or the front gates of the Maze. Screws were often separated from their weapons in the most bizarre circumstances, but almost always involving alcohol on some level. The screw who took his gun out of his pancake holster and set it on the shelf of a public telephone box whilst he made a call became the butt of many a joke for weeks after. In his spirit-induced stupor, he had forgotten to replace the gun in his waistband after making his call, and had left it there for a member of the public to find some time later. It was a serious enough incident, but I don't remember much more than a reprimand being administered by the authorities. He did, however, have to endure numerous cartoons appearing in and around the jail depicting his caricature depositing a firearm in a telephone box with the word 'ARMOURY' clearly displayed above the door. There would be no space left to write anything else in this book if I took the time to recount just some of the more enlightening incidents and, in fairness, there would be equally as many, if not more, involving police officers as well. I believe it was not in the public interest to wash the dirty linen in full view of the public during what could only be described as difficult and trying times for anyone working in a security-related job in Northern Ireland.

The continuing troubles on the streets of the Province had opened up a monumental divide between Loyalist and Nationalist communities. The various paramilitary groups who claimed to represent these two communities did, however, appear to have common enemies in the shape of the RUC, the Army and often times the Prison Service staff. It always seemed unfair to me to be continually the 'piggy in the middle'. Our job was one of containment, and we had to abide by the type of regime that the Northern Ireland Office deemed fit to enforce. As far as we were concerned, a terrorist prisoner was a terrorist prisoner regardless of his affiliations. Nevertheless, we had been ruled in as 'legitimate targets', whatever they were, and over nearly a twenty-year span, from 1974 to the early 1990s, twenty-nine prison-related employees lost their lives through terrorism from both sides. When Francis Curry and Joe Nellins went on hunger strike in Magilligan in 1986, they did so in an attempt to highlight conditions which they thought intolerable inside the jail. Jim McDonald, the Loyalist prisoners' welfare spokesman at the time, warned the NIO that there was mounting pressure on the outside for more militant action to be taken against prison officers. They were strong words, and some even considered them incitement. The action eventually came in the form of a letter bomb delivered to the Coleraine home of a screw, and then incidents of car bombs at Limavaddy addresses where other officers lived. There were no placard protests or strongly worded letters. Terrorism had been the proven method when pressure needed to be applied for any changes to be implemented, and actions spoke louder than words.

I was at a slight disadvantage around the time of Curry's incarceration as he hailed from an area just up the road from my own house. He was a controlling figure in the jail at the time and had a reputation as a vicious and uncompromising individual. Bangor had its fair share of Loyalist paramilitaries who had influence both in North Down and East Belfast, and they chose to live in areas all over the town, not just in Loyalist controlled housing estates. Curry was one of those to opt for a private house in a quiet residential area of Bangor from which he could control his illegal dealings. Unfortunately, the Assets Recovery Agency did not exist then, and Curry amongst others were living in what some considered circumstances beyond their means. They would quite happily socialise in the Loyalist run clubs and bars but often strayed further afield. I knew that it wasn't going to be long before I would bump into one of them in a pub in the town. When it did happen, I was given the shock of my life.

One particular weekend when home for a few days, myself and my future wife went to the cinema and then popped into our local for a drink before home. We couldn't have been sitting more than ten minutes when one of the better known personalities came in, along with another male who I didn't recognise. He deliberately chose a seat across from ours, and smiled over. I nodded over, and then continued in conversation with my other half. Only a minute or so later, he walked over to our table and called me by my first name, asking if he could buy us both a drink. I was taken aback as I had no idea how he knew my name. I declined his offer, stating that we were only there for one drink, and one drink only. Undeterred, he then called my partner by her first name and said that he would be most disappointed if neither of us took him up on his offer of a drink. I knew then that he was there to make a point. He obviously knew quite a bit about me and was reminding me in no uncertain terms that my card was being marked.

I was rattled by the encounter, and made a point to approach the security PO when I returned to work in the next day or two. I didn't have to. My name, my address, and the make and registration of my car were being shouted from the windows of the block I worked in most by Loyalist prisoners at lock-up times, and it was considered that I was under threat. On the strength of that, I began to take my personal security more seriously. I immediately became wary about socialising in particular pubs or clubs, and avoided forming any sort of patterns which would have earmarked me as a 'soft target'. A lot of screws were in the same position as myself, and some were worse off, as they already lived in Loyalist areas, right amongst the very people they were locking up on occasion. The prison officer's lot was an unenviable one at times. Every other security job in Ulster saw you come in contact with undesirables, but only for the short time when you were either arresting them, or prosecuting them through the courts. The screws, however, would have to face these men day in, day out. There was no escaping them. That was the nature of the job. It wasn't difficult for them to find out where you lived, who you were married to, and how many kids you had. When they eventually brought this to your attention, emphasising just how vulnerable you and your loved ones were, it could be a bitter pill to swallow.

But it was how you coped with this added pressure as an individual, along with the other day to day challenges of the job, which would set you apart. Alcohol was recreational as far as I was concerned, and I kept it that way. It was never a crutch for me. I may on occasion have shown up for work nursing the mother of all hangovers, but it was a rare enough occurrence. The key to identifying the seasoned drinkers in the job was to look for the ones who always smelled of alcohol, but never had a hangover.

In the Crum as well as Magilligan and the Maze, there were also small groups of daytime drunks who breakfasted from a bottle, and continued topping up the rest of the day. When I say breakfasted, I literally mean they broke the seal on a bottle at breakfast time, and substituted booze for food. Working alongside one of these men was particularly difficult, as the cons could smell drink a mile away and would often use this to their advantage. You were always two men down when an alcoholic screw worked in a busy wing, as your time was divided between watching the cons and keeping an eye on the screw in case they upset the equilibrium. Drink made them either aggressive or plain obstinate, and often led to confrontational behaviour towards the inmates. Whenever a drunk screw turned up for association time, they were nearly always taken off side into the class office where they couldn't do any harm. It was hard to hold your tongue sometimes and not tell the senior staff on duty.

That, however, would have been to commit the cardinal sin of touting on your mates, and life would not have been worth living.

I recently spoke to an ex-prisoner who I remembered from Magilligan in 1985, and then again in the Crum when he returned in 1988 on remand. I had known him since he was a teenager, as he had grown up in Bangor and our paths had crossed on more than one occasion. In his early twenties his life had taken an unfortunate twist and he had ended up in prison. Circumstances for him have changed considerably since his release in 1991, and he has become a skilled worker in the motor trade and a dedicated family man. He was happy enough to share his recollections of the Crum, but wished to be known only by his first name, Eddie. I was curious how Eddie had felt about the staff in the jail, particularly the Crum, and I knew him well enough to probe a little bit deeper than I would have with a stranger. I knew his reply would be open and honest:

> Like most others, cons I mean, I never really thought much about the screws. They were there, and that was that. There were some now who had a real attitude problem, and you would have never got tired of punching them. They were the ones who were always on your back. They were also the ones who you saw one day and then it might have been a couple of days later before they came back on to the wing. You could tell that they got a real kick out of winding you up. One bastard I remember well always seemed to appear at mealtimes to do the sliding doors into the dining hall in A-wing when I was on remand. I remember him well. He was a small guy with glasses and thin face and a moustache. He was really insignificant. When we were going through the gates into the dining hall, he would try and slide the door across to catch you as you walked in. You knew he was smiling when he did it. If there hadn't been a cage and screens between him and I, the story may have ended differently. I have never been a violent man, but as far as I was concerned I was getting on with my punishment . . .

and this prick was intent on making life difficult. It was always the small things which wound you up, never the bigger ones. I hated my visitors being kept waiting whilst I was told late about the visit, and I hated watching screws standing laughing and chatting outside the class office whilst I had been asking for at least ten minutes to get out of my cell for a shit. The thing I hated most, though, was the drunk screws who wandered around giving you a touch or two, and then fucking off to leave someone else to pick up the pieces.

I realised Eddie was talking about getting wound up by temporary wing staff, some of whom were known to have gone to the club for a pint or two before association. The frustration he must have felt was natural. Not only were these screws mixing it up when they were on the wings, but they were also constantly reminding the inmates just what they couldn't have—alcohol. I know that alcohol abuse was contributory in many ways to some of these men offending, and it was only their incarceration which was managing their addiction.

I really think these guys thought that once they put on a uniform, nobody was going to touch them. They thought they could get away with anything. Frankly I wouldn't have given a shit what uniform they were wearing, and neither would any of the other cons. If one of them had really pissed me off, I would have knocked his bollocks in. It's one thing acting like a hard man, but if you can't back it up, then you deserve everything you get. I know the same men wouldn't have given the big UVF or UDA men any grief. Oh aye, they were always a bit more subdued when they were around. For any man to gain my respect, they have to respect me as a person regardless whether I was a prisoner or not. In fairness, I believe that there were a few screws who were genuinely only interested in doing their jobs as best they could and not making life difficult for us in the process. For that reason and that reason alone, I would

Another McGuinness leaves the jail after a short stay for not paying his fine. (Pacemaker Press International)

Nearly free. Republican hardman Dominic McGlinchey makes it to the gate, only to be re-arrested pending extradition to the Republic. (Pacemaker Press International)

Loyalist prisoners' roof-top protest in 1981, demanding changes to the prison regime in Northern Ireland. (Pacemaker Press International)

Picking up the pieces: scene of the gun battle during the June escape in 1981. (Pacemaker Press International)

WANTED

These men, who were in custody charged with serious terrorist offences, escaped from Crumlin Road Prison, Belfast on the afternoon of Wednesday 10th June 1981.

SLOAN, Gerard,

FUSCO, Angelo

McKEE, Michael A.

DOHERTY, Joseph P.T.

MAGEE, Paul Patk.

SLOAN, Anthony Gerard

CAMPBELL, R.J.

If you have any information on the whereabouts of these men or if you can help in any way - please get in touch urgently with any Police Station or ring the Confidential Telephone BELFAST 652155.

Any information will be treated in absolute confidence.

WANTED

Issued by the Royal Ulster Constabulary

On the run: a 'Wanted' poster, depicting seven of the eight escapees. (Pacemaker Press International)

The net widens in the search for the escapees. Soldiers from the Royal Highland Fusiliers stop vehicles on the Antrim Road. (Pacemaker Press International)

Closed for business: the jail falls into decline after its closure in 1996. (Pacemaker Press International)

The glass door: the air-lock system of gates, controlled by an officer in the 'bubble' directly beside it.

Spiral staircase in the circle area. The walkway above would have been used by inmates going to and from chapel.

C-wing as it is today. The cones at the far end mark the staircase descending to the drop room.

never hold a grudge. I know that some screws would question that, and they think that all of us would like to trail them up an alley and give them a good hiding, but it's their own paranoia. Over the past few years I have bumped into a couple of faces whom I remember as screws from the Crum. When you look in their direction, and a few seconds later it clicks with them where they remember you from, you can see the panic set in. One time I went into a service station in Newtownards, and on my way up to pay for my petrol I spotted this big PO, and nodded at him. When I went back out to my car, I could see him hiding at the magazines at the back of the shop and sneaking wee looks into the forecourt. He must have stayed there for about ten minutes. Just for badness, I parked out on the road, and when he eventually got back into his car and drove away, I made sure he seen me waving at him. He couldn't take his eyes of the rear view mirror. He was shitting himself. I had no intention of doing anything, I was just winding him up. Now if it had been that wee shit I remember from A-wing, I probably wouldn't have been able to help myself.

I found it reassuring that Eddie had adopted an attitude of tolerance in the face of his experiences with twisted individuals who were on some kind of persecution trip. He was level-headed enough not to have tarred everyone with the same brush. I am not sure that would be the case, though, with every ex-inmate. For some cons, a screw was just as bad as a peeler, and given half a chance they would do their worst.

* * *

There were particular screws, though, for whom the idea that they were the common enemy never quite sank in. On more than one occasion, I witnessed prison officers verbally siding with Loyalist inmates on issues which were ongoing in the jails. It was even scarier to hear a colleague turn around and tell you and others around him that if there were to come a day when the IRA's campaign escalated beyond control, to a near civil war perhaps, then his conscience would force him to open the cell doors and let his Loyalist 'brothers' out to fight the war. I was astounded, to say the least, but in no way surprised as to where his sympathies lay. The Ulster flags and 'No Surrender' tattoos on his forearms were clear indicators of his political viewpoint. It was his assumption that no one would take offence at this comment that was the hardest part to take in. It was also the fact that he actually believed that if his scenario was indeed played out exactly as he had described it, that he would not himself be a target for the Loyalist prisoners. I know that the Loyalist inmates had difficulty coming to terms with what they considered a contradictory situation, i.e. being imprisoned by the very State they believed they were defending, and being locked up by people who should recognise them as comrades. One influential Loyalist in the late 1980s and early 1990s, John Gregg, had commented on just that idea, stating that he could never have done such a job for any amount of money. He actually used the terms 'lock up my own people'.

That particular screw was not the only one who had strongly held views and who made no bones about it. There were several who openly pinned their colours where all could see them. The prison authorities themselves didn't appear to take issue with emblems, badges or tattoos that could be construed as sectarian. This apathy gave out a very mixed signal, and one which allowed the behaviour to go unchallenged. I admit to sometimes finding it difficult to work alongside these men when they made no attempt to mask their bigotry and narrow-mindedness. Regardless of my religious beliefs, or lack of them, I expected a degree of consideration. To take issue with the problem would have opened up a whole can of worms, and there would have been few willing to take the repercussions as the person behind any such complaint.

The issue also had more sinister implications, as you could never be sure if these men would go as far as to traffic items into the jail for paramilitary prisoners. Because of the nature of the job, and the ever-present risk of violence on the wings, you expected your colleagues to watch your back, just as you would for them. When the person you were working with was someone you couldn't trust, then you were very much isolated. It is not a comfortable position to be in. I do not know if any officers of the Protestant persuasion had come across Republican sympathisers in their time, and can only comment on my own experiences, but I am sure that there were some amongst the prison staff somewhere. The majority of prison officers did come from Protestant backgrounds, however, with the Catholics being somewhat under-represented at that time. With no measures in place to address sensitive issues like this, the problem was one which was dealt with by the individuals involved. I do know that today, the Police Service of Northern Ireland amongst other employers has adopted a 'zero tolerance' approach to sectarianism in the workplace. Their policies reach far beyond just religious discrimination, but cover any discrimination, whether it be sexual, racial or lifestyle. The era of accountability and political correctness has arrived, and there is a huge emphasis on 'good and harmonious conditions' in the workplace. It is the employers themselves who will fall foul of the law if they have not addressed any issues which could lead to an allegation of harassment.

To be the whistle-blower must still be the most difficult position to put yourself in. If you choose to remain in your job after making a stand for whatever reason, rest assured the stigma will undoubtedly follow you wherever you go. I never had any great difficulty when dealing with anyone who brought their own brand of discrimination to work. I had already grown skin as thick as a rhino's, and knew that to rise to the bait was the biggest mistake you could make. That we had to deal with problems such as these from colleagues at all was an awful indictment on the working conditions within the Service at the time.

*   *   *

This was meant to be a professional body of men who carried forward a tradition of good reputation and standing, dating back to the previous century. There was an expectation of certain behaviour, dress code and sobriety. Thankfully I do remember most as being diligent and worthy of that tradition, but sadly others I remember as a collection of misfits and social pariahs.

An example of the bravery and dedication of prison officers came in World War Two during the Belfast Blitz over the period of 15 and 16 April 1941. Belfast had already been attacked over 7 and 8 April, and it was a reality check for everyone concerned. The city had not been prepared for such a raid, with the docks being extensively damaged as well as reports of thirteen dead. Throughout the early hours of 16 April, the city was to suffer a major onslaught from Nazi bombers whose targets again included the shipyard and various factory sites. Casualties in terms of loss of human lives were huge, over 900 believed dead, with even more people being affected by the loss of their livelihoods as mills and workshops were reduced to rubble. The German command had committed around 180 bombers to the raid, which lasted over a four-hour period. The Crum was close to many of the heavily targeted areas, yet prison officers were still carrying out their duties during the persistent air raid, with little regard for their own personal safety. They didn't have to be coerced into remaining at their posts, and did so even when the Republican inmates of the time gave them little incentive to do so. Even those on a rest period turned out for duty when conditions became stretched to near breaking point. The A-wing Republicans had refused to avail of the air raid shelters supplied, stating that they were being provided by an 'alien government'. When the raids became heavier, however, and several prison officers were standing on the roof of the jail directing fire teams to the numerous falling incendiaries, the Republicans made a request to leave their cells to take cover in the shelters. When unlocked, however, they ran around the wing shouting 'Here come our allies', obviously referring to the Luftwaffe planes overhead. It must have been a sickening display, and put severe pressure on the already struggling members of staff to recover control of the jail. It wasn't an easy task, as prison numbers at that time had risen to accommodate a further two hundred more than usual. With everything taken into account, the officers coped incredibly well. In recognition of their contribution, a letter was drafted by the Right Honorable J.M. Andrews, DL, MP of Comber, suggesting that a sum of £5 be paid to each staff member who attended work over this period in appreciation of their diligence and bravery. The sum of money was irrelevant, although £5 was considerable in those days. The recognition of their personal sacrifice would have meant more than any amount of money.

All through the 1940s, the Crum was bursting at the seams, to the point where even one more inmate could be the straw that broke the camel's back. I found a letter on record from 1944, whereby an ex RAF member, Robert Maxwell MacDonald, who had been serving a sentence at Camphill Prison on the mainland for theft and arson, had wished to be transferred to Belfast to be near his wife and child. The answer was short and not so sweet, with his request being refused on the grounds of the prison already being overcrowded. It was always the staff who proved they could keep the prison in check over the years. Regardless of the financial restraints and the failure to appoint more officers, or the practical limits of accommodation in the wings, the staff were the people who kept the prison running as close to clockwork as they could.

*   *   *

You could always tell the ex-services element in the ranks as they paraded in the circle prior to commencing duty. They stood out a mile, with their highly polished boots, razor-sharp creases in their trousers and shirts, always looking clean-shaven and buffed. They took pride in wearing the uniform, and even though in many cases they were no better at the job than their 'Paddy' counterparts, they gave the impression through their attention to detail that they were on the ball. It was a 'bullshit baffles brains' type approach.

The majority of officers working in the Crum up until the late 1960s and 1970s would have been ex B Specials and servicemen from both here and the mainland, and a few transfers from the

Republic of Ireland Prison Service. There were those who entered
the job directly, but preference was given to those who came from
a services background, where they would have been accustomed
to a discipline regime and a structured chain of command. All
would have been required to be educated to a standard befitting
relevant academic benchmarks of that particular era. As
standards of education developed and improved over the middle
of the twentieth century, the requirements for a position in
uniform jobs in the Province rose in turn.

In 1922, for example, the Ministry of Finance made reference
to new recruits having to be 'sufficiently educated in writing
(copying manuscripts and spelling), arithmetic (the first four
rules), money, and avoirdupois weight'. Hardly extreme, but these
would have excluded many people from the position who had
not been privy to a formal education and had joined the factory
workforces early in their teens. Although the prison population
was fairly consistent, always in or around 200 to 250, the number
of officers working in the jail fluctuated. Staff numbers in
September 1922 consisted of the following:

CHIEF WARDER	1
PRINCIPAL WARDER	7
PERMANENT STAFF	30
TEMPORARY STAFF	22

It is incredible to think that the prison could have been run
successfully by this mere handful of men, having to accommodate all manner of shifts and association periods, and to still
make allowances for sick leave and holidays. Although in the
middle of the 1920s the jail was locked at 5 p.m., from 7 until
8.30 p.m. all convicts staying longer than three months would
have been unlocked to attend chapel, lectures or concerts. At this
point there were still only twelve staff on duty, a clear indication
of general well-being in the jail at the time. On reading through
the Board of Visitors' monthly reports from the 1920s to the

1930s, it appears that there were very few complaints from either staff or inmates. The reports would usually state that the visitors 'saw all convicts at work and exercise', and that good order prevailed. There were times when they would have had to preside over disciplinary matters relating to inmates and impose some type of penalty befitting the breach of good conduct. These instances were few and far between during this particular period, and the lapses in behaviour which were addressed and documented were strange to say the least. One particular letter from the Board of Visitors to His Grace the Governor of Northern Ireland dated 4 January 1928, outlines the case of two convicts, Canning and Wright, who both received seven days' loss of remission and a further seven days on what was described as no. 1 punishment diet, for having 'swallowed needles'. The type or size of the needles is not made clear, but it alludes to the fact that this was an attempt at self-harm by both parties, which was of course punishable under prison rules.

Of course, the harmonious attitude and reliability of the prison officers during such times could have been directly related to pay and conditions. Pay scales were continually being discussed during the early part of the twentieth century, in an attempt to bring the Northern Ireland Prison Service in line with the mainland. The North was seen by many to be treated by the Government as a backwater, with no direct correlation between rates of pay for identical jobs. In 1927, the pay scales in the NIPS were as follows:

WARDERS	41/– per week (43/– after five years)
PRINCIPAL WARDERS	53/– per week
CHIEF WARDERS	69/– per week

The Governors were on approximately £500 per annum, depending on whether they held positions as Deputy or Class I Governors. The difference between these figures and those of mainland staff were in some cases shillings. But the tasks performed by both bodies of officers were identical. Bearing this in mind, and the fact that the working conditions were no less or more perilous, complaints were frequent.

The police force of the day, regardless of where they were stationed in the country, were being paid slightly more than the prison officers, a distinction which some will argue remains even today. When screws became 'legitimate' targets during the recent Troubles, and some were to lose their lives at the hands of terrorists, the question was frequently asked as to why there remained any difference in pay and conditions. There is a slight gap in records in relation to police pay scales in the time of the transformation from the old RIC to the RUC around the 1920s. In 1921, however, the RIC constables were being paid around £3–10 per week. Many prison officers posed the question to some of their police colleagues as to which they would prefer to do: walk up and down a wing full of life-sentence prisoners all day with a wooden baton in their pocket, or travel in the back of an armoured Land Rover up the Falls Road, carrying a Ruger revolver and a longarm. There was always a certain amount of consideration given to the eventual answer, and then the argument would perpetuate.

The many police crews who visited the Crum to lodge their prisoners had to agree on occasions that they would not have traded places with us for anything. They could always offload their 'problem child' at the jail and carry on with their patrol as before, having been relieved of the responsibility of looking after the arrested person from that point on. This was always the case when depositing some of the better known alcoholics in the city, who lived rough most of the time and who often engineered a stay in jail so they could avail of three square meals a day and a warm cell at the expense of the taxpayer.

My first encounter with one of these gentlemen was early in my service, when I was working in the large forecourt area of the jail, through which all vehicular and foot traffic coming into and out of the prison had to pass. My post on this particular day was to control visitors as they walked through the forecourt and facilitate their entrance into the legal visits area. When a police vehicle was allowed entry into the forecourt, all movement stopped, and the prisoner or prisoners were taken from the vehicle and searched in a little box structure, before being allowed into reception for processing. One of the screws on duty in the forecourt area, whoever was free at the time more or less, took it upon themselves to search the incoming prisoner. On this particular day, I noted that the police crew who drove into the forecourt did not hesitate when they parked the car, and all three of them exited their respective doors and stood alongside the vehicle. I looked around me and it was obvious that my colleagues had scattered in double quick time. I could only imagine that this prisoner, whom I could barely see seated in the rear of the car, was going to be trouble. I moved over to the car and leaned inside to tell him to climb out. My nose was just inside the door jamb and no more, when I was confronted with the most hideous smell I have ever had the misfortune to encounter. The little man in the back then stepped out onto the concrete and stood for all to see. He was about 5'4 in height, with closely shaven hair and about two days' worth of stubble. He had applied a hair colour to his head, of a deep copper tone, which on anyone else may have been attractive, and looked to be wearing at least five or six coats. This was 'Pepsi' McNally.

I put on two pairs of gloves, one pair over the top of the other, and began to search amongst the many layers of clothing which Pepsi was wearing. As he disrobed, it was clear that he had been sporting no less than five outer coats, two shirts and two vests. His body weight was halved by the time we stripped him down to what most people consider normal dress. Throughout this charade, which was providing my work colleagues with endless amounts of fun, Pepsi presented himself as the most foul-mouthed, obnoxious little man I have ever come across. He was ranting and raving at the 'fucking peelers' and grinning maniacally like a demented James Young. It was the smell, however, which gave me the most problems. I have always been an advocate of the wholesome breakfast: eggs, bacon, sausages and toast, washed down with a strong coffee, and I believe it fully prepares you for anything during the day. Not on this occasion, however. He was rank beyond belief and had no embarrassment about being so. When I eventually completed the search and took him down towards reception, it was all I could do to stop myself gagging and regurgitating £1.20 worth of starch. For the rest of the day I itched and scratched, and showered in the gym at every opportunity. It was a lesson well learned. If you were cute enough, you made sure that you were wired off by the screws at the main gate as to who was being brought in. I was never caught out again.

Although the likes of Pepsi were tolerated on the wings, by both staff and prisoners alike, there were episodes I witnessed which, if they had happened today in our undoubtedly 'politically correct' society, would have been considered abuse. I have to say that although he had questionable personal hygiene problems, Pepsi McNally did not deserve to have scouring powder poured over his head whilst taking a shower, in what was considered a witty attempt to aid him towards cleanliness. It was downright dangerous, to say the least. It was not just the other cons who took part in these high jinx, but the class officer on the wing at the time had more than a hand in it. Pepsi took it as well as could be expected, laughing and taunting the cons as they came near, even taking a swing at one as he left the area of the showers. I don't think I really ever thought much about the incident at the time. It was only later, when I saw myself as being complicit in this treatment, albeit as an observer, that I considered just how borderline the behaviour was.

My time in the Crum saw many a visit by Pepsi and other alcoholics, who were the scourge of city centre police. The majority of them were compliant whilst serving their short sentences and knew exactly what side their bread was buttered on. The officers on the wings in which they were staying were, to them, permanent hoteliers, whom they may have the fortune, or misfortune, whichever way you care to look at it, of meeting again. It was prudent therefore never to upset prison staff, assuming a return some time in the near future.

When one grasped the concept of just how much control one's position as a regular wing officer had over the inmates under your charge, it was fairly easy to create a workable atmosphere.

You had the power to control every con's access to toilets, showers, meals, visits and just about anything. I was able to witness many an introductory speech from various class officers to new prisoners coming on to the wing, and the gist was generally the same. Life was going to be a lot easier and sweeter for them if they behaved themselves and co-operated with the staff. The threat was more than just an implied one.

From unlock to lock-up, the movement in the wing was the responsibility of each class officer on each landing. Regulations and good practice, from a security point of view, were to restrict prisoner movement on the landings to four prisoners at a time. If this rule had been strictly adhered to, the system would have been damn near unworkable. There was always more than four out, between someone taking a shower to two or three taking a cup of water from the large water boilers set out on the crossover points between each side of the walkways. The idea of four out at a time, or 'controlled movement', was implemented in order to reduce the risk to staff of being overpowered due to being outnumbered. We all knew that if the cons wanted to take over the wings, it was just a matter of when and not how. We were always outnumbered.

The logistics of life on the wing required you to wash and breakfast all the prisoners as soon as was physically possible, and have some ready for court appearances, visits, work, dentist, doctor, and anything else which may be required. It wasn't easy. It was further complicated by the fact that the wing was made up of both Catholic and Protestant prisoners who had to be segregated. Whilst the RCs breakfasted, the Prods would be washing and using the ablutions, and vice versa. Also when it came to the obligatory daily exercise of the prisoners, the arrangement between the two factions was that they would take it in turns. There would always be an atmosphere between the two sides, but restrictions within the prison made it imperative that certain things be negotiated. It was a clear case of self-segregation.

No one, especially the screws, would have complained, as it effectively made their jobs easier. No system which we imposed would have worked if the cons did not want it to work, and that was worth remembering. They had the power to turn things around to suit themselves if they felt strongly enough about it. Thankfully they rarely had any major complaints other than changing cells or problems at visits, or overzealous letter censors. When they did kick off about something, it was seldom as a collective body, and we could cope with it without too much bother.

*   *   *

The class officer was always the point of contact, and dealt with prisoners' welfare issues as well as running the wing as efficiently as possible. He was invariably an experienced screw, with a good grounding in prison rules and standing orders. As general duties officers, visiting almost every landing in the jail at one time or another, we could clearly see that there were two types of class officer. The firm but fair kind, and the 'prisoners' friend'. We all hated the latter, and were ill at ease with the first-name, all sweetness and light approach which they adopted on their landings. They were downright dangerous to work with, as they had created, of their own volition, an environment in which it was difficult to staff normally; the cons being used to pampering and an unhealthy degree of familiarity between them and whoever was on duty. I could hazard a guess as to why the prisoners' friends decided upon that approach to the job. The tensions between prisoners and staff could be all-consuming at times, and like most screws, I would dread the return to the wing after a break away from it. There was almost constant whinging and bickering, and the outward aggression of some inmates could be unnerving. I suspect that they thought by presenting themselves as someone who was a friend, someone who placed the inmates' welfare and happiness above all other things, they would not become the focus of aggression. If that were the reason, then how wrong they were. The line was clearly drawn, and for most of us, there was no ambiguity. Prisoners and screws were, and always would be, on different sides of the fence. It was a them-and-us mentality. If they were frustrated and angry at something, maybe a personal relationship issue from outside the jail, then you were the ones who got it in the neck. It stands to reason. You were the ones who were keeping them from the outside, there to close the big green door behind them at night, locking them away. You were the ones who took their freedom away, full stop.

I know that even the prisoners in the care of a 'prisoner's friend' were somewhat embarrassed at the closeness of the relationship. But why ruin a good thing. They were regularly allowed to trip in and out of each other's cells and to roam unchallenged about the landing. During lunch periods, when all cons were meant to be locked when not in the yards, you could find a little group of four or five playing cards in a double cell with the door locked back, and not a screw in sight. The security implications of this type of behaviour were bad enough, but you had to wonder what other breaches were taking place. These friendly screws were setting themselves, and oftentimes others, up for a huge fall. The thirst for intelligence-gathering amongst the collective factions in prisons is well documented, and I am sure that these men were a great source of information of a delicate nature, whether unwittingly or not.

Another explanation for their manner of running the wing may have been attributed to the age-old problem of conditioning. The Prison Service could identify the chinks in the physical security of a prison quite easily and address those problems as they appeared. They could implement airlock systems at certain through areas, or revise particular working practices to minimise risks to staff. The biggest risk to safety and security, however, came from the attitudes of staff.

Human nature as it is, when we accept certain behaviour or take it for granted, we are less likely to challenge any small deviances in that behaviour. Firstly we accept the behaviour because it is nothing new to us, having been carried on for some length of time. Our comfort is in the length of time it has been considered the 'norm'. This acceptance of what may in fact be small breaches in security is due to conditioning. It is nothing new; it has been used ever since people have been held captive and have had to manipulate their captors whilst making plans to escape.

The Prods and the RCs have honed their skills at conditioning officers over a number of years, and with dramatic results on occasions. Almost every escape ever made from jails relied in some part on screws having adopted a relaxed routine due to careful conditioning.

The 'prisoners' friend' may have fallen foul of one form of conditioning, allowing the boundaries of behaviour to be stretched to a point where he no longer had control over the inmates on his landing. Take for instance a simple rule of lock-up during a lunch hour, when staff were always at a bare minimum. It may be the case that one of the cons, someone who had never been problematic, would ask the class officer if he could be let out to make a trip to the toilet as his piss-pot was not going to be sufficient for his requirement. When he returns to his cell, the class officer asks him to close his door behind him. This he does, but only to the point where the door is pulled over and the lock is not engaged. When the class officer during the next unlock sees that the door has been open and the con has not taken advantage of the situation, he begins to place a certain amount of trust in him. The next time this situation arises, when the con is returning to his cell, he may even linger and talk with the screw, finding some common ground and building some rapport. It may take some time, but eventually, if the con were to ask for his cell door to be left unlocked during the whole of the lunch period, the likelihood is it will be done. The officer will have reached a point where he cannot in effect backtrack, and instead chooses to place his trust in the inmate. He has been conditioned.

When the Maze escape took place on 25 September 1983, it relied heavily on conditioning for various aspects of the plan to work. In one particular part of the plan, arguably the most important part, the escapees had to find a way to overpower the screw at the front gate of the block they were in, namely H7. The distance from the exit door of the block to the front gate, which was a set of two vehicle gates and two pedestrian gates, was about twenty yards, give or take. Any sign of something amiss was sure to raise the suspicions of the front gate officer, who could sound the alarm and lock the compound. One prisoner, Brendan 'Bik'

McFarlane, had made it his practice to sweep the yard area outside the front door to the block, down to the main gate and then within the sterile area. He had progressed this over a period of time, pushing the boundaries of his work area ever so slightly each time. It was no surprise then, that the screw on duty at the H7 main gate area the day of the escape took little notice, if any, of McFarlane as he approached, flanked by two uniformed screws. It was a familiar event. The screws working at the gate had been conditioned to accept this behaviour as routine, an assumption which was to have dire consequences.

During my conversation with veteran Republican Martin Meehan, he explained that part of the reason for his own successful escape came from the fact that he had constantly watched the screws on a Thursday lunchtime, when he states they received their pay packets. He had observed how the screws were clearly pre-occupied with investigating their wage slip, and took little notice of what was happening around them. It wasn't rocket science by any means. All he did was observe and take advantage of human nature. The human element would always be the weakest link in any secure environment, and the prisoners had all the time in the world to watch it unfold.

The day to day conditioning of officers in the Crum was often for a purpose far less drastic than an escape. Their aim was to try and make life a little easier for themselves, less disruptive and certainly more comfortable. They would hope to bring themselves within the officers' circle of trust. This in itself may exclude them from constant cell searches, or less thorough ones at least. In turn, this would make them of use to other cons on the landings, who, having seen the way they could move freely with little suspicion, made them obvious mules to move and store contraband.

There were some screws and cons who gradually formed not necessarily a relationship as such, but more of an understanding. It was very much a taboo to fraternise with each other, totally frowned upon by prison authorities and paramilitary leadership alike. So, often these 'friendships' were kept covert, and rarely witnessed by others. When I met Gusty Spence, he told me of his alliance with a particular officer, who he would not refer to by name, but only by the code name 'Minister'. This man was a Catholic, and they had engaged in the odd conversation over a period of time. On finding that they had certain things in common, they developed a deep respect for each other. When Gusty was unsure about a certain officer on duty, his willing accomplice would draw the man into a conversation and, with a few well-chosen words, gauge if he posed any particular threat to Spence. This would have been reciprocated by Spence, when the 'Minister' had his own concerns about certain inmates. It was a civil arrangement between two individuals, and in Gusty Spence's opinion, he owed the man a great debt of gratitude.

When I first started in the Service, I was given the best bit of advice by a veteran screw who said very little at the best of times. When he did eventually engage me, he imparted little gems such as his single most important rule of 'trust nobody'. Unfortunately he went on to complete the sentence with 'including me'. The gist of his message was true, though, and over time I found that it served me well to question everyone and everything. Those cons who went out of their way to ingratiate themselves to me I trusted less than those who were continually confrontational. At least you knew where you stood with the ones who longed to take a swing at you and made continual remarks about your parentage.

In fairness, there were not that many screws who could have been identified as prisoners' friends, but there were several who could have been classed as 'prisoner shy'. It was a term which was applied to those whose job never brought them within spitting distance of an inmate. These men walked around the extremities of the jail, nearly always in twos, but never with a prisoner attached. They appeared to have engineered 'jobs for the boys'. The suggestion was that these were the 'rubber' officers; the ones who had not been able to cope with the stress and strain of the wings, and had thrown a 'wobbler'. The said wobbler may have been an incident of emotional breakdown, usually involving drink, or a prolonged spell of sick leave accompanied by a line for stress from their General Practitioner. The Prison Service, I suspect, may have been obliged to reduce the stress on these men in their working environment, therefore creating a position for them which didn't really exist.

It is understandable how anyone could have suffered from stress whilst working in this often hostile workplace. However, the effect the pampering of these individuals had on the morale of the rest of the men who had no choice but to work in the wings was clearly evident. They often referred to these cosseted individuals as 'dead wood', and failed to acknowledge them as fellow screws. When the opportunities arose each year for a position in a permanent post within the jail, you can bet your bottom dollar that their jobs were never at risk. I can honestly say that there were some men wandering about the jail who I could never quite marry up with any job or job description. These men could be seen pacing about the place with a little folder or a few pieces of paper under their arm, but never really going anywhere in particular. They did this all day. Occasionally they would be seen in the company of other 'dead wood', and, to the untrained eye, both of them would appear to have some purpose. Most of us had jobs to do, and frequently ones which we did not like, but at least we retained some self-respect.

* * *

The prison officer's job was reasonably well paid in comparison to many in the workplace, and afforded us all a moderate standard of living. It seemed ridiculous to me then, that there were those who tried to squeeze as much as possible from the public purse if they could get away with it. We all knew who they were. Some were more blatant than others, but the method was almost always the same.

Each prisoner had an issue of toiletries whilst they remained in custody, namely toothpaste, toothbrush, soap and towels. Some entrepreneurial screws realised they could save a few quid on their weekly shopping bill by dipping into the stores of these items. The wife may never need to buy toothbrushes or toothpaste again. Why go to Dunnes Stores for your towels when hubby could bring home nice blue ones which he would always replace when they wore out. I wouldn't have been surprised if some had even taken away enough toiletries to sell them on a market stall. It was a standing joke that you could always tell a screw's house by the blue towels or the white shirts on the clothes-line. Disposable razors were another big desirable item. It was common for many screws to arrive at work looking slightly dishevelled, only to be found at breakfast time in the staff toilets on the wing, shaving and washing with the prisoners' issued kit. It must have been a practice which cost the taxpayer thousands. On the odd occasion when I had been training in work and had forgotten a towel, I dipped into reception and borrowed one. When I was finished, however, I left it back, and it was included in the general laundry. These screws took the perk too far. However you dressed it up, they were stealing.

There were other screws who almost never brought a lunch or evening meal into work, as they survived on prisoners' meals in the dining halls. These men were happy to eat whatever the cons were eating, as long as it was free. Anyone who has ever served time in the Crum will agree that the food which was dished up to them was bordering on inedible, and in no way bore any similarity to what was described on the daily menu. Their meals were 'created' by screws who were described as cooks, ably assisted by cons detailed to work in the kitchens. As often as not it was the 'old hands' who thought nothing of taking advantage of the excess food, and never questioned the quality.

Like many other men in the job, I always had a problem with the cons working in the kitchens that provided food for the officers' mess. I was never comfortable with the idea that they were often unsupervised during the preparation times. I hardly ever took so much as a cup of coffee offered by a wing orderly, even when I was assured by the permanent wing staff that they were sound. I may have been cynical, but I believed they would try their best to put one over on a screw in any way possible, and 'gobbing' in their coffee, or worse, was a perfect way to do it. The ease with which they could tamper with the breakfasts, lunches and evening meals in the Mess made me opt for a packed lunch most days. It is arguable then that the safest place to eat food from was the cons' kitchens, where it was unlikely they would contaminate their own food. The thought of eating the cons' version of cottage pie, however, was a bridge too far for most of us.

I recently sat down with Dessie O'Hagan, a well-known Official Republican and member of the Workers Party of Ireland, and was entertained and enlightened by his own unique memories of the Crum. He remembers the food well from his first stay in the late 1950s, and was surprised, to say the least, when he returned during the onset of internment in 1971. He also had surprisingly few complaints about the screws he encountered during both his stays.

> I was first in Crumlin Road Prison in 1957. I did four years there on a charge of trying to remove a prisoner from Her Majesty's custody in the City Hospital. I didn't succeed and was arrested subsequently, and I think I was sentenced in May of 1957. Crumlin was a very harsh place to serve time in, I think. In some senses it was good and in some bad. I was later interned in the 'cages' of Long Kesh during internment, and thought back to the Crum with nostalgia almost. For one, you had a single cell, and for instance you could read in peace and quiet. I did a lot of studying in Crumlin. I had been at St Malachy's College, and I had said to myself if I was going to be here for a year or so, with remission as it was, then I wasn't going to waste my time. So, I applied to do an external degree with London University, but they wouldn't accept me at the time because they didn't recognise Senior Certificate as being the equivalent of their A levels. So, I first had to sit two A levels, which I did within the jail, and passed them. And that stays in my mind as a very important decision, and I got no interference from the jail authorities whatsoever. I'm not going to name any of the screws in question, and one in particular comes to mind, but let's just say one significant gentleman, a senior screw in the jail, came to my cell at about eleven o'clock at night with

a bunch of forms. He was applying for a post, and I wrote his application for him. On different paper of course, so he could copy from it. But yes, I wrote the lot. I got twenty 'blues', and a quarter bottle of whiskey. I'll not mention his name, because he has a family, and I wouldn't want to embarrass them. And there was another screw who was in two separate Masonic Lodges. He and I got to know each other fairly well. A decent man in my opinion, and most of the screws I found to be decent men. I know there are people who would cut me for saying that, but that's the way I feel about it. Well, he got me to pen a resignation from one Lodge so he could stay in the other. I remember those two incidents very well. And a third benevolent interest, towards me anyway, was a screw who was in A-wing on a regular basis. On this occasion, my father took ill, and a particular 'gentleman', and I use that term loosely, came to me saying that I had to sign a form so that I could get out to the hospital to see him, which I would have done if he was dying. But I spoke to this other screw, and said, 'Do me a favour, go over to our house and see if my father is dying or not.' Well, he looked at me and said, 'Do you want to get me the fucking sack!' Nevertheless he did it. When he came back, I was then able to tell the guy in question to fuck off, and that my father wasn't dying. Of course they wondered how I had got to know that.

The downside to the experience was the food. The food was crap, and I mean crap. The porridge which was served in the morning was usually prepared the night before. It was in little round tins, and, eh, there was a skin on it, and quite often had mouse shit over the top of it. I think you got one fry a year. There were also about three parcels a year coming in. They weren't much but they saved the day in respect of sugar and what not. There was a shop in A-wing, run by, quote, 'a Christian gentleman', and some of our prisoners discovered through reading the paper that all was not right. Say you bought a tin of beans off your man in A-wing for ten old pence. Well the boys reading the papers were seeing that a tin of beans was rarely more than sixpence for instance. I don't remember exactly what the prices were, but this 'Christian' man was making a nice profit from his little enterprise. Thompson was the Governor at the time, and when he became aware of this he went ape shit. But anyway, the food was typically foul, and the one decent meal you got was on Christmas Day.

The other harsh part was the lock-up. You were locked at night at seven, and that would have been until seven in the morning, twelve hours. You were again locked after breakfast, from about half eight until half nine. Again you were locked up at lunchtime for about two hours. That would have accounted for about fifteen hours. You would typically have had an hour's association at night if you were there up to six months, and then a further hour if your sentence ran past that. From five until seven. You also got a third of an ounce of tobacco a week, which increased to two thirds after a few months, and to a glorious ounce after a year.'

I was interested as to whether the culture of using tobacco as a trading item was prevalent back then in the late 1950s, or if the Republican prisoners of the time had similar structures in place where a quartermaster was in charge. From his answer, it appeared a rather informal arrangement, and he didn't dwell on it. His recollection of one particular episode he experienced whilst alone in his cell did strike a chord with me, however.

Tobacco was used as currency, by some anyway, but not really by us. I think that in some cases these details are somewhat exaggerated. We did have our own structure as such, and when cigarettes or something came in they were evenly distributed. We also did a bit of smuggling and whatever. When my sentence finished, I was glad to see the end of it. There was only one night I remember where I nearly flipped my lid. I don't recall what happened exactly. I was reading, and suddenly I felt this tremendous sense of panic. I really thought I was going to lose it. I held on to the end of the bed tightly as the sweat poured off me, but it eased away as quick as it had come. This was close to the end of my sentence, as I was to get out around Christmas. I overcame it anyway, and I didn't experience it again. When I did get out, I went straight across to the pub on the corner, I think it was on Agnes Street.

He may have been miffed at this sudden onset of panic, but I assured Dessie O'Hagan that it was not an uncommon phenomenon, and one which the screws called 'gate fever'. Many inmates, when approaching the very end of a sentence, suffered from gate fever, particularly after serving a long sentence. I remember one particular inmate explaining to me as we spoke briefly on a landing one day that he knew he was being irrational, but that he couldn't quite help himself. He told me that he had done the best part of three years without a problem, and had only a few weeks to push. He went on to say that because he could nearly taste his freedom, because it was in sight, time seemed to be moving at a ridiculously slow rate. He agreed that a 'fever' was an apt description for the condition. Some of those who suffered gate fever had been model prisoners who, from out of nowhere, became agitated and aggressive towards both cons and screws alike. Their behaviour would have been totally out of character. And like O'Hagan, just as soon as it appeared, it would pass.

The next time I was back in was at the start of internment in 1971. I was taken from Girdwood Barracks through a hole in the wall. Again, when I came in, I came into reception. I always thought that was a great name—'reception'. There was half a dozen cops with me at the time, but the two screws on duty at the time knew me from my visit back in the 1950s, and quickly told me to go into one of the wee rooms, saying, 'Lock that from the inside Dessie'. They were telling the peelers to fuck off in other words. It was early morning, about half three or so, and they saved me from a beating. Now I thought Crumlin Road had changed. I remember in the morning the screws coming down to the cell where I was with another man, a fella from Ardoyne, a fucking 'Provo', one of these stupid people. The screw opened the door and said, 'Right lads, downstairs and get your tray for breakfast.' I thought he was taking the mickey, as there were no trays in my day. So I went out after him into the hall and shouted, 'Are you trying to make a cunt out of me?' But he wasn't. When I went into the hall, there were two dividers set up with the breakfast tables laid out, and the boy serving said, 'Porridge, Cornflakes or what?' I just looked at him in amazement. The sausage and eggs and bacon were over there, and the toast was across the way. I just couldn't believe this. I'm not sure what wing I was on at the time, I just can't remember, but it may have been C-wing. But that for me was entirely different, even more so when the cook came out and asked what you thought of the grub. But then internment was different. You were free all day in the jail, right up until lock-up. There was free movement in the wing, it was more relaxed.

I asked Dessie if he could remember any of those he was interned with, and if he had formed any lasting friendships with fellow internees. He struggled to recall any names other than Jimmy McGuffin, who he knew had later penned a book on internment in 1973. It seemed to me that Dessie didn't mix with others in any great way, very much enjoying his own company, so I didn't labour the question. He continued.

I did try to escape during my time on internment. They were starting to move people, which wasn't good. We actually broke up the ends of the chairs and made them into hooks, and then we had cut up a number of blankets and made ropes out of that. I think we had four, or maybe six, ready to go. There was a football match taking place, and the signal to go was when the screws had all moved to the side to have a yarn. The referee was to give a very shrill blast on the whistle. So it was and they made a dive for the wrong wall, and went for the St Malachy's wall. I must say, though, that the guys with the hooks, about five or six of them, threw them up and all bar one of them held tight at the top of the wall. The last one landed right on the second attempt. Then each man was counted on to the ropes and all I heard was 'Ah fuck'. The Brits were on the other side. It was probably my fault, cause I knew St Malachy's was on the other side of that wall. If they had have gone for the other wall they would have escaped.

It is clear that O'Hagan is referring to the documented incident which occurred just before the 'Crumlin Kangaroos' made the headlines when they went over the wall. However, O'Hagan never witnessed that particular escape. Shortly after his own attempt he was sent to Long Kesh, or as he likes to refer to it, 'the cages'.

The use of the term 'cages' was, according to O'Hagan, a memorable propaganda tool, in that it implied the inmates were being treated like animals. In his time as civil rights movement co-ordinator in the compounds, he recalls using the term on several press releases, which he was surprised the newspapers actually picked up on and printed. When he starts talking about those turbulent times in the early 1970s, he is more animated and aggressive. He is unequivocal when he states that in his and many others' opinions, the propaganda war was being well and truly won. The blame for loss of ground in respect of swaying public opinion he lays fairly and squarely at the door of the Provisional IRA, in particular the escalation of their campaign of atrocities. There was certainly no love lost between the Officials and the Provisionals, and this was true whether inside or outside of jail.

The food was obviously a sore point for O'Hagan, more so on his first visit to the Crum back in the late 1950s. The memory was so vivid that he kept reiterating his disgust time and time again throughout our chat. He also told me that there were always rumours throughout the general population that most of the good rations were being carried away by some of the screws before it got as far as the kitchens. I didn't doubt that for a second. Although he had found the majority of screws he had personally encountered to be reasonably fair individuals, he did have reservations about corruption within the jail at a higher level. He was slightly guarded when he recalled a particular sentenced prisoner he had known back in the late 1950s. He told me that this man had been jailed for causing the death of a person when driving his car, and was sentenced to six months in all. He went on to say that this individual did not serve one day of his whole sentence inside, as he was in fact out every day. I couldn't quite get my head around this and asked him how that could be possible. According to O'Hagan, the arrangement was facilitated by a person or persons at a very high level within the Prison Service. He explained that this man was transported in a prison lorry or van to his place of work every day, and again picked up in the afternoon to return to the Crum to spend the night in his cell. He assured me that this was well known by other inmates at the time, but for obvious reasons he declined to go as far as naming the person in question.

* * *

The words of a wise old principal officer in Magilligan stayed with me during my time in the Service. He shook my hand heartily when introduced, and whilst still holding on to my hand in both of his, imparted this nugget: 'In your time in this job you will come across murderers, rapists, thieves, conmen and general scumbags, and then there are the prisoners.' He was absolutely serious. He was also not far from the truth. There was always a whiff of some scandal or other involving a member of staff, concerning their actions either inside or outside of the jail. More often than not there was some substance to these rumours. Invariably the internal matters involved misappropriation of monies or funds. Question marks over monies taken in the staff canteen were often raised, and it seemed prudent to remove yourself from any position in the jail which involved handling money of any sort. The prisoners' 'tuck shop', and the officers' 'tea boats' were worth avoiding at all costs. I don't remember the Crum having that many scandals, certainly not in comparison to Magilligan.

In Magilligan, in the large open 'phase' area amongst the work compounds and football fields there stood a pre-fabricated cabin which I have fond memories of. This decrepit little temporary erection was a virtual oasis to all who had the misfortune to be detailed at a post anywhere nearby. It afforded its patrons a welcoming Styrofoam cup of hot coffee or tea and an assortment of snacks and cold drinks, but more importantly a brief refuge from the inclement weather. I became an avid fan of the pickled eggs which were always on offer and, like most, was a regular patron. It was very much a meeting place as well as a refreshment stop, and the world was put right there on many a day. The 'tea boat', as it was known, was run by prison officers, one in particular, and the profits were ploughed back into the business or diverted into the recreation club . . . or so it seemed. From what I can remember, that one particular officer managing the tea boat was actually detailed by the duty office to attend to the day to day running of this facility. He usually made you feel about as welcome as a turd floating in a swimming pool, but after a while you became used to his thran manner and gruff exterior, and in some strange way I found him entertaining. The tea boat appeared to be a sort of official/unofficial arrangement. He wasn't running this enterprise out of the goodness of his heart. No, this man was getting paid to oversee the management of the tea boat on a prison officer's wages. When one day the doors remained shut, and rumours of misappropriated funds swept through the jail like a bush fire, we were all taken by surprise. An internal investigation was launched and, without any real clarity, we were told that several thousand pounds had gone missing. I can't remember exactly how much was involved but it was considerable. The matter was brought up at several POA (Prison Officers Association) meetings held in the officers' mess, during which tempers were frayed and allegations were plenty. These meetings were often hi-jacked by certain individuals to rally support for some personal vendetta or to point accusing fingers at innocent individuals. They would often descend into full-blown arguments and verbal abuse, but were consistently divisive. Days went to weeks and weeks to months, and eventually the matter was resolved in some way, which in today's culture of accountability and transparency would be neither satisfactory nor acceptable. The officer who had clearly been at the centre of the scandal returned to normal posts within the jail, and the door was firmly closed on another incident, swept well and truly under the carpet. It was never mentioned again—well, not to his face anyway.

The untimely demise of the tea boat did, however, provide an opportunity for expansion for one Prison Service entrepreneur, who went by the most politically incorrect nickname of 'the white Paki'. I am sorry if this offends anyone, but he had been christened some time before I ever set foot through the gates of Magilligan. Darren, which was his actual name, had a habit of taking a suitcase or two to work with him, the contents of which were all sorts of consumables and bits and pieces. He would set up his stall at whatever post he was given, selling items ranging from sweets and cigarettes to body warmers, to any hapless passers by. I remember his most profitable pitch being the tally lodge in the main prison. Everyone had to pass through the tally lodge at some stage during the day, and it was impossible to ignore his efforts at window dressing, as he opened the lid of his suitcase to reveal his wares laid out in an attractive array. None of us back then worried too much about expiry dates or excise infringements. He was a walking convenience store, providing a service which was much needed. Who cared what rules he was breaking.

The chief officers and the governors at Magilligan could hardly have been oblivious to Darren's activities, and I believe they chose not to disrupt his little venture. Their relaxed attitude towards such eccentricity was just one of the differences between the regimes at the Crum and Magilligan. I had heard it said before that there were two Services in Northern Ireland, and only one was the Northwest Prison Service. I was eventually in a position to comment on that after having worked in both places, and I believe it is a statement with some degree of accuracy. After a few months working in the Crum, it was apparent that the authorities were slightly anal, and rules and regulations were all that mattered, and to hell with levity and morale.

*   *   *

There was always a good rumour circulating about something or someone, and if there wasn't, you could be sure someone would start one maliciously. The targets of many of the rumours in the Crum would often be a group of self-proclaiming Christian officers, many of whom appeared to have made an almost overnight conversion. These men had backgrounds which were jaded to say the least, with their personal 'road to Damascus' having come at a particularly poignant time. As was the norm, these individuals were branded with a witty if slightly irreverent nickname—'the Velcro angels'. It was a reference to the impermanent nature of their adherence to the Christian ways which they professed to hold precious. The Velcro was the material with which it was proposed they attached themselves to the 'Cross', as opposed to the permanency of nails. They could then attach or detach themselves at will, metaphorically speaking of course. It was always difficult to narrow down who exactly had arrived at this humorous yet outrageously blasphemous pigeonholing, but whoever it was had created a monster which only grew in stature daily. The Velcro angels could be the equivalent of reformed alcoholics or recently quit smokers. They embraced their newly found faith with an enthusiasm which was both sickening and scary at times. I am afraid that I found it hard to suppress my natural turn of phrase when in the company of an angel, with my every third word being an expletive of sorts. This was after all a jail. It was a workplace where every weakness would have been exploited by the inmates, and it was safer in some ways to speak in a language which they understood and identified with.

The prize for the rank and file rabble who were beyond redemption was to witness the fall of one of the Velcro angels. As a particular rumour involving one of them unfolded into truth, then slowly the angel would peel away from the rigidity of the Cross, falling into the crowd below, and once again taking his rightful place amongst the other miscreants. It was an elaborate metaphor to use to describe this common enough transformation, but it was hilarious. It was very much in the psyche of screws in Belfast to thrive on the hypocrisy of people, and cut them to the bone when they overstepped the mark. There was no hiding place from anyone when you were the focus of an indiscretion or a compromising story. You just had to hope and pray that some juicier rumour would become the focus of attention, and you became yesterday's news.

I myself made a fatal mistake whilst socialising one evening at a friend's house party, one that I paid for, for some time after. On this particular evening, I had one drink over the usual eight, and cornered a young lady who often visited the Crum in a civilian capacity. Had I been thinking straight, I wouldn't have done this with the witnesses that were there plotting my progress with great interest. For the next few weeks I became the topic for discussion and abuse, with numerous references being made to my sexual prowess, or lack of it. I soldiered on, seldom rising to the bait that was being continually cast in my direction.

Some time later, when a colleague let slip to a friend and confidante that his on/off girlfriend insisted that he wear a gun belt and his loaded Walther pistol whilst having sex, I knew the heat was off me. Nothing would ever be considered sacred by your mates, and they would relish the fact that they had been able to supply a tasty morsel for the rumour mongers to feed on.

Surviving the Crum was all about learning not to take anything seriously. Those unfortunate enough to acquire nicknames would have to endure much more abuse than was normal, both from cons and screws alike. The cons could get away with calling these screws by their adopted titles simply because they rarely heard their actual names being used by other officers. I can still remember cons referring to certain individuals as 'Busted Sofa', and 'Jimmy Five Bellies'. They were both fairly accurate descriptions of the two gentlemen in question, but it must have stung that little bit more when used by inmates. Everyone was guilty of using nicknames instead of their proper titles, but it had a habit of catching up with you sometimes. When I first started dating my wife, she took me to a house party which was being hosted by her cousin and her husband. I had been told to be on my best behaviour as other members of my wife's family were there, and I was glad when I got on well with her cousin's husband, who was called David. We sank a few tins, smoked a few cigarettes, and found that we generally had a lot in common. He eventually got around to asking me what I did to earn a crust. Armed with the knowledge that he was a policeman, I had no hesitation in telling him where I worked. He seemed genuinely interested, and asked me if I knew this particular senior principal officer, giving me the surname. After scratching my head for a few moments, I clicked my fingers and replied that of course I knew him, but had not recognised his proper title, as at work he was generally known to everyone as 'Pigs in Space', purely because he held a striking resemblance to the character from *The Muppet Show* who captained a spacecraft in the sketch by the same name. David tipped his glass and calmly said, 'Yip, that's my dad.' I hadn't seen the family resemblance, and the next few minutes saw me frantically trying to fill in the hole which I had just dug for myself. Thankfully, David was gracious in accepting my apology and was able to see the funny side of it. My girlfriend was less forgiving.

The one phrase which was to become the ultimate 'put down' was thought up by a screw whose identity will forever be a question for debate. He was to take two simple words and apply them to almost any sentence, immediately turning it into an insult. The words in themselves were harmless enough, but when applied with a twisted sense of humour, they were to get many a reaction. I can remember when I first heard it being used. I had inadvertently parked my car in a slightly tighter parking space than usual in the staff car park one morning. On gingerly opening the door to get out, I remember saying something like 'that's a bit of a tight fit' to one of my travelling companions. Almost immediately he replied, 'Yer girl knows all about a tight fit.' I couldn't believe what I was hearing. Here was someone who I knew little about, having just started car sharing the previous week, throwing an unprovoked insult at me. The other guy in the back seat started laughing, and it was all I could do to stop myself rounding the front of the car to confront both of them and ask them just what they meant and why they found it so fucking funny. I let them walk on ahead of me, and continued into work shell-shocked. I had just been insulted, or rather my girlfriend had just been insulted. But I knew they didn't know my girlfriend, and she didn't know them. How could they say such a thing? As the days went on, I caught up with the rest of the jail and no longer felt as if I had been singled out. They were all at it. It was 'Yer girl' this, and 'Yer girl' that. You only had to mention something as mundane as a pencil sharpener, and some witless tube would chirp up, 'Yer girl knows all about a pencil sharpener.' Yes, I know, it's a bit of a stretch, but in some twisted sense it did seem to apply to even this innocuous phrase. 'Yer girl' became the two most used words in the screw's vocabulary. It was introduced into conversation at every opportunity, and was even borrowed by the cons and turned against staff when they thought they could get away with it. Like a lot of things, though, the culture of the screws in the working environment was wholly removed from life outside. Often the unique sense of humour did not translate into normal circumstances. You can imagine then how the taunt of 'Yer girl' was responsible for many a black eye and fat lip when used in the local pub. It had to be used carefully and in controlled conditions to avoid insulting anyone. There were a few instances when it was innocently used on fellow screws who were unfortunately experiencing domestic turmoil. The last thing you want to hear from a colleague is 'Yer girl knows all about Chelsea football team', when you are still trying to come to terms with revelations about her recent infidelity. The consequences could be dire.

* * *

One of the most compromising and difficult moments in my time at the Crum came shortly before I made the decision to resign. After parading for work in the circle as usual, I was detailed to work down in base reception. On arrival, I was handed a set of keys and told to start unlocking the new arrivals to be washed and breakfasted. When I opened the first cell door, the look on my face must have said it all. There, looking back out at me, was someone I was more used to seeing in my living room at home, drinking coffee from one of my mugs and watching my television. Lenny was a close friend of my flatmate, and a cheerful, happy-go-lucky guy who I knew had a cannabis habit, but one which I believed to be recreational only. Until that moment, I hadn't realised just how out of hand his situation had become. Fortunately for me, he was totally switched on and never acknowledged me in front of the other con he had shared his first night with. It was much later in the day when I was able to share a few words with him out of earshot of anyone. He had been sentenced to a short term for the possession of cannabis with the intent to supply, and his world had just been turned upside down. I could sense his panic, and heard the tremble in his voice as he spoke. I felt totally powerless and tried as best I could to reassure him that he would get through this. I knew the words were hollow, but I had to say something. Lenny knew I was going home at five o'clock that night, and every other night after that, and he wasn't. I could not tell him what his time inside would be like, because I was on the opposite side of the fence, as it were, and had never experienced so much as one night in a cell.

There were other more serious implications for Lenny and myself, and after serious consideration, I took a course of action which would impact greatly on both of us. When he was taken up to D-wing and put in general population, I was horrified to find that he was sharing a cell with a notorious paramilitary from Bangor. This man had a long history of terrorist involvement and general criminality, and I feared that Lenny would become tainted in some way, or worse, would be coerced into doing something which could get him involved in something more serious. As well as that, I would never know if Lenny would inadvertently compromise me, and I had to remove that risk. My only realistic course of action was to approach the security PO and make him aware of my circumstances, and insist that Lenny be moved. Within the week Lenny was moved to Magilligan Prison. I know that he was less than happy at first, but he did secure a job at the jail which kept him outside for most of the time. At first, I felt guilty because I had alienated him even more from his friends and loved ones, as Magilligan would mean a one hundred and sixty mile round trip for his visitors. In my mind, though, the move was justified, and I have no regrets. He has since admitted that time passed a whole lot quicker for him when he was working, and in some way I feel better about manipulating his move.

Len wasn't the only person who I knew and would bump into as an inmate. I had kicked about with various groups of guys when in my teens, from all parts of the town, and knew a lot of people. One of those I also knew from being in the form below me in grammar school, as well as episodes of underage drinking in the shelters on a Friday and Saturday night. Again it was a shock when I turned the key in a cell door in D-wing one morning and he was standing there to greet me. I will not reveal his name, because I still see him on occasion and would not like to compromise him in any way. The strange thing was, I knew that he had joined the police some years previously, and he was the last person I expected to see in jail. I couldn't help but feel sorry for him when he explained just how he had arrived at this point in his life. His marriage had collapsed over a period of time, and as he had considered the blame lay fairly and squarely at the door of his wife, he had refused to pay her any monies as directed by the court. He was in effect breaching a court order. He had continued to ignore the order on point of principle, knowing fine well that he would almost certainly lose his job as well as his freedom. He stood there inside his cell telling me his story without a hint of regret in his voice. He was a proud man who had paid an unusually high price to retain the moral high ground, and I felt slightly guilty that I would in a sense be a party to his misery. My further concern for him was that his time in prison could be made more difficult if details of his job were to be revealed. Thankfully that didn't happen, and I know he put his head down and walked out the front gate in one piece when his time was served. I have since seen him in rather less bleak surroundings, and it looks for all intents and purposes that his life has moved on. For his sake I hope it has.

I know that my observations of prison life in the Crum will conflict with other people's experiences, and not everyone will share my negativity in relation to the job itself. The NIPS will not be using my mugshot on any recruiting posters anytime soon, and in fairness, I wouldn't expect them to. For a brief moment, I had to stop myself writing and consider if I was being too scathing in my comments about colleagues and the regime at the time. So, when I cornered another ex-prison officer, Mike Porter, it was in some ways comforting to hear him confess that he hated every day he spent in the Crum. Mike had came into the Prison Service almost directly after leaving the Army, with a brief spell as a civilian scenes-of-crime officer in between. He remembers the two-week familiarisation period very well, although his particular squad, around thirty men in all, were also able to visit Magilligan, Maghaberry and the Maze, to experience the atmosphere of the more modern approach to offender confinement and rehabilitation. It was no surprise to learn where the majority of them would have preferred to be posted.

> Everybody wanted to go to Magilligan, because the atmosphere was completely different and much more relaxed than the Crum. But, it was the travelling. In spite of that, of the thirty or so who were in my squad, they secured about six or seven willing to go to Magilligan there and then. A lot more than that wanted to go. The Crum was to all of us a dirty stinking hole. That said, it was considered the 'mothership' of the service. I know in some ways it was horrible, but the tiered system was great in the sense that you could see exactly what was going on around you on the ones, twos or threes. In contrast to Maghaberry for instance, which was horrible. Everything seemed to be on top of you. If the place went tits up, you would have nowhere to go. There would be no way out.
>
> My first memories of the Crum were that it was so dark and dingy, and everywhere you went it was so black. Only when you walked up the admin corridor were you anywhere near the real jail. Remember, you had to change outside, then go through the tally lodge with the airlock system, and then you had to queue up to change your pass. It was almost

like dehumanising you. And the first time you went into the circle it was unbelievable. It was a unique experience. I would say that I have experienced quite a bit in my life, but nothing like that. People were going by you as you stood there, constant movement, constant noise. I also remember that when I got home at night, my shirt collar would be black with dirt. I couldn't wear a shirt any more than one day, although some did. There was a chief officer once who, when they would have paraded staff in the circle, had his eye on this one boy who was a fucking mess. So to check if he had changed his shirt, he would come up behind him and put a tick with a biro on his shirt collar, and then check the next day to see if it was the same one.

The humour as always shone through in spite of the circumstances within the Crum. Those of us who had a sense of humour exercised it as much as we could, to preserve what sanity we had. The enemy within, or other members of staff, were often responsible for causing anguish and stress. Mike Porter believed that because he had hailed from across the 'shuck', an Englishman no less, he was always treated differently, forever to be the outsider.

I know it is not true nepotism, but a type of nepotism exists in any organisation, whether it is the police or the Prison Service. The cliques that existed there were unbelievable. In my first week in D-wing, the PO there hated me with a passion, just because I was English. I didn't even know the man. So I got the root patrol, the crap patrol in other words, every day without fail. Other people who had far less service than me were class officers, and I was still on crap patrol. And crap patrol meant exactly what it said on the tin. I had to take some sex offender along with a bin bag to pick up the mystery parcels which had been thrown into the sterile area of the yards below the wing. I always got the crappy towers as well. But if you were in the right clique, you were elected. The right drinking club perhaps, or you played golf with the right person. It wasn't fucking fair. I mean the Crum was the first place I heard the word 'dipso' or 'dips'. These were guys who would come back from lunch and they were pissed. I hated them with a passion. One of them I remember was called by his nickname mostly, 'Big Bird', I think it may have been, but he would turn up for associations pissed. We would normally have put him in the slider, the air lock control into the association room. And he would have to control the movement by keeping one grill shut and allowing four people into the space in between the grills, slide the first one shut and then slide the other one open. That's all he had to do. Of course he was that drunk on occasion he would fall asleep and the cons would come up to the screen and bang on it as hard as they could, causing him to wake with a jolt and fall off his chair.

He would also keep the sliders open and nearly cause a disaster by letting the Prods out into the middle of the RCS. Of course when you went down to see the PO about this, all he would do was send him home. There was never anything done about it.

As far as cliques were concerned, the security department was the real inner circle. They ran the whole prison. Unless you were in the circle of trust, you couldn't get anywhere near it. As an ex-SOCO [scenes-of-crime officer], I was amazed at just how haphazard investigations were in jail. I mean people died there. But apart from that there were searches and finds which were being dealt with in a very unprofessional way. So I submitted a paper to a number 2 Governor, outlining a suggestion that we should have a SOCO liaison who would, in the event of an incident, come in and bag and tag the items in the proper manner. Of course the attitude of security was something along the lines of 'Who was I to make comment on their handling of situations?' And that was that.

Although Mike started working in the Crum some three years after I left, very little seemed to have changed. He continued working there right up to 1994, just two years before it was to close. In truth, he was negative in many of his comments, but he did refer to the prison as being 'alive'. I knew exactly what he meant when he used this term. The jail when full of cons and screws was almost like a living organism, with the people in it the lifeblood surging through its veins. It may have been dirty and smelly, and was anything but sterile, but it possessed something more than the blocks of the Maze or Magilligan, or the houses of Maghaberry ever would. From the moment it awoke in the morning at unlock, it lived and breathed, and only slumbered when the last light was turned off by the night guard. It had a personality all of its own.

The only relevant change from my time in the Crum that Mike could recall was that B-wing became a paramilitary wing, and C-wing became populated by ODCs. He was very verbal when I asked about A-wing, and screwed up his face as if he had just eaten something particularly sour.

I hated that wing with a passion. It was a really dirty, dingy, black horrible hole of a wing. Thankfully I didn't have to spend any time in either of the paramilitary wings at the start of my service, as I was still a SOCO witness for a trial where the defendants were awaiting trial in the Crum. When that was over, the only time I ever went in there was on overtime.

I didn't mind B-wing, and when working there perma-nently, would only give prisoners exactly what they were entitled to, and nothing else. You see, there was always a 'yes' man, who would give them everything. And he would always be busy, because they never came near me. The only time they came near me was when they knew they were entitled to something. When they did approach me, I would check up on it and give them it if they were right. Now the 'yes' man, he was busy all fucking day. I do remember a lot of 'prisoners' friends', but there were also a lot of men like myself. In fact there was a boy I remember in A-wing, who had an attitude the same as mine. The only thing was, he had upset them in some way. And then one day, three of them ran across the landing, attacked him and broke his leg. There had been three or four screws on duty not far away, and they all saw what was coming, turned their backs and walked away. They turned their backs on a colleague getting a kicking.

The divisions in the ranks were clear when an incident like this took place. It wasn't an isolated occurrence either. There are many more reports where it is believed certain officers turned their backs as men they were working alongside were being assaulted. It is shameful, but true. With most other uniform jobs, teamwork and solidarity are key elements which bind people together as a unit. Some screws chose to live by the rule of self-preservation, and to hell with the rest. You would have thought that such a betrayal would have played on their conscience, but I suspect the same men didn't possess much in the way of conscience.

Mike's attitude just confirmed to me that I wasn't being too harsh in my judgement of the service at the time. I am sure that it has moved on since then, keeping pace with other demanding uniformed jobs. If it hasn't, the authorities owe it to the staff to provide them with as much in the way of welfare consideration as the modern day Police Service provides for its members.

Chapter 6
Over the Wall

The opposing factions during the Troubles, although often from similar social backgrounds and living geographically almost side by side, were clearly poles apart. Their politics and religion were, and continue to be, defined by emblems and flags, with the various colourful and taunting murals on gable walls marking out their territories, which they defended with vigour and venom.

As a prison officer, one of the most blatant differences I found between the two factions was in respect of their imprisoned volunteers, and more specifically their military structure, or lack of it. The Loyalist prisoners did not seem to retain any definitive rank or order within the jail, although I do know that they had commanding officers and a loose chain of authority of sorts. Outwardly they appeared slovenly, and undisciplined, which could be seen simply by opening the doors of their cells. The general appearance within was unkempt and disorganised, untidy beds and page three girls everywhere. They were often hot-headed and extremely verbal individuals, and definitely more predictable in their actions.

The Republicans, however, were much more organised and focused. They always appeared to have another agenda and would rarely react individually to any matter with which they took issue. The response was usually co-ordinated and measured, and on most occasions was taken up and presented by the commanding officer. Quite simply, the Republicans behaved more like prisoners of war than their Loyalist counterparts. They had reached the stage where they were fully aware that their value was as part of a collective consciousness which in itself was certainly more effective than a singular voice. I believe the Loyalists could and should have learned a lot from the way the Republicans conducted themselves in jail. From my own memory, the Loyalists' appointed leaders were often arrogant and totally self-obsessed, and lacked the 'craft' of their opposites. The only exception to that would have been in the late 1960s and early 1970s, when Gusty Spence insisted the internees behaved just like the soldiers he believed they were. During his time, polished boots and constant drill would have been the order of the day. Unfortunately, this ethos dwindled away as the paramilitary factions within Loyalism underwent significant changes in the late 1970s.

Most of us will be familiar with epic World War Two movies depicting allied soldiers languishing in prisoner of war camps preoccupied with only one thought. That being, that the duty of every prisoner of war was of course to escape. It is no surprise then that the Republicans spent a considerable amount of their time, in various jails, planning and indeed executing escapes. Every volunteer captured by forces of the Crown would have been expected to try any means possible to escape and, when appropriate, return to active service. With any well-structured command unit in jail, there was always an individual appointed as an escape officer. It was he who would consider any escape ideas put forward and, along with the commanding officers in the wing, either sanction or veto the proposal. I would be surprised if any of the escape attempts uncovered over the years by the prison authorities or security services which bore the hallmark of Republicans had not been sanctioned by whatever escape committee had been in place at the time. Successful escapes were a major propaganda victory and usually helped to swell the ranks with young volunteers, itching to sign up for active service. On the other hand, foiled attempts were many and only helped to lower morale both inside the prisons and out. There was a fine line between what was a good, feasible idea and what was pure fantasy and totally unachievable.

The Republican prisoners had a wealth of experience to draw from when considering plans to break out. Over the years many among their ranks had been incarcerated in various prison establishments around the island of Ireland and had frequently made headlines with successful and often dramatic escapes.

When Great Britain went to war in 1939, and countless young men and women from Northern Ireland made their own valuable contribution to the war effort, there were those intent on turning the situation to their advantage. The enemy within was just as dangerous and often times more unpredictable than the Nazis. The British in effect were fighting two wars with very different rules being applied to both. Those combatants who were determined to disrupt and undermine the British Armed Forces in Northern Ireland wore the uniform of the everyday man in the street, but were anything but. They were ruthless and singularly focused individuals, bent on waging their own very personal war. Four such men were Hugh McAteer, James Steele, Patrick Donnelly and Edward Maguire. The four found themselves in Crumlin Road due to different circumstances, and were anything but content to sit and wait for their release to come about in the form of time served. All four would make a successful escape from the Crum on 15 January 1943, causing such concern to the authorities that a £3,000 reward was offered for information which would lead to their recapture.

McAteer was described as the 'ring-leader' or Chief of Staff of the IRA by Justice Brown, as he handed him down a sentence of fifteen years imprisonment in November 1942. He was arrested and tried for the offence of Treason Felony, although he was also being sought by the authorities in the Republic in connection with the murder of a police sergeant. Steele was also a seasoned IRA campaigner, and had already served five years in jail for another incident linked to the famous arms raid on Campbell College in the late 1930s. When he was later found in possession of a revolver and sensitive documents, he was sentenced to a further ten years in jail in February 1941.

Donnelly, a Portadown man, had been arrested after a gun battle with police at Cullyhanna in South Armagh in July 1940. He, along with several others, had been in possession of at least two machine guns, sixteen revolvers and two rifles when they were eventually arrested at the scene. He was to get twelve years for his involvement in the engagement, starting on 23 November 1940. Lastly, Maguire had received a sentence of six years for his part in what was described as an armed robbery. He may have deemed himself lucky not to have been given a heavier sentence, as he had in fact robbed two soldiers of their issue rifles.

Reports differed as to exactly how the four escaped, but what was known was that at around 8 o'clock in the morning of 15 January 1943, whilst still relatively dark outside, the men came across the roof of the prison laundry to the outer wall. There they scaled the wall with the aid of a rope ladder made from sheets, and dropped into the street below. With the general confusion that followed, all four disappeared into the surrounding streets and were clean away. The prison authorities in the Crum at the time were stretched to the limit, having to look after almost 600 inmates, nearly 300 of whom were internees. Conditions imposed upon the internees were less rigorous than those of the sentenced prisoners, affording them considerably more freedom of movement. This may have contributed to the escape in 1943, and indeed an escape two years earlier in 1941, when five internees made a successful bid for freedom.

Gerry Docherty, Liam Burke, Eddie Keenan, William Watson and Phil McTaggart had all climbed through a hole in a corrugated fence, and scaled the outer wall, also by means of a hastily constructed rope ladder and hook. They reluctantly left behind another inmate as he was pulled back by warders on duty, whilst another two inmates had been caught coming through the same hole in the fence. It was believed that there were more than just seven or eight due to take part in the escape, and that the numbers may have been upwards of fifty or more. One of the escapees, though, Gerry Docherty, was to become famous for his involvement in a further two escapes from other jails, in both the North and the South.

As a result of the escape, Chief Officer Holmes and Principal Officer Johnston were severely censured for not ensuring that there were adequate numbers of staff on duty to suppress the attempt fully. There were also certain amendments implemented in relation to standing orders, and agreed alarm procedures were put in place. It was almost always a case of shutting the barn door after the horse was long gone.

*   *   *

The Crumlin Road may have seemed a gift to some who had spent time in temporary detention centres, especially floating ones such as the *Maidstone*, the *Argenta*, or the renowned *Al Rawdah*, as these had proved almost impossible to escape from, regardless how elaborate a plan may have been.

The *Argenta* was a purpose-built prison ship which was used during the turbulent early 1920s, when approximately 500 men were held on board in a number of wire cages. Internment on this occasion included a few Unionist activists, but reports suggest that their stay on board was short in contrast to that of the many Republicans. The ship was anchored in Belfast Lough, just offshore below Carrickfergus, and remained there until the last of its occupants were released in 1924. Conditions aboard the vessel were reported to be basic and harsh, with poor rations and continuing health problems. As a prison, however, the *Argenta* proved to be one from which no prisoners ever escaped. This was a fact which was certainly not lost on the Government at the time, and may have influenced the use of the *Al Rawdah* prison ship when internment was re-introduced in December 1938.

The importance of reducing any risk from within during World War Two was a key factor in rounding up Republicans whom the authorities believed posed a significant threat to homeland security. Several of them were sent to the *Al Rawdah*, which was moored amidst the beauty of Strangford Lough in County Down, yards from Killyleagh village. The ship was rather inadequate, however, and conditions aboard were even more cramped and unacceptable than those on the *Argenta*. On 5 February 1941, there was an attempt made by a handful of detainees to escape using a rowing boat. An engineer of a coal boat moored beside the *Al Rawdah* saw a slight commotion in the area of the boat and raised the alarm. He received a few cuts and bruises for his troubles, but was praised for his vigilance. In fairness, the ship was only used for a short period of time, the remaining detainees, about ninety in total, being bussed from the sleepy village of Killyleagh to the Crum on 11 February that same year. Yet again, though, the ship had proved a deterrent to any escapees.

The *Maidstone* was the last and most recent attempt at reducing the overcrowding during the times of internment. As a ship it had a proud history, having served the Royal Navy well during World War Two. It had been built in the shipyards at Clydebank back in 1937, and saw active service throughout the war, having initially been stationed at Rosyth, and then later at Gibraltar in 1941. It took part in 'Operation Torch', the allied invasion of North Africa in late 1942, until eventually dropping anchor in Algiers. After the war, the *Maidstone* became the flagship of the Home Fleet, and underwent various refits before eventually ending up as temporary troop accommodation at Belfast in 1969. When internment was re-introduced in August 1971, the ship was converted to accommodate prisoners and moored at Coal Wharf in Belfast Lough. There was a good stretch of around 500 yards between the ship and the shore, and barbed wire had been placed in the water around the vessel to deter any would-be escapees. It was, nevertheless, the sheer determination and attention to detail which saw the eventual escape of seven prisoners on 17 January 1972, under cover of fog and darkness. As with other famous escapes, the participants were instantly entered into the realms of Republican folklore and forever became the 'Magnificent Seven'. The seven men— Thomas Gorman, Tommy Toland, Seamus Convery, Martin Taylor, Peter Rodgers, Tucker Kane and Jim Bryson—were all competent swimmers, and confident that they could swim the stretch of water between the *Maidstone* and the dock. During the course of that winter's afternoon, all seven men stripped down to their underwear and socks and greased themselves with margarine and black shoe polish. They had cut through a bar across one of the portholes, and were able to squeeze through the gap. Fortunately for them, a steel cable (hawser) was left hanging from the deck of the ship and they were able to use it to drop into the freezing water just beyond the barbed wire. All seven made it to the shore, although things didn't quite go as planned when they did. Like any well-laid escape plan, they had relied on assistance from outside, and were expecting to be met by armed volunteers in two separate cars laden with warm clothes for their getaway. It was not to be the case, as they had landed in the wrong place, and had to improvise. Events took on an almost surreal turn, and the seven made their getaway in a hijacked bus, heading straight across town into the staunchly Republican Markets area. From there, they were spirited away to other areas in the west of the city before the security forces had time to organise a credible search.

The sheer determination of the Republicans to escape from jail was often due to the presence of someone in their midst who possessed a single-minded determination to make a bid for freedom. Martin Meehan was such an individual. When we met during the summer of 2006, I knew that this would probably be the only opportunity I would have to speak with a successful escapee, and I wanted to hear every little detail. I had read conflicting reports of the circumstances surrounding the escape, from both newspapers and Internet websites, but only Meehan was qualified to give the definitive account.

I imagined that he never got tired of telling it either. It is possible he still regarded it as a great personal victory against an aggressor who he believed had held the upper hand on most occasions. I didn't need to prompt him to begin:

The very first time I was in prison was August 1969. There was an incident where a young lad, who has in fact just died recently, he had his legs severed by a police jeep during a riot in Ardoyne. And during that incident I threw a concrete slab at the windscreen of a police jeep. But there was that grill on it, and so it didn't break the window, but the police all jumped out and hammered me. So me and him was anointed from the beating, plus he . . . got his legs severed. I was later charged with taking part in the riot. Come 22

August 1969, I was jailed for two months. Now prior to that I had got an absolutely fantastic job at the docks, working with containers, and the money was phenomenal, well over £100 per week some weeks. With the overtime and all, I bought my own house, my own car and a telephone in the house, which was something in them days. Life was looking up. When this incident happened that was the catalyst for me, and getting put into Crumlin Road Prison. I was sentenced to two months, and out of them two months I done six weeks with remission. And, eh, I was a star prisoner, never having been in prison in my life. I came into the base just for overnight. But they never told you that you would only be there overnight. You thought you would be there for the duration of your sentence. And I kept looking round this big black dungeon cell, and the first thought I had was what have I got myself into here. And then the next morning you were told to move, and you were brought up and given a brown suit with a big star on it, like the Jews would have had in the Second World War. And you were processed, sort of, and given your number. I think mine was 72 or something. And they referred to you by your number, not by your name. They would just have said 'number 72' so they could take away your identity. Then they brought you up to your cell, and you were told to keep your cell clean, and every morning you had to be out for work, and I was told I was going to be working in the woodyard. I didn't know what the woodyard was or anything about it. So when they brought me out there they put me on a big saw along with another prisoner, to cut big logs of wood. I had blisters on my hand, and you weren't allowed to stop sawing. There were one or two prison officers walking up and down who would have turned and said, 'Keep them saws moving' and this auld craic.

I confirmed with Meehan as to the location of the yard at the rear of the prison just below the prison hospital. He continued.

There were about thirty working there sometimes, working all day from early morning. I think we got a break at dinner time and then you were back out there say at one o'clock, and you worked until about four o'clock, or half four. And then you were back in again . . . it was a very restrictive regime, you know! I remember when you were out on association, you weren't allowed to congregate in groups of more than two. If there was any more than two congregated, there was a sort of hassle over that. I think you had just one letter a week, and wages were . . . I think at the end of the week, they gave you a very small amount of money to buy sweets and stuff—I didn't smoke so tobacco was no benefit to me. I remember saying to myself at the time that this would be the last time I would ever be in jail. It really sickened me because I thought I would lose my job, I was worried about my mortgage and all those things, and there was another baby as well, you know! So with all those worries, I was absolutely ecstatic about getting released after the six weeks. Says I, 'I'll never be back here again, that's my first and last time in jail.' Little did I know that I'd be back more than just once.

I was curious as to whether he was able to continue working after his first stint in jail, and asked if he had kept up payments on his mortgage.

Yes, thank God, I got my old job back. We [Catholic dockers] were deep sea dockers, looking after the foreign boats, as it were. The Protestants as they were, looked after the cross-channel boats. So that was 1969. I wasn't in jail in 1970 at all, even though the honeymoon period for the Brits was over, and there was all sorts of rioting and escalations in violence. I think it was March or February 1971, in or around that time when the first British soldier was killed. Then Barney Watt and Jim Sanders were killed from our area. At their funeral there was a Tricolour put over their coffins, and the Loyalists attacked us on the Ballygomartin

Road and stole the Tricolour. It was alleged that I produced
a gun and pointed it at the boy who stole the flag. I wasn't
even at the front of the cortège, I was right at the back. I
didn't even know this had happened until I was arrested.
They stood up and testified that I had produced the gun,
and I was then remanded in custody in Crumlin Road
Prison. At that stage there were only about seven or eight
Republican prisoners, Billy McKee and a few others. So
there was no real command structure as such, although Billy
would have been recognised as the more senior Republican,
and the prison officers unofficially recognised it. He would
have been the unofficial channel they went through. At that
stage we hadn't got political status, and the 'ODCS', ordinary
decent criminals, were mixed in amongst us. We sort of kept
to ourselves with our own identity. I can remember a boy
coming in from Queen's University, a fellow called Jim
McCann. Jim was a sort of a radical, he wouldn't have been
a Republican. He was along with a Jew and an American
student, and they were charged with petrol bombing
Queen's University common rooms, and I think they were
caught with a shotgun. So these three were remanded in
custody, and Jim was put in the same cell as me. And this
was some character, he kept saying things like 'This place
isn't big enough to hold me' and all this type of thing. He
said, 'I'm going to break out of here,' and I thought he was
spoofing, you know! The next thing he arrived in the cell
one morning with hacksaw blades stuck down the sides of
his socks, and I realised then that he was serious about
trying to get out. I thought he was a Walter Mitty. So me
and him sawed the bars for what must have been two or
maybe three weeks. A wee bit at a time and then a wee bit
more. Eventually we had near enough sawed through the
bars, and I went to see Billy McKee about this and told him
that there was a chance here of me getting out. So McKee
instructed me not to participate, saying, 'This man's a
balloon, don't be having anything to do with him. You will
get yourself shot.' And all the rest of it. He reminded me that

there was a good chance of beating the charge I was in for, as they had very little on me. He strongly advised me not to go with him, so I moved out of the cell the day before, with an excuse that I wanted to be doubled up with another prisoner I knew, a guy from Lurgan. Well, the next morning McCann went. And he done it by sawing out the rest of the bars, dropping down at seven o'clock in the morning into C-wing yard, and he had a hook made out of iron and he had a rope made out of sheets and he made his bid. Now the soldiers were in the pill boxes at this time. He timed it well, because he watched the soldiers in the boxes, and what time they went in at, changeover of the staff and that whole point of confusion. That's when he went. I have to say that it was some individual achievement. I had watched him from my cell. He had climbed up the gates that led into the football pitch, holding on until the top of the gate, and then climbed up on to the top of the wall. He had got away. I had given him an address to go to, which he did, and at eight o'clock, whenever the doors opened, he had left a message on his cell mirror to all the screws. The whole thing about it was a few weeks after, around June 1971, when he escaped, then I was acquitted in the High Court. That all took place about five weeks before internment.

I had read press reports about the McCann escape, and in comparison, Meehan had provided an accurate account without embellishment, although in fairness, the dates of the escape were slightly conflicting. The press had pointed out similarities in the details of McCann's lone flight to that of a Republican prisoner by the name of Daniel Donnelly, who had himself gone over the wall back around 1961. It appeared that Donnelly had also never been recaptured. Meehan began to paint a rather more bleak picture of events around that time as he continued.

Everything had gone from bad to worse. We knew internment was coming along, but we didn't know exactly when. On the morning of internment they hit my house, but I was at another house, which they also hit. The problem for them at the other house was they were after the individual who lived there, and I was lying on the settee, totally out for the count, and, to cut a long story short, they didn't arrest me because they had no idea it was me lying there on the settee. But they got the man of the house and took him out. It was only later that we found out he had been arrested. His wife or nobody else knew where he had gone. I hadn't seen his arrest . . . as I say, I was out for the count. I had woken up and all the doors of the house were lying open. So effectively that was me on the run.

Then in November 1971, the ninth, that was the night I was arrested. I got a terrible hammering.

At this point Meehan refers to the BBC television programme recently aired, 'Facing the Truth', in which he claims an ex-Army officer taking part in the broadcast was the same person who had been involved during his arrest back then. He continues:

They brought me back to Flax Street mill, and they actually had a photograph of me with all the injuries I received, which were pretty bad. So I was detained then, and eventually returned to the Crum, heading for C-wing. When they had brought me in a stretcher after Flax Street mill, they had taken me to Palace Barracks (Holywood), and brutalised me there. They put me in front of a firing squad, and done all sorts of brutality to me. And that was all after the initial arrest. They even dressed me up in a British Army tunic with holes in it and a cap with a feather coming out of it. After three and a half days or so they brought me to Crumlin Road Prison. The police and Army were still digging at me at this stage, the whole way down in the jeeps. The soldiers were spitting at me and kicking me. So I arrived into reception of the jail, hanging on to the rail getting processed. And I was sort of conscious, but half out of it. And as they were digging at me, a prison officer came over to me and said, 'I'm in charge here, leave him alone.' There was a bit of verbals between this officer, he was a principal officer in fact, and these soldiers and police. I always admired him for doing that. It always stuck in my mind that he actually stood up for me. He brought me in and got me a bath and all. I had forty-eight stitches in the back of my head, bruised from head to toe. And he tried to be as conciliatory as possible. Then I was put into the prison hospital for a while. The name of that officer was Tug Wilson. He had been on reception for years. I always remembered him. Even in times after that. I remember later in the H-blocks, his son being an assistant governor. The shame was that Tug Wilson was shot dead going into a club on the Crumlin Road. I think that was around '79, around the time I was on remand. I remember hearing it on the news about this prison officer Wilson being shot dead. I felt a wee bit aggrieved at that, as he had been decent with me, you know! I remember saying to his son, the same story I am telling you, and how he had went out of his way to help me at that particular stage. I don't even know if his son is still in the Service, as that was some years ago. So two weeks after that I escaped.

I was surprised at just how close to his capture his escape attempt had been, and asked him what had made his mind up so quickly to try and make a bid for freedom. He was clear in his mind that he believed that he wasn't going to get out of prison for some considerable time, and why wait.

The remand prisoners had escaped during a football match, and I was in the prison hospital at this stage. The first thing hit me was I'll never get out of here again. So when I came back to the wing, everything was closed down for nearly two weeks. They wouldn't let us out for those two weeks until they got their security all tightened after the big escape. Eventually they did let us out, and I was still on a walking stick from the beating I had got during my arrest. So they let some of us do referees and linesmen during our daily match. You didn't actually do much other than walk up and down the lines. As I walked up and down, beside Mickey McGuire, a manhole rattled underneath me. And the next thing was, I said to Mickey, 'There must be a way out of there'. He replied that he didn't think so. He thought it was bolted down, but we both said we would have a wee 'duke' at it. So when we lifted it up, there was six foot of a drop, with water at the bottom. In seconds, I had my mind made up. I knew there was no way out of the manhole cover other than when we had a Gaelic match at half past twelve every day, when we could probably get down into the hole at half time and wait. As well as that, Thursdays were the day that prison officers got paid, and they were always more interested in counting their wages. I had observed this for some time and knew that the wages were usually given out around dinner time. So we arranged for the teams to stand out in a half circle, to distract the various officers on duty. I then went to see the OC, a fellow called Burns, and he said it was madness, telling me that we would never be able to do it. He told me that he thought we would be shot dead by the soldiers on duty. I think 'ludicrous' was the word he used. He wouldn't give us permission. So we pounded him all day, until he eventually said, 'Right, I'll concede. If it's a success we will claim it, but if you'se are caught, you done it off your own bat.' So we went to bed to wait for the big day. And the next thing I remember was someone came up with the idea to put a pound of butter all over me, because the water was freezing, bearing in mind this was in the winter. We reckoned we would be six hours, maybe longer, in this freezing water. In truth we had no idea how long we would be. So we put the butter all over us and went out the next day to the match. We had our sheets made up in a rope, and a hook made from a chair. It was a chance in a million. So at half time the teams stood around eating oranges, turning their backs to us so we could drop down into the manhole. I stood up to my neck in the water, with another four feet to go until the top, and I remember there was wee steps inside. In fact I was down there a few months ago, getting a photograph taken next to the manhole cover, as it's now in the car park of the Mater Hospital, the same spot where the football pitch used to be. So anyhow, everything went according to plan up until then. There was only two of us designated to go. Dutch Doherty was dropped down on top of me, and three would have been an impossibility. But little did we know that another prisoner who wasn't even authorised to go had decided to jump in too. You can imagine what this was like. It was like a sardine tin. The other two were above my head. I didn't know where I was, and I nearly passed out on several occasions. And then eventually at about half past six that night we lifted the manhole cover up, and the steam that came out of it from our body heat was something else. As luck would have it, there was fog outside, and you couldn't see ten feet in front of you. It had just dropped that night. We climbed around under the barbed wire, cut to pieces, and moved towards Girdwood Barracks and Clifton Park Avenue. All of a sudden I said, 'Hold it'. I saw what looked to be a soldier sitting down in front of us. I had come this far, however, and I decided to make a run for it. Away I went, and I actually had to pass this soldier side on. As I did, I realised it was a cement mixer with a shovel sticking out of it, which had looked just like the silhouette of a squaddie and his rifle. It had definitely looked like a soldier, but the laughs of us was something shocking. I had to tell the other two to keep their voices down, because we were right beside the barracks. So we got to the wall, and threw the rope up, and although it caught several times, it didn't catch right. Eventually then it did catch. We had taken care to put sheets around the hook itself to drown any noise. As we were climbing up the rope, the disadvantage of the butter on our arms and legs became apparent, as we kept sliding back down again. It was like something from the 'Keystone Cops'. So we had to re-tie knots into the rope, and then we were able to scale the wall and drop down the other side. I had arranged for a car to be parked close by. A green Avenger it was. It was parked in

Clifton Park Avenue, with the keys under the mat. Anyone sitting in the car at that location would have been suspicious to police. So that's the way everything worked out. We had to climb over a couple of smaller walls, and by the time we did that we were absolutely exhausted. I drove the car, and we crossed over the Shankhill, and into the Falls Road to a safe house. That was it. We had got away.

I had read some reports about the escape, and how people believed that he had crossed the Border almost immediately after the escape. He was able to put the record straight on that issue.

No, I didn't at that time. That was a Thursday night, and I didn't go across until Sunday. There was a girl in the car with me and one small child. She was driving actually until about Banbridge, and I turned to her and said, 'Let me have a wee drive, I want to get used to it.' So I jumped in to the driver's seat and drove on towards Newry. As we were coming outside Newry, there was a big, massive road check, with UDR and police. I remember it was a windy day. As we moved forward in the queue I could see that they were asking almost every driver to get out of their car and open the boot. I was wearing a big wig, and had false identification on me. When I got to the boy stopping the cars, I rolled the window down slightly, and the guy said to me, 'That's a terrible auld day, where are you going?' And I replied that I was going into Newry. I produced my identification, and he said, 'I'll not ask you to get out in this weather, with the child in the car,' as he looked past me into the back seat. I then asked him what the problem was, and he replied, 'Them three bastards who escaped the other night. It's a waste of time as they are probably long gone.' I said, 'You never know your luck.' He then waved us on. I was then over the Border.

Meehan finished that sentence with a wry smile on his lips. The memory of his escape was indeed a sweet one, and I am sure he has dined out on it on many an occasion.

There is no doubt that luck played a great part in all aspects of Meehan's escape, bearing in mind that there appeared to be little time between the initial plan itself and the actual event. He admits himself that the blanket of fog which had fallen over that part of North Belfast on that night was totally unexpected, and without it things may have been somewhat different. His escape was obviously hailed as a major victory for the Republicans, and it was even suggested that the press had been alerted to the escape before the prison authorities had known anything about it, adding insult to injury. The then Prime Minister, Brian Faulkner, was outraged at the obvious holes appearing in the prison's security and embarrassed by yet another successful escape. Just weeks prior to Meehan's escape, nine Republican prisoners had gone over the wall with a little help from people on the outside, and seven had managed to evade police and Army and cross over the Border. They became known as the 'Crumlin Kangaroos'.

The 'Kangaroos' were made up of Christopher Keenan, Peter Gerard Hennesey, Bernard Elliman, Terence Clarke, Thomas J. Maguire, Seamus Storey, Daniel A. Mullan, Thomas Kane and Thomas Gerard Fox. Their particular escape must have been even more embarrassing to the authorities because it had been preceded around a month earlier by an almost identical failed attempt, which was thwarted only by sheer luck. On that occasion, five prisoners had actually made it onto the top of the outer wall during a football match, only to be met by an Army patrol below them, who had reacted to the sound of a nail bomb exploding in the general area. They abandoned the escape and returned below to be swallowed up by the other participants in the football match. I suppose the authorities would have considered it foolhardy to use the same ruse twice in a row, not to mention only weeks apart. But that was probably the beauty of the plan. No extra security provisions had been set in place as a result of the first escape attempt, and the plan had worked up to a point, so why revise the idea.

All nine of the prisoners were being held on remand for various terrorist offences, and were deemed to be amongst the most dangerous in the prison population at the time. Both

Thomas Kane and Peter Hennesey had been arrested in the early hours of 28 June 1971, in a warehouse in Devonshire Street with an array of bomb-making materials and arms and munitions, which made an impressive haul for the security forces at the time. Recovered at the scene were gelignite, detonators, eight nail bombs, five flares, 90 feet of sump fuse, and 500 feet of pentaflex detonator fuse. As well as that, there was a quantity of sugar chlorate, a .45 revolver, a .22 rifle, and over 300 rounds of various calibre ammunition. The warehouse had been doubling up as both a Celtic Supporters Club and a bomb-making factory. Both men were interviewed at the Police Office, and were then remanded in custody on 30 June of that year. The other escapees had been remanded for similar offences and must have realised that, if convicted, they stood to serve a considerable amount of jail time.

When 16 November came around, the football match was taking place as usual. The team were playing in a green football strip, and when a signal was given, rope ladders were thrown over the exterior walls from the outside, and the escape began in earnest. Only nine eventually got over the wall, and were met by two cars, one of which was described as a white Ford Cortina which had been parked in Clifton Park Avenue. The nine who made it over the wall were believed to be only a third of the men actually planning to make the prison break. It seems that although the security measures around the external wall were less than adequate, the prison officers inside the jail managed to restrain another sixteen inmates from following their comrades out onto the street.

Some time later, six men who claimed to be amongst those who had escaped from the Crum appeared at an organised press conference at the headquarters of Sinn Féin in Kevin Street in Dublin. The press were told that although they could attend the conference, they could not photograph all six men, but would be restricted to taking photographs of one man only, namely Bernard Elliman. They did, however, name the others as Storey, Maguire, Fox, Hennesey and Kane. It was also mentioned that Clarke was unable to attend as he had to greet American relatives at Shannon Airport.

Bernard Elliman then told reporters how the escape had been planned for some weeks from both outside and in. He described the escape as it had been reported, but stated that after scaling the wall, each man went his separate way, and all were able to cross over the Border into the South shortly after. He took the opportunity to complain bitterly about the alleged abuse he and the others had suffered at the hands of the Army and the RUC during their detention and arrest, and admitted that all six men had walked freely about Dublin City with little if any attention.

It is clear that the Republican movement, in particular the IRA, stood to benefit greatly from the positive propaganda the escape had provided, and therefore they made the best of the press conference. There is another explanation, of course, as to why they insisted that all six men be identified but only one photographed. Two of the nine escapees were known to have been recaptured in the North, but the other seven still remained at large. It was not known, though, if all seven had actually crossed into the South. By claiming that the six men at the conference were actually the escapees, it may have persuaded the security forces in the North that any further searches for the missing prisoners would be fruitless. I suspect that Special Branch and Army intelligence would have had an inkling that they were being thrown a 'red herring', and not for the first time.

Both the Meehan/Doherty escape and the 'Kangaroos' were music to the ears of the IRA, and like most major triumphs, immortalised in song. I was able to find lyrics to a Republican ditty which rejoiced unashamedly in the inadequacies of the measures put in place to hold their volunteers. I can't be sure of the tune used to accompany the lyrics, but I suspect it was equally as unimaginative.

In Crumlin Road Jail hall the prisoners one day,
Took out a football and started to play.
And while all the warders were watching the ball,
Nine of the prisoners jumped over the wall.

Over the wall, over the wall,
Who could believe they jumped over the wall.
Over the wall, over the wall,
It's hard to believe they jumped over the wall.

Now the warders looked on with the greatest surprise,
And the sight they saw brought the tears to their eyes.
For one of the teams was not there at all,
They all got transferred and jumped over the wall.

Over the wall, over the wall,
Who could believe they jumped over the wall.
Over the wall, over the wall,
It's hard to believe they jumped over the wall.

Now the Governor's came down with his face in a twist,
Said, 'Line up these lads while I check out me list'
But nine of the lads didn't answer the call,
And the warder said 'Please Sir they're over the wall.'

Over the wall, over the wall,
Who could believe they jumped over the wall.
Over the wall, over the wall,
It's hard to believe they jumped over the wall.

The security forces were shook to the core,
So they barred every window and bolted each door.
But all of their precautions were no use at all,
For another three prisoners jumped over the wall.

Over the wall, over the wall,
Who could believe they jumped over the wall.
Over the wall, over the wall,
It's hard to believe they jumped over the wall.

When the news reached old Stormont, Faulkner turned pale,
When he heard that more men had escaped from his jail.
Said he, 'Now we'll have an enquiry to call,
And we'll get Edward Compton to whitewash the wall.'

Over the wall, over the wall,
Who could believe they jumped over the wall.
Over the wall, over the wall,
It's hard to believe they jumped over the wall.

The prison Governor at the time, Major Albert Mullin, had little to reproach himself about. He was struggling to retain control of a prison population which should have been between 400 and 500 inmates, but had swollen to over 800 prisoners and another 100 detainees under internment. His staff could only be praised for managing under such extreme pressure. The security forces in general were finding it difficult to cope with bombings and shootings on a daily basis. Providing a permanent guard for the perimeter of the Crum would be a drain on already stretched resources, and would also bring with it more problems in relation to attacks on that guard force from elements outside.

It was no surprise to anyone that the jail itself would eventually become a target for the terrorists. On Sunday 23 August that year, a ten-pound gelignite bomb was tossed out of a moving car and directed at the front gates that opened on to the Crumlin Road. The force of the blast lifted the gates off their hinges and damaged some linked fencing on either side, but did not cause any great disruption. Windows in the surrounding area, including those of the Crumlin Road Court-house, were smashed, and passers-by were shocked at just how blatant the bombers had been. That particular weekend was a busy one for the Army and police, with several incidents of bombings and shootings taking place all over the North. The campaign was becoming both ruthless and co-ordinated, with little regard for innocent members of the public or the damage to the local economy. The escapes were a further blow to the Government, and it was clear that measures had to be taken to reduce the overcrowding at the Crum and on the *Maidstone*.

A quick solution at the time was to move around 219 internees to Long Kesh to be housed in the compounds. The urgency with which this was done is evident, as they were moved by helicopter in groups of around ten at a time, securely handcuffed. The use of Long Kesh may have seemed a perfect solution to the problem at the time, but considering that there were over fifty successful escapes recorded there between 1971 and 1975, the record speaks for itself. The sheer determination of the prisoners to make a bid for freedom at any cost continued to rock the authorities.

During September 1971, a young man by the name of Phillip Larkin was shot in the back during a gun battle between British Army troops and a local IRA unit. Larkin had been part of the unit, and on his capture he was admitted to the Mater Hospital to receive medical treatment. Larkin went missing from his hospital bed a week later, having made an attempt to evade his Army guard by posing as one of his own visitors. His bid for freedom was short-lived, however, and he was cornered just three hours later in the basement of the complex. Little wonder it seems, as he was anything but fit at the time.

*   *   *

The period during the 1980s saw the Troubles still gripping the Province and striking fear into innocent people in both communities. Although there were fewer attacks on police and security forces than in the 1970s, the IRA's methods were becoming more and more sophisticated. The brutality of some of the murders carried out by both sides was also becoming worryingly gruesome. Despite the security forces making major advancements in infiltrating the various organisations, and notching up success after success, there was also no shortage of recruits to step up and take the place of those who had been captured or killed. And still, those who found themselves in jail were committed to rejoining this bitter campaign.

In June 1981, the then Secretary of State, Humphrey Atkins, had to face some of the harshest criticism ever from MPs across the political spectrum regarding the latest breach in security at the Crum. The timing of this latest most daring escape from one of Ulster's jails couldn't have been worse, as the Maze hunger strike was in full swing. All eyes had turned towards the fate of those still refusing food, and tensions outside had been building towards major civil unrest. The escape of eight Republican remand inmates from Crumlin Road was deemed to be a major victory to the IRA, and in some ways drew more support for the plight of the hunger strikers in the Maze.

There was nothing unusual about eight Republican prisoners availing of a consultation with their solicitors, especially as seven of them were involved in a high-profile court case dubbed 'the M60 trial', because of the involvement of some of the accused in earlier machine-gun ambushes. Judgement in respect of the trial was expected the following day, and it had been normal for the accused to speak with their counsel frequently throughout the month-long trial. At around four o'clock on this quiet July afternoon, the legal and professional visits area of the Crum was full of the eight prisoners and three solicitors, Oliver Kelly, Ciaran Steele and Joseph Rice. As the consultations began to take place, the inmates produced three handguns and directed everyone present to stay quiet. There were around ten prison officers present held at gunpoint. Two of them were told to strip, and two Republican inmates put their uniforms on. At this point, they were only yards from the main gate, but still had to negotiate the air-lock system. They split into two groups, each with one of the uniformed imposters, and took along some of the visits staff as hostages.

There are varying reports as to the resistance they met at the main gate area, but it is known that shots were fired at any screws who stood in the way of their escape. Other reports were of hand-to-hand exchanges and batons having been used on escapees and screws alike. The first group to make it to the Crumlin Road through the wicket gatewere able to get to a waiting getaway car and make good their escape. The second group came under fire from the guard squad at the jail and a police patrol. Numerous shots were exchanged as the group of men legged it through the health centre beside the Crumlin Road

Court-house towards another waiting getaway car. There was confusion everywhere as innocent passers-by took cover and scattered in all directions as bullets rained down on the fleeing men. The security forces had to take a step back from a full-on engagement, as they were unsure exactly who were legitimate prison officers and members of the public, and who were hostages. Eyewitness accounts were of total panic, with people running around, and cars which were parked in the health centre being riddled with bullet holes. One of the escapers had even tried to hijack a vehicle on the Crumlin Road, which to his surprise had three plain-clothes police inside. He thought better of it when one of the policemen fired a shot in his direction.

All eight men got clean away, with injuries to prison staff surprisingly minor, considering the amount of shots fired during the incident. There was an air of total disbelief at just how co-ordinated the escape had been. According to Republican sources, the three guns had been smuggled into the jail some weeks prior to the escape. They also stated that active service units had been present on the day outside the jail to assist their comrades as they fled. Both getaway vehicles were later found near Unity Flats at Hopewell Crescent, one of which bore several bullet holes in the bodywork.

The security forces were put on full alert to try and recapture all or any of the eight men, as both the daring nature of their escape and the offences for which they had been tried at court suggested they were extremely dangerous. The press were given photographs of all eight, and within hours their faces were all over the newspapers and the television. The eight men were named as Angelo Fusco, 24, of Slieveban Drive; Joseph Patrick Thomas Docherty, 28, Spamount Street; Robert Campbell, 27, Ballymurphy Crescent; Anthony Gerard Sloan, 26, Summerville Drive; Gerard Michael Sloan, 27, Westview Pass; Michael Anthony McKee, 24, New Barnsley Crescent; Paul Patrick Magee, 33, Glenalina Gardens, all from the Belfast area; and Michael Ryan, who hailed from Ardboe near Coalisland in Tyrone. Ryan was the only one of the eight who was not involved in the M60 trial, but instead was accused of the murder of a UDR member in Omagh the previous December.

The M60 murder case was significant in that the weapon itself had been used again and again, and was a powerful machine-gun which had struck fear into police and Army alike. It had been used in the murders of SAS Captain Herbert Westmacott on the Antrim Road in 1980, and Police Constable Stephen Magill in Andersonstown, amongst other shooting incidents. The conviction and further imprisonment of all seven men would have reassured people that those men capable of using this substantial piece of firepower were now off the streets for good. The escape was to turn everything around and the fear gradually returned.

Shortly after the escape, 21 June to be exact, Paul Patrick Magee made an appearance at the Wolfe Tone commemorative rally at Bodenstown, Co. Kildare. It was almost customary now to flaunt an escapee in front of the media at such a high-profile event. The Irish Government were under pressure to show expediency in tracking down the fugitives and returning them to custody. Only six months after the escape, Gardai arrested Michael 'Beaky' McKee along with three other men, and for his part in relation to the escape he received ten years in Portlaoise Prison. Even when he was released, a bitter battle for his extradition was again fought in the Dublin courts, but to no avail. McKee did, however, make his own way north of the Border, only to be arrested hiding in the roof space of a house on Ballymurphy Road on 1 November 1991.

Of the others, Joe Docherty was fighting extradition from the United States, whilst Michael Ryan, the only one not connected to the M60 trial, was shot dead by security forces in Coagh, Co. Tyrone, along with two other men.

The outrage at the security blunder at Belfast jail brought forward suggestions by James Molyneaux, the Official Unionist leader, that a 'fifth column' had in some way infiltrated the service and assisted in trafficking the weapons used during the break-out. There were possibly elements of truth in the statement, as some degree of internal assistance may have taken place. But in fairness, every time an escape attempt from any prison was successful, there were always fingers pointed at staff. It had been a well thought out and audacious plan, and had required luck as a key element if it were to be a success. Luck was indeed what they had.

*   *   *

Security measures at any prison are always under review, regardless of whether there has been an escape attempt or not. Every now and then matters come to the attention of staff which need to be addressed as they present a risk to the general security in the jail. Measures are then put in place to reduce the risk, and are duly adopted as good practice. The human element, though, still remains the weakest link in any such equation. It will always be difficult for the authorities to be sure that every eventuality has been taken into account and factored into any system they choose to implement. The fact that in Northern Ireland the prison population has always had various collective factions comprising the main body of its inmates has made its prison system almost unique, and difficult to deal with. The structures which existed in these collective bodies of prisoners provided the perfect support system for escape plans and disruptive protesting. As they adapted to their surroundings, and explored possibilities, then so the Prison Service had to do the same. It was always going to be a cat and mouse situation, but played out with real lives and real consequences.

Chapter 7
Trial and Error

When I was detailed court duties, I always dreaded what the day would bring. It wasn't so bad when you had to take a prisoner out to a court in another jurisdiction, but courts at the Crumlin Road were anything but pleasant. I hated the waiting around, and the hustle and bustle of the holding area below the Crumlin Road Court-house. Most of all, I hated the tunnel. The tunnel ran from below the jail, underneath the Crumlin Road, and eventually into the bowels of the court-house. There was an entry door at the beginning of A-wing and a staircase leading you down below the level of the forecourt and out in the direction of the front gate. After descending a few more steps, you eventually came to level ground where the tunnel stretched out in front of you, arcing away to the right. The ceiling of the tunnel was a permanent arch, and the many heating pipes gripped the walls to your side, encaged in mesh. There was barely enough room for two people to walk side by side, which was exactly what you had to do when handcuffed to a prisoner due for court. It was unbearably humid, and just small enough to make me edgy and slightly claustrophobic. All the inmates who were due to appear at the court that day had to be escorted through the tunnel and into the holding cells to await their case being called. It was always a long wait. Those screws who were lucky enough to be directed into the dock of a particular court could while away the day listening to various cases being heard, and it was always cooler up there. When the trial for the Maze escapers came around, it was one which most of us on general duties had an opportunity to attend, and did so gladly. There were always interesting cases going on in other courtrooms, but the more juicy ones were saved for number 1 court.

The stairs up to the dock in number 1 court were steep and narrow. You almost had to take side steps when negotiating them, and on each tread you would hear the creaks and groans of the age-old timbers straining beneath you. The wooden panels and handrails at the top were the first indication that you would be emerging into the type of courtroom straight out of a period film. In normal circumstances, the court did have all the pomp and circumstance one would have expected. The judge in his finest robes and wig, and the barristers buried beneath piles of official-looking documents, and bowing to the Crown as they entered or left the court. The room itself boasted high, heavily corniced ceilings and elaborate light fixtures, with richly grained hardwood bench seats throughout. It was all you would expect of a courtroom of yesteryear. I often imagined how the room would have looked during one of the famous murder trials which it had hosted, in particular the final moments when the judge would have donned the black cap to pass a sentence of death upon the accused. In reality, it had changed little since then, only twenty odd years having passed since McGladdery's hanging.

There were other trials at the court, of course, which had resulted in life imprisonment or acquittal for the defendants, and they were numerous. In particular during times of civil unrest and any upsurge in the Republican campaign, incidents of homicide were frequent enough.

In 1922, for instance, John Porter was arrested and tried for the murder of Michael Crudden, during what was described as sectarian trouble in the Oldpark area of the town. Another man by the name of David Duncan also appeared at the court that year charged with the murder of James McIvor at Little Patrick Street and attempting to murder Patrick McMahon the very same day during civil unrest. I knew the 1920s had been a period in the history of the North which had been marred by trouble, but by all accounts, there were running gun battles in the streets of Belfast. For the soldiers unfortunate enough to be garrisoned

here during those years, they faced much the same
those who were to come back fifty years later.

In September 1921 two young Belfast women had come out oi
to the street outside their homes to talk with each other. It was a
day like any other for Maggie Erdis, aged just nineteen, and
Evelyn Blair, her senior by only three years. They may have been
discussing work at the mills that day or making plans for the
forthcoming weekend, but neither would see the end of the day.
As luck would have it, an Army patrol was passing the bottom of
Vere Street, where both girls were. As they did, two gunmen came
out of a house further up the street carrying two rifles. They
engaged the Army foot patrol, firing towards the bottom of
Vere Street and Cross Street, but were unable to hit any of
their intended targets. They did, however, hit both girls as
they attempted to take cover, fatally wounding them. Herbert
Woodhouse, a corporal in the 1st Battalion of the Norfolk
Regiment, and part of the foot patrol on the day in question, gave
evidence at the trial of John Corr, who had been arrested after a
follow-up search of the area. His evidence was clear in that he
stated that although the gunmen had fired several rounds in the
direction of the patrol, he had been unable to return any more
than one round. It was a tragic case which drew condemnation
from all sides, highlighting the sheer disregard for human life
that these fanatics appeared to have. Maggie and Evelyn were to
join the long list of civilian casualties caught up in the continuing
Troubles, and headlining the court list for trials at the time.

There were, of course, domestic murder trials at the court
where the circumstances, although just as tragic in respect of the
loss of life, were as a result of a 'fair dig'. When I say fair dig, I
mean two people engaging in an altercation with each other
which would not normally have ended in one or the other party
dying. Such was the case of John Matchett, who was accused of
the murder of James Megarry in August 1922. Both men had
known each other for some time, and had worked at the famous
St George's Market at May Street. On this particular day,
witnesses said that there was tension between the two men,
culminating in Matchett having thrown a tomato at Megarry,

nitting him on the head. Megarry had crossed the distance to where Matchett stood, and a fight ensued. Matchett was reported to have thrown a punch at Megarry, catching him on the left side of the face. At this point others present broke up the fracas, and Megarry returned to work. Matters didn't lie there, however, as shortly after, Matchett returned and again hit Megarry, who fell backwards, hitting his head and causing a fatal injury to his skull. The market was busy that day, and there was no shortage of witnesses coming forward. Some, it appears, had their own agendas, stating that they knew Matchett had always carried a small hammer with him, although there was no evidence to suggest a weapon had been used. It was itself a tragic end to Megarry's life, and a blight on Matchett's own, having taken matters further than he would have wished. Alcohol had undoubtedly played some part in the lives of both men, and had shaped the outcome of the day's events.

In more recent years, the Crumlin Road Court-house constantly flirted with controversy, with the Government and the judiciary introducing various methods with which to slow down the terrorist express train, which appeared to be gaining momentum. One tactic that drew more criticism than most was the introduction of the Diplock Court. It was introduced in 1972 in an attempt to eradicate potential tampering with any formally elected jury. The Troubles had nurtured networks of terrorists on both sides, all capable of obtaining information on jurors and their families and pressurising them into swaying the outcome of various trials. The disadvantage the court service had was the fact that Northern Ireland was anything but a large country, with everyone knowing everyone else's business, and secrets were hard to keep. There was the added possibility that details of jurors' identities could have been passed by sympathisers within the system.

Lord Diplock's report went towards forming the British Government's policy of criminalisation, whereupon paramilitary elements were treated as common criminals and not politically motivated individuals. As you can imagine, it was not a popular policy.

It didn't just stop there either. Just around the corner came the use of the 'supergrass'. I can only think the Government had reached a brick wall when the thought of accepting the tainted evidence of one man against others became grounds for a successful prosecution. Nevertheless, they proceeded with recruiting these men, with the promise of financial remuneration in some cases, and immunity against prosecution in others. It was flawed right from the start, but I suspect the British Government was prepared to face the criticism of political parties across the board in return for the continuing remand of several hundred suspected terrorists. Many had in fact labelled the supergrass system as 'internment by another name'. In many ways it was. When Christopher Black was arrested in 1981, and only after securing immunity from being prosecuted himself, he supplied information and statements which resulted in the arrest and remand of over thirty-five men. Two years later, the solitary judge at the Black supergrass trial found twenty-two men guilty of various offences connected to IRA terrorism, and passed a sentence totalling 4,000 years imprisonment on them. One had to remember that there was often no corroborating evidence to support the statements given by Black, and that he was in effect being coerced in no uncertain terms. How he could be conceived to be a credible witness by any stretch of the imagination was beyond the belief of any reasonably thinking individual. The supergrass was in effect an accomplice of those accused, and should have been a co-defendant instead of a star witness.

The system continued, however, with those who had the finger pointed at them languishing in jail for long periods awaiting trial. In some cases this was a stretch of more than two years. To be remanded for this length of time purely on the word of someone who may have had a grudge against you would have been worse than internment itself.

The last supergrass trial to be heard was late in 1985. I remember that the name Harry Kirkpatrick was anything but popular amongst the Republican inmates, especially those who were affiliated with the INLA. In December of that year, twenty-five INLA members were convicted as a result of his evidence. It only took another year, though, for twenty-four of those to have their convictions overturned by the appeal court. Most of the others convicted in the same way walked free from prison as soon as their appeals were heard.

The 'grass' was the most unpopular man around, having sold out his comrades for money or freedom or both. When in jail awaiting the trial, these men were housed in the rear of D-wing, in a secure annexe, and waited upon by experienced screws, who had to remain indifferent towards them. They were cosseted in many ways; kept sweet so that they would not retract their evidence at any stage. Their families and friends would often desert them, or would themselves become victims of violence by association. It was not an easy decision to make to turn Queen's evidence.

It will always be a contentious area, with the majority believing that there was always another agenda to be met from accepting the evidence of a supergrass. The British Government was quite happy to accept criticism on the basis that the ends justified the means. Literally hundreds of people were taken off the streets for long periods of time without any physical evidence having to be presented to a court to empower them to do so.

The Diplock Court system still remains today, but recent reports suggest that it too will be phased out in the very near future.

*   *   *

One of the dangers of working in the Northern Ireland Prison Service was that it was a certainty that at some point on the outside, you would cross the path of one or more ex-inmates. They would seldom forget the faces of the men who shut the big Belfast door at night, or continually walked up and down the wing keeping an eye on their every move. They would recognise you fairly quickly. That is not to say that they would be aggressive in any way, but there was always the risk that they would. If you were able to place them yourself, it was a natural reaction to avoid eye contact and walk away in the opposite direction. It happened to me on many occasions, but only once did I feel uncomfortable. On this particular day, I had reason to visit Clonard Mill in West Belfast to pick up an item for a close friend who didn't drive at the time. After about ten minutes messing about at the bottom of the Springfield Road, I eventually found it and drove into the small car parking area. I found the workshop I was looking for, collected the item which had been left aside, and returned to my car a few minutes later, ready to drive out the gate. It was only then that I became aware of a car in front of me, the driver seemingly eager to take my space. When I looked up at the driver, I knew exactly who it was. He seemed to be glaring at me through his aluminium-rimmed glasses, with absolutely no sign of emotion on his face. I fumbled with the keys, and stalled the car as I let out the clutch to move off. Still his countenance hadn't changed. When I did move off, his stare seemed to follow me the whole way out of the car park, his eyes burning into the back of my head.

The tall, dark-haired man I remember as a red book prisoner on D three had changed little, other than a few grey hairs and a reasonably priced suit. Gerry Kelly was one of the Maze escapers who, for me, stood out amongst the rest as he waited for the trial to commence in the early part of 1988 at the court-house across the road. It was to be a significant trial in all respects, not only for those who had been involved in the escape (who had at various stages been returned to custody), but also this trial was of personal interest to the prison officers who had worked alongside James Ferris, the officer who had lost his life as a direct result of events that day in 1983, when thirty-eight Republican prisoners staged the mass escape.

Kelly appeared to most of us who worked in the Crum as the epitome of what we believed a terrorist was or should be, and was therefore regarded as a very high-risk prisoner. He had a stern countenance, and would rarely answer any questions in anything other than monosyllables. He carried himself with an air of defiance which verged on total arrogance. It was a given that he was to be watched closely at all times, whether it was during visits, or trips to the prison hospital, or even to chapel on a

Sunday. Being the lapsed believer that I was, and still am, I felt somehow out of place at Sunday Mass in the chapel, but attended regularly enough through indifference, as some screws (on religious grounds) actually objected to putting a foot near a Catholic service for fear they would be contaminated. I am quite sure that they would not have received second degree burns from the holy water in the fonts, but they wore their ignorance like a campaign badge. The authorities in those days did not compel them to attend as part of their duties. Those Catholic officers who expressed a wish to attend were usually accommodated.

The Mass was more of an excuse for a giggle and a laugh amongst the ranks of the Republicans, although there were those whose piety shone through in their adherence to every word the priest uttered. They gladly took communion, and entered into the spirit of it all, if you pardon the pun. Gerry Kelly, I remember, sat alone on most occasions, relaxed and reclined, and looking around him, as if sizing the place up for a possible escape attempt. He appeared to pay little attention to the order of service, and maintained this aloof, almost reclusive persona, as if he had to maintain his distance from the others by virtue of rank. He came across as cold, emotionless and dedicated, and I wondered just how much of this 'hard man' image was bravado. When I read reports about the parts the various inmates had played during the escape from the Maze, I could see that Kelly was a ruthless and single-minded individual, and worthy of his red book status.

The Maze escape was carried out on 25 September 1983, and was the largest prison break in terms of escapees ever recorded in Northern Ireland. Thirty-eight Republican inmates took over a H-block from staff, and hijacked a food lorry with which they made their way to the main gate and escaped. During the escape, weapons that had been smuggled into the jail by various means were used against the warders, directly causing the death of James Ferris, and leaving Officer Adams with a gunshot wound to his head. The escapees were brutally determined, and willing to kill to achieve their objective. Gerry Kelly had played a major role during the escape, which had been meticulously planned for some weeks by himself and McFarlane, who had been the IRA Commanding Officer in the Maze at the time. Kelly was never convicted of shooting officer Adams in the control room of H7, but was almost certainly there when it happened. Whether he did pull the trigger or not is immaterial. He was part of a ruthless team of men with nothing to lose, who were hell bent on returning to the armed struggle on the outside; so much so that for some considerable time afterwards, the security forces failed to catch up with any more than nineteen of the original thirty-eight.

When Brendan (Bik) McFarlane and Kelly were arrested in Holland two years later, the flat they were in had in it several items which were of use to terrorists, and it was apparent that their war was anything but over. Kelly had remained a dedicated Republican volunteer even whilst on the run. His active service record was well documented, right from the time when he, along with the Price sisters, had bombed the Old Bailey and Scotland Yard back in the early 1970s, killing one person and injuring 250 more. On his conviction for those offences, he was committed to prison in England in 1973. He was transferred to the Maze three years later, having already proved a handful for the Prison Service on the mainland by embarking on a self-imposed hunger strike which lasted in excess of fifty-five days. McFarlane was cut from the same cloth as Kelly, and had put aside his studies for the priesthood in favour of joining the IRA. He was convicted of killing five people in the bombing of the Bayardo Bar on the Shankill in 1975, and was serving five life sentences for his involvement. The travesty would be that, of the twenty-five years he was due to serve, he would complete only eight before escaping. When returned to Belfast for the Maze escape trial, it seems he did not have to serve the remainder of his sentence. In fact, Kelly's circumstances were fairly similar. There is no doubt that Gerry Kelly was an active volunteer, and after an interview with a local newspaper as recently as 2004, when he stated that the death of Ferris had been 'unfortunate' but that he had no regrets, it would be hard to convince some people, especially those who remember James Ferris, that Kelly is now a man committed to brokering peace through negotiation.

My first days at the Crum after moving from Magilligan saw me undergoing a one-week familiarity period. During that time I remember being told about the significant amount of red book prisoners in D-wing, with a certain emphasis being placed on McFarlane and Kelly. They were still considered extremely high-risk individuals, although part of the extradition deal thrashed out with the Dutch authorities had returned them to legal custody with the proviso that the sentences which they were serving prior to their escape would in some way be considered time served. It did make the likelihood that they would attempt a further escape a bit of a far-fetched scenario. The Dutch Supreme Court had taken some convincing that both men had acted as combatants during a divisive political struggle. As late as 2 July 1986, McFarlane's plea to fight extradition was thrown out by the Supreme Court on the grounds that they thought there was 'too broad an interpretation of political motives'. That decision was to be reversed some time later with Kelly and McFarlane faring quite well indeed from the deal. Both men had been returned to the Crumlin Road to await trial for escaping from lawful custody in September 1983. Neither was to stand trial for the murder of James Ferris during the outbreak. Kelly, however, also had to answer to the charge of attempting to murder prison officer Adams, who had been shot in the head during the escape. They weren't the only ones to face trial for their part in those events, and were accompanied by fourteen others in the dock for one of the most bizarre spectacles ever to be witnessed at the Crumlin Road Court-house. Standing alongside them on various days were Hugh Corey, J.J. Burns, Denis Cummings, William Gorman, Paul Hamilton, Robert Kerr, Brendan Mead, Henry Harrison Murray, Marcus Murray, J.P. McCann, Sean McGlinchey, Martin McManus, Edward O'Connor, James Gary Roberts, Joseph Simpson and Bobby Storey.

When I first attended the Maze escape trial, and escorted Bobby Storey across the tunnel and up into the dock in the number 1 court, I was confronted by a totally bizarre scene. There were about eight defendants already seated in a haphazard fashion on three or four benches facing the judge's bench. As you looked across towards the seat where Lord Lowry would eventually be presiding, you could see that there had been sheets of bullet-proof glass erected to protect him from any possible assassination attempt. Taking up vantage points in the same area, facing the dock and the public gallery, were two or three RUC officers, armed with rifles, and occasionally scanning the benches in front of them. Security could not have been tighter.

One must remember that just prior to the beginning of the trial, on Saturday 25 April 1987, the IRA had blown up and killed Lord Justice Gibson and his wife Cecily at Killeen outside Newry as they were returning from holiday. There was great outcry at how vulnerable he had been to this attack, considering he had just been left by a Garda escort in readiness to be picked up in the North by his RUC escort. There were questions asked as to how information about his route, vehicle and time of return had been acquired. It was clear that the IRA would go to any lengths to assassinate prominent members of the judiciary who had involvement of any sort in terrorist trials. Lord Justice Gibson was seventy-four years old when he died. Clearly pensioners were fair game in this bloody war, and during the escape trial nobody was taking any chances.

The trial had started in earnest on 28 April 1987, and there were due to be eighteen seated in the dock, with the promise of others to follow if extradition plans went ahead. However, two men failed to answer their bail to appear at the court, and the number was reduced to sixteen. There were seventy-three charges in all being put to the various men in the dock, who seemed oblivious to the fuss, talking and chatting amongst themselves as the proceedings continued. The most obvious charge related to the escape from lawful custody, but others included hi-jacking and of course the murder of James Ferris. In answer to the charges read out at court, all of the accused returned pleas of not guilty.

On the second day of the trial, matters were adjourned in respect of the demise of Lord Justice Gibson. The trial was in reality going to last for some considerable months, and a day would make no difference to the public purse. In all, there were about 1,000 pages of evidence to be put before the court, and at least 100 prison officers as witnesses who may be called.

On Thursday 7 May the Crown counsel were dealt a blow by the Dublin High Court, when Patrick John McIntyre was released, another of the escapees who had been in custody in the Republic for some time. McIntyre was due to be extradited to the North to stand trial alongside the other eighteen, but instead was released and whisked away through the streets of Dublin on the back of a waiting motorcycle. According to the Dublin High Court, McIntyre had been held unlawfully by the Gardai in Ballyshannon, and should not have been further detained. Again this incident caused fury amongst politicians in Northern Ireland who were convinced the Government in the Republic would never be committed to working together with them towards a singular purpose, i.e. getting rid of the terrorists.

The trial continued day after day, with accounts of the various events of the escape being covered again and again by both defence and prosecution. The officer who had been shot in the head during the escape, Officer Adams, stood before the court on 6 May and told how, when he had tried to close the control room door and raise the alarm, he had been shot in the head by one of the escapees. He said that he had been only two feet away from his attacker and that he knew him to be Gerry Kelly. It would have been intimidating standing in the witness box at the best of times, but at such a high-profile trial, with the defence counsel constantly picking holes in your evidence, it would have been ten times worse. A few of those who had come in direct contact with the escape as it unfolded, and had then to give evidence some three and a half years later, admitted that they were still suffering from disturbing flashbacks. The trial meant that some of them had to almost relive the experience, causing real pain and anxiety.

On 8 May, only a week or so into the trial, another of the original thirty-eight escapees made the news. Patrick McKearney, whose address was given as Benburb Road, Moy, was one of eight IRA men shot dead by the British Army as they attempted to carry out a bomb and gun attack on Loughgall police station. Kearney had been serving a fourteen-year sentence for the possession of a loaded sten gun, when he had joined the others on the escape from the jail in 1983. The incident at Loughgall was hailed as a major success for the security forces, despite the fact that one innocent passer-by was caught up in the hail of bullets and later died from his injuries. There had clearly been inroads made into the infrastructure of the IRA, and important intelligence had been received which had laid the active service unit bare during the raid. It was a deflating time for those standing accused at the trial.

All in all, the escape trial continued until October 1987. It wasn't until 27 April the following year that Lord Lowry acquitted all sixteen of the murder of James Ferris. It was a black day for prison officers throughout the Service. Lord Lowry had ruled that Ferris had died from a heart attack, and not as a direct result of the stab wounds he had received at the hands of the men escaping. It beggared belief. Had James Ferris not been stabbed, he would likely not have suffered a heart attack. It was a desperate 'chicken and egg' scenario, and it was hard for many of us to believe that there was no political motive behind the decision to acquit.

To add further insult to injury, those who were convicted of escaping from lawful custody, in particular Gerry Kelly, received just three years imprisonment. As Kelly, amongst others, had already spent time on remand and awaiting trial, he was virtually time served, having had his 50% remission taken into account, and he was released.

* * *

With the profile of Belfast City ever changing in preparation for the new millennium, the criminal justice system too had to undergo a makeover of sorts. The new courts at Laganside were constructed opposite the Royal Courts of Justice, a stone's throw from the Waterfront Hall. With the impressive views from the third floor lobby, looking out over the Lagan and beyond to the Odyssey Arena and the Holywood Hills, you could be forgiven for asking why such valuable real estate was chosen as the site for a court. There is no expense spared either in the quality of build or the fixtures and fittings. There is nothing imposing about the building, and certainly nothing intimidating. Everything about Laganside is in total contrast to the Crumlin Road Court-house.

As times change, so too does our attitude to the law. There is no such thing as accepting your punishment for a crime without first challenging every aspect of the system. The solicitors and barristers of today thrive on a protracted set of procedures that ensure they appear in court many times before very simple cases are settled. Their fees are often phenomenal, and of course their clients are more than likely availing of legal aid. In terms of cost, we as taxpayers are supporting a deeply flawed system which has arguably regressed in its duty to maintain law and order on our streets. The courts are no deterrent for today's offenders. In years gone by, one look at the Crumlin Road Court-house, and across to the Crum itself, could have been enough to keep you on the straight and narrow.

Chapter 8
Looking Back

Just recently I was lucky enough to be invited back to the Crum by Jane Campbell from the First Minister's Office, the person largely responsible for researching the prison and its history. It came as a complete surprise, as I was aware that there was a long list of people, about 8,000 in fact, who had expressed an interest in taking the warts and all tour. I jumped at the offer, and on 19 September 2006 I was able to wander through the jail with Jane as my guide. She pointed out ongoing restoration work and informed me about the ideas and plans for this vast site.

The sight which greets me when the large hydraulic gates swing open is a rubble-strewn landscape, with the skeletal hulk of the jail spreading its limbs towards the outer walls. Whilst waiting for the gates to open fully, I could see the people around me, who had been visiting the Mater Hospital and were now returning to their cars, turn their heads and stop to stare. I drive my car a few feet inside the gates and am greeted by Jane, who has just arrived herself. From the reactions of the permanent security staff, she is a frequent visitor, and has the virtual run of the place. Such is my enthusiasm, the introductions are done as we begin walking around the access road leading from the rear gate at the Mater Hospital past the D-wing visits entrance and into the forecourt. With a little imagination, I begin to see the place exactly as it had been nearly twenty years before, with some of the parts which have survived the stripping out providing me with reference points. I am more than surprised when I look up at the far wall beside A-wing gate, and see the 'Tardis'; the annoying box with its bright orange warning lamp, which when activated controlled the movement in the forecourt. It was an awful post to have been detailed, and only on a wet day did it have any redeeming qualities, offering some shelter from the rain at least. Surprisingly, it had fared rather better than some of the more permanent structures. The majority of the iron gates and grills are missing, having been taken down when they were surplus to requirements, and in preparation for grander plans. The very razor wire which lined the walls and gates like tinsel is almost non-existent, little patches remaining here and there in less accessible places. The façade of the main building remains much as I remembered it, apart from the accumulation of dirt and pigeon droppings on the sills and ledges. As we pass through what had been the main gate and the tally lodge, the extent of the decline becomes more obvious. We have to pick our way carefully through the blanket of shit lying at our feet, and avoid the many obstacles, some of which have been highlighted with brightly coloured hazard tape.

It is a welcome relief to the nostrils when we step out through the foot gate which leads to the front of the old cottages adjacent to the Crumlin Road and towards the pedestrian wicket gate. The first thing that strikes me is that the doors to the cottages retain their numerals, counting upwards in the 1960s as you move countrywards. I had never been aware of this detail before, and when I point it out to Jane, she herself is not altogether sure if the door numbers actually relate to the other properties on the Crumlin Road. Outwardly the general structure looks to be the same as in the 1980s, but she quickly assures me that this is not the case, and they are all in a very poor and somewhat dangerous condition. We continue up to the Officers' Club, and the odd broken pane and curtain shifting inside the first floor windows have a ghost-like quality. When Jane describes to me what has been suggested to improve the frontage of the jail, her great enthusiasm for her work and the project in general is infectious. She explains that the proposals suggest removing any security trappings which would have been added later in the prison's lifetime. All the barbed wire and ugly metal fencing will be torn down, and the iron railings, which run the length of the jail along the footpath, will be restored to their original glory. The entrance gate will be cleaned and restored, and the general area along the outside of the cottages landscaped with trees and shrubs. She paints an attractive picture, and I can see that in carrying forward these proposals, it will go a long way towards changing people's attitude towards the jail, which some currently regard as an eyesore.

We make our way back through the main gate and into the admin block through the double black doors. As I step onto the black and white tiled floors, and look ahead of me down the brightly lit corridor towards the glass door, I am slightly confused. All the doors off either side of the hall are black and glossy, the walls are freshly painted, and there is a Queen track belting out from a radio somewhere off to my right. As we walk forward, I hear voices, and realise there are a few men working in the building, and they have convened in one of the old offices to have a cup of tea. Jane leads me on to the office at the top of the hall on the left, which would have been the Governor's. I only ever remember being in it on three occasions, but I have a picture in my mind's eye of it being rather grand and austere. When we walk inside, there are still aspects of its original state, but in the far corner, the ceiling has a rather large hole in it and the floor joists above are exposed and rotten, affording one a view up to the room on the next floor. When we walk out of the room and through the glass door area into the circle, I am able to identify the room above the Governor's as part of the prison chapel.

It is here in the circle that the memories come flooding back. I turn around and around, looking everything up and down and reminding myself what went where, and pointing out things to Jane which I myself had forgotten until that moment. It all seems a lot smaller than when I had to move between wings with a bunch of keys, back and forwards at a rate of knots. What strikes me first is the spiral staircase which leads onto the walkway around the circle at first floor level. It has been moved from its original position at the left hand side of the entrance to A-wing, to the middle of the circle between B- and C-wings. Here would have stood the chief officer's box, from which he controlled the unlocks and paraded staff. It has since been taken away, leaving behind an ugly raised plinth serving no purpose whatsoever. What is testament to the few people who are working inside the prison on a casual basis, is the fact that they have managed to keep a respectable shine on the heather-brown tiled floors of the circle area, and that of the only wing which Jane explains is safe for us to walk around in.

The fact that we will be visiting C-wing is a bonus to say the least, and as we pass through the circle grill, I know that I am going to see something special. I can hardly believe my eyes that the little half door at the class office is still there, and on walking inside, the white board which would have held information about all the inmates on the landing is fully intact. There is no furniture in any of the cells, which all have their doors locked back into the frames, and the red paint on the floors is peeling and flaking. The lights all appear to be on in the wing, and with the natural light streaming in from the roof lights, the atmosphere is anything but oppressive. I find it strange to walk along and not hear any of the sounds I would have associated with the jail. It is eerily silent, as if the building itself is sleeping, waiting to be once again awakened by the jangling of keys and the banging of doors. I can only liken it to a church interior, and as we move further into the wing, we do so with the same reverence we would normally reserve for such places. I can see ahead that there is an area taped off in front of me, and as we draw closer, it becomes apparent that this is the original stone staircase which would have led down to the drop room and the punishment cells beside it. Jane explains that although it has been recently opened up, there are a few structural problems which need to be addressed before it can be used as the access to that area. She does, however, invite me down to view the drop room by using the same route I had taken nearly twenty years before. Even after my last experience, I have no hesitation, and she wanders off to collect some torches. As she leaves me alone, I take the opportunity to stand in the middle of the condemned cell, which is to the left of the staircase, and see if I can conjure up any of the atmosphere of my last visit. Whether it is because it is the middle of the day, or that the space is brightly lit, I am not sure, but I feel none of the fear or anxiety I did before. If anything, there is a peacefulness which is both engaging and reassuring. I do not feel threatened in any way, and remain standing there until Jane soon returns with two flashlights in hand. Whilst standing beside me, she points out the fractures in the plaster wall and tells me that this marks the position of the original doorway through to the little ablution area which was only used by the condemned man. Beyond that again lies the execution room.

The steps leading down to the drop room are around the side of the wing, and as we descend, there are a few lights wired on an extension to guide our way. I am slightly embarrassed when Jane tells me she has been down here on countless occasions, and has no problems at all doing so again. She is relaxed and comfortable as we edge our way through the arched tunnel and into the small landing area. The floor is damp here, and the air slightly less musty than I remember it being. The draught emanating from the open stairwell up to C-wing appears to have breathed new life into this dungeon of a space. It no longer feels oppressive, but still has an element of something sinister which I can't quite put my finger on. When we walk into the drop cell, the memory of my last visit comes flooding back. It was here I had felt the most negative of feelings. It was here where I had wanted to turn around and run away. I had stood then and looked up at the trapdoor mechanism and had experienced something which I found hard to explain. A totally irrational response, maybe, but very real and troubling to me at the time. It is very different this time though. I am able to pick out more of the detail of the room, which I didn't back then. I can see where the doors of the trap would have been hinged, and the outline of a staircase on the far wall, which would have descended from the execution room above. The room is empty save for the wooden apparatus above us, and, allowing for the time during which it has stood unused and almost airtight, has survived as well as any of the cells above. I feel like I could stay down here for ages, confident in my newfound bravery, but Jane has already mentioned a stroll along the tunnel, and I know that I can't resist.

The walk back through C-wing and the circle to A-wing grill brings more memories back to me. I had been unable to remember clearly how the tunnel was accessed until we arrive at the Perspex-covered grill beside the entrance to A-wing. The jail is a myriad of tunnels and stairwells, and until you had walked around it a few times it wasn't uncommon to get lost on your way to a particular post. My guide is sure we are heading in the right direction, though, and when she opens the padlock and we walk down the first part of the stairs, I have total confidence in her. We again have to use our flashlights, particularly after we unlock one of the heavy iron doors which gives access to the main part of the tunnel. As we walk along, Jane quips about 'Bob', the ghost of a warden who died of a heart attack in or near the tunnel, and who, it is said, haunts this part of the building. Although she has not seen Bob herself, she isn't particularly worried if he makes himself known or not. Our progress is slow, as the space is tight here, and the torches are our main source of light. There is no heat coming from the pipes beside us, leaving the tunnel cold and damp, with the muted rumblings above our heads of the morning traffic as it moves up and down the Crumlin Road. The space is claustrophobic, but I feel no panic, as we are the only two people here. When we reach the other end of the tunnel at the court side, the iron door is firmly locked and Jane explains that there is no access through to the holding area. Although the jail has had twenty-four hour security since its closure, the court-house has not. The current owner has chosen to let the property sit as is, and unfortunately it has fallen into serious decline. Understandably, there are health and safety issues in the building which would need to be addressed before anyone would be allowed to venture inside. It is a shame, as I can still picture the grandeur of the number 1 court and the ornate plasterwork of the entrance hall and adjoining courtrooms. As we walk back towards A-wing, Jane tells me of the plans which are being proposed by the new owner of the court-house.

The need for further hotel accommodation in Belfast has been apparent for some time, ever since our tourist trade has seen a steady increase over the last five to ten years. Barry Gilligan, having purchased the site for a meagre sum of money, has earmarked the court-house as a future luxury hotel location. The building will, of course, have to retain some of its original features if the planners are to agree to such a proposal, and any changes would have to be sympathetic, to say the least. The development of a hotel at the site could be complemented by any plans to turn the Crumlin Road Jail into the tourist attraction which most believe it should be. The tunnel adjoining both the jail and the court-house may once again echo to the sound of voices as they pass from one historic site to another. The walk from the court to the jail completes a unique picture of crime and punishment, and would offer the visitor an opportunity to follow this thrilling and thought-provoking trail. The collective redevelopment of these two buildings, in part at least, has the potential to create a whole new lease of life for this area of the city. It is a place which is seldom visited by the tourists who come here on the cruise ships or by their own steam, and at present, offers little in the way of interesting architecture or places of note. Any change to these buildings should be positive, and when I listen to Jane Campbell enthuse about the plans which are currently being considered for funding, I can't help but be convinced that they will come to fruition as she promises.

*   *   *

The journey through the jail that day wasn't one full of sentimentality. I am, and always will be, in awe of the Crum and the sense of history which is wrapped up in its past. But it is no lost love. You will have gathered by now that I did not particularly enjoy my time as a screw, less so when I returned to Belfast from Magilligan. Four years for me was more than enough time to make up my mind as to whether I had any future in the Service. The job itself was sedentary and unrewarding, but the experiences were life-changing and unique. Had I realised this at the time, I would have opened my mind more and may have opted to serve in the Maze, purely for the experience. There were work colleagues from back then who today I still consider friends, and others who I would cross the street to avoid. It was far from an everyday job, and even further from an ordinary workplace.

Part of that unique experience, I realise, is that for a small part of my life, I may have touched upon other people's lives, some of whom would have an impact, positive or otherwise, on my generation and generations to come. I have walked daily in places where hundreds if not thousands of different people have tread during more turbulent times. Many tears of sadness and despair have been shed in the cells and walkways of this sinister place of hopelessness, where both men and women dreaded the heavy thud of the green door as it closed behind them. The echo of their footsteps may have faded years ago, but it is said that 'with every contact, there leaves a trace'. I am convinced that those who lived and worked here have left a part of themselves behind, and I believe that their energy is channelled through the very fabric of the building. I also believe that the Crum in turn has left its own trace upon anyone who had reason to cross its threshold, whatever the circumstances.

I would like to think that in years to come, the Crum will be restored to a condition which affords others a chance to experience the atmosphere inside this historical gem. There are few positives to take from the Troubles in Northern Ireland, and I find no reason why we shouldn't look upon the jail as an opportunity. We cannot remain forever just being considered the birthplace of the *Titanic*, intent on celebrating the construction of one of the world's most spectacular disasters. If the peace process continues forward with the same momentum as in recent times, then we could all soon benefit from a healthy tourist industry which instead celebrates the successful journey of a country, once torn apart by conflict, into one where exists a peaceful and lasting democracy.

Index

Agha, Zara, 68
Aiken, Bella, 67
Aiken, James, 67
Aiken, Maggie, 67
Al Rawdah, 191–2
Allen, Harry, 74, 76
Anderson, Gerry
    'Gerry's Ghost Hunt', 46–52
Argenta, 191
Atkins, Humphrey, 208–9

Barry, Peter, 93
Belfast
    Blitz, 152
    Falls Road area, 17
    history of, 16–17
Bentham, Jeremy, 24
Berry, James, 57–8, 76
Bertram Mills Travelling
    Circus, 68
Billington, James, 77
Black, Christopher, 217
Blair, David, 11, 12–13
Board of Visitors
    report on security, 26
Bratty, George, 75
Breckenridge, Mary, 27–8
Bridewell Palace, 18
bridewells, 18, 23

Brown, Corporal Robert, 54
Browne, Brendan, 11
Browne, Michael, 11, 12, 13
Bryson, Jim, 192–3
Burke, Liam, 190

Cahill, Joseph, 71–2
Caldwell, Colin, 127–8
Campbell, Jane, 73, 79, 227–33
Campbell, Robert, 210
Campbell, T.J., 60–61
Carroll, James Joseph, 19–20
Clarke, Terence, 203–8
Coates, Warren, 47–9, 50–51
'conditioning', 5, 160–64
Connor, Mervyn John, 112
contraband, 6–7
Convery, Seamus, 192–3
Cordner, Harry, 71
Courtney, Harold, 69–70, 73
Crum, The, *see* HMP Belfast
'Crumlin Kangaroos', 203–8
Crumlin Road Courthouse,
    213–18, 226
Cullens, Eddie, 67
Curren, Bob, 47
Curry, Francis 'Pig Face', 115,
    144–5
Cushman, Samuel, 65–7

Daly, John, 56–7
Daly, Mary Ann, 56–7
Dartmoor Prison, 20
Democratic Unionist party, 85
Diplock Court, 216–17
Docherty, Gerry, 190
Docherty, Joseph Patrick Thomas, 210, 211
Donnelly, Patrick, 189–90
Dornan, Thomas, 67

Elliman, Bernard, 203–8
Ellis, John, 76
Ervine, David, 110–16
Executioners, 75–81
    boxes of, 79
Executions, 53–75

'Facing the Truth', 198
Farrell, Mairead, 130
Ferris, James, 219
    ruling on death of, 225
Fox, Thomas Gerard, 203–8
Fullerton, Maggie, 61
Fusco, Angelo, 210

Gallagher, Patrick, 75
Gamble, Pearl, 74
Gardner, Lyle, 58–9
Gilmore, John, 58–9
Gorman, Thomas, 192–3
Graham, Marshall Colin, 11, 12
Gregg, John, 150

hanging, 53
Hanna, 'Bunky', 20–21
Hennesey, Peter Gerard, 203–8
Hermon, Jack, 91
Home Truths, 12
HM Prison Belfast
    Belfast Blitz, 152–3
    C-wing, 43–5, 59
    D-wing, 2
    design of, 23–6
    early inmates, 29–30
    future plans for, 228–9
    general duties, 10–11
    labour, 22
    'M60 trial' escapees, 209–12
    overcrowding, 207–8
    register of births, 33
    register of deaths, 30–32
    staff alcohol abuse, 146–7
    zip gun, 22
HM Prison Maze, 35
    1983 escape from, 162–3
    trial of escapees, 220–25

Inside Out, 46
Irish Republican Army, 15–16, 34, 71
    and Michael Pratley, 61–2
    as inmates, 187–91
    'Crumlin Kangaroos', 203–8
    'M60 trial' escapees, 209–12
    Meehan escape, 193–203
Irwin, Mary, 59

Jebb, Colonel Joshua, 24
Justin, Richard, 60

Kane, Thomas, 203–8
Kane, Tucker, 192–3
Keenan, Christopher, 203–8
Keenan, Eddie, 190
Kelly, Gerry, 93, 219–25
Kelly, Justice Basil, 12
King, Tom (warder), 91
King, Tom (Secretary of State
    to NI), 93
Kirkpatrick, Harry, 217–18
Knight, Charles, 31

Lanyon, Sir Charles, 23–4
Larkin, Phillip, 208
Leech, Nelson, 63
Lindsay, Joe, 46
Long, Mary J., 30

MacDonald, Robert Maxwell, 153
Magee, Paul Patrick, 210, 211
Magill, PC Stephen, 211
Magilligan Prison, 7–9, 173–5
    hostage crisis, 9
Maginnis, Ken, 87–94
Maguire, Edward, 189–90
Maguire, Thomas J., 203–8
Maidstone, 191–2
Marwood, William, 76
Mawhinney, Dr Brian, 129
McAteer, Hugh, 189–190
McCaffrey, James, 128
McCann, Danny, 130

McCann, James, 66
McCarthy, John, 36
McCauley, Maggie, 64
McCauley, Sarah, 64
McCormick, Daniel, 32
McCrae, Reverend William, 86–7
McDowell, Minister Wesley, 9
McFarlane, Brendan 'Bik', 162–3,
    221–5
McGeown, Simon, 61
McGladdery, Robert, 74–5
McGivern, Bridget, 60
McIntyre, Patrick John, 224
McKearney, Patrick, 224
McKee, Jack, 115
McKee, Michael Anthony, 210,
    211
McKeown, Arthur, 57
McLaughlin, Nellie, 74
McLaughlin, Samuel, 73, 74
McMullan, John, 27
McNally, 'Pepsi', 157–8
McTaggart, Phil, 190
Meehan, Martin, 95–103, 163,
    193–203
Millisle Prison Service College, 7,
    138
Ministry of Home Affairs, 29
Molyneaux, James, 211
Morteshed, Francis, 63
Mullan, Daniel A., 203–8
Mullin, Major Albert, 207
Murdoch, Kate, 64
Murphy, Constable Patrick, 71
Murphy, James, 30

Murphy, Lenny, 112
Musa, Achmet, 67–9

Nellins, Joe, 115
Newsletter, 55
Northern Ireland Office, 29
Northern Ireland Paranormal
    Research Association, 46–7
Northern Ireland Prison Service,
    1, 37
    Millisle Museum, 79
    resignation from, 135

O'Hagan, Dessie, 34, 107, 167–73
O'Keefe, Christopher, 28
Oliver, John, 71
One Flew Over the Cuckoo's Nest,
    125
O'Neill, Robert, 54
'Operation Torch', 192

Paedophile prisoners, 122–5
Paisley, Dr Ian, 83–5
    imprisonment, 86–7
Pavis, William, 112
Pentonville Jail, 24
Perry, James, 71
Phillips, Mary Jane, 57
Pierrepoint family, 75–7
    Albert Pierrepoint, 77–8
    Henry Pierrepoint, 76–7
    Thomas Pierrepoint, 77
Porter, Mike, 182–6
Porter, Robert, 90
Pratley, Michael, 54, 61–3, 73

Prison Act 1865, 18
Prison design
    panopticon, 24
    telephone pole design, 24
Prison Officers' Club, 141–2
Prison Rule 32, 120–21
Prison system
    in Victorian times, 17–19
    rehabilitation within, 18–22
Progressive Unionist party, 108

'Red book' prisoners, 94–119
Redvan, Assim, 67
Reid, Minnie, 69–70
Rodgers, Peter, 192–3
Rodham, Leslie, 22–3
Ryan, Michael, 210, 211

Savage, Sean, 130
Simpson, Patrick, 71
Skey, Robert, 127–8
Sloan, Anthony Gerard, 210
Sloan, Gerard Michael, 210
Smiley, William, 64–5
Spence, Gusty, 20, 103–10, 126,
    163–4, 188
State of Northern Ireland
    establishment of, 16
Steele, James, 189–90
Stephenson, Jason, 32
Stone, Michael, 129–35
Storey, Seamus, 203–8
suicide, 39–42
'supergrass', 217–18
Symington, Olive, 70

Taggart, 'Swing', 21

Taylor, Martin, 192–3

Telegraph, 85

Thompson, Annie, 60

Toland, Tommy, 192–3

Troubles, the, 15

Twaddell, W.J., 62–3

Ulster Folk and Transport
  Museum, 79

Watson, William, 190

Westmacott, Captain Herbert,
  211

Whisker, Charlie, 12, 13

Wormwood Scrubs, 24

Wylie, Edmond, 32,
  40–41

Ward, Daniel, 55–6

Whitley, Margaret, 56

Wilgar, Charles, 55–6

Williams, Thomas, 54,
  71–3

Willis, William, 76

Woods, William, 59–60

Wright, Billy, 127

Young, Bernard, 31–2